Comments on other *Amazing Stories* from readers & reviewers

"Tightly written volumes filled with lots of wit and humour about famous and infamous Canadians."
Eric Shackleton, *The Globe and Mail*

"The heightened sense of drama and intrigue, combined with a good dose of human interest is what sets Amazing Stories *apart."*
Pamela Klaffke, *Calgary Herald*

"This is popular history as it should be... For this price, buy two and give one to a friend."
Terry Cook, a reader from Ottawa, on ***Rebel Women***

"Glasner creates the moment of the explosion itself in graphic detail...she builds detail upon gruesome detail to create a convincingly authentic picture."
Peggy McKinnon, *The Sunday Herald,* on ***The Halifax Explosion***

"It was wonderful...I found I could not put it down. I was sorry when it was completed."
Dorothy F. from Manitoba on ***Marie-Anne Lagimodière***

"Stories are rich in description, and bristle with a clever, stylish realness."
Mark Weber, *Central Alberta Advisor,* on ***Ghost Town Stories II***

"A compelling read. Bertin...has selected only the most intriguing tales, which she narrates with a wealth of detail."
Joyce Glasner, *New Brunswick Reader,* on ***Strange Events***

"The resulting book is one readers will want to share with all the women in their lives."
Lynn Martel, *Rocky Mountain Outlook,* on ***Women Explorers***

AMAZING STORIES

VANCOUVER CANUCKS

AMAZING STORIES

VANCOUVER CANUCKS

Heart-Stopping Stories from Canada's Most Exciting Hockey Team

HOCKEY

by Justin Beddall

PUBLISHED BY ALTITUDE PUBLISHING CANADA LTD.
1500 Railway Avenue, Canmore, Alberta T1W 1P6
www.altitudepublishing.com
1-800-957-6888

First published 2004

Publisher Stephen Hutchings
Associate Publisher Kara Turner
Editor Joan Dixon

We acknowledge the financial support of the Government of Canada through the Book Publishing Industry Development Program (BPIDP) for our publishing activities.

Altitude GreenTree Program
Altitude Publishing will plant twice as many trees as were used in the manufacturing of this product.

National Library of Canada Cataloguing in Publication Data

Beddall, Justin
Vancouver Canucks / Justin Beddall.

(Amazing stories)
Includes bibliographical references.
ISBN 1-55153-792-3

1. Vancouver Canucks (Hockey team)--History.
I. Title. II. Series: Amazing stories (Canmore, Alta.)

GV848.V35B42 2004 796.962'64'0971133 C2004-903748-X

Printed and bound in Canada by Friesens
2 4 6 8 9 7 5 3

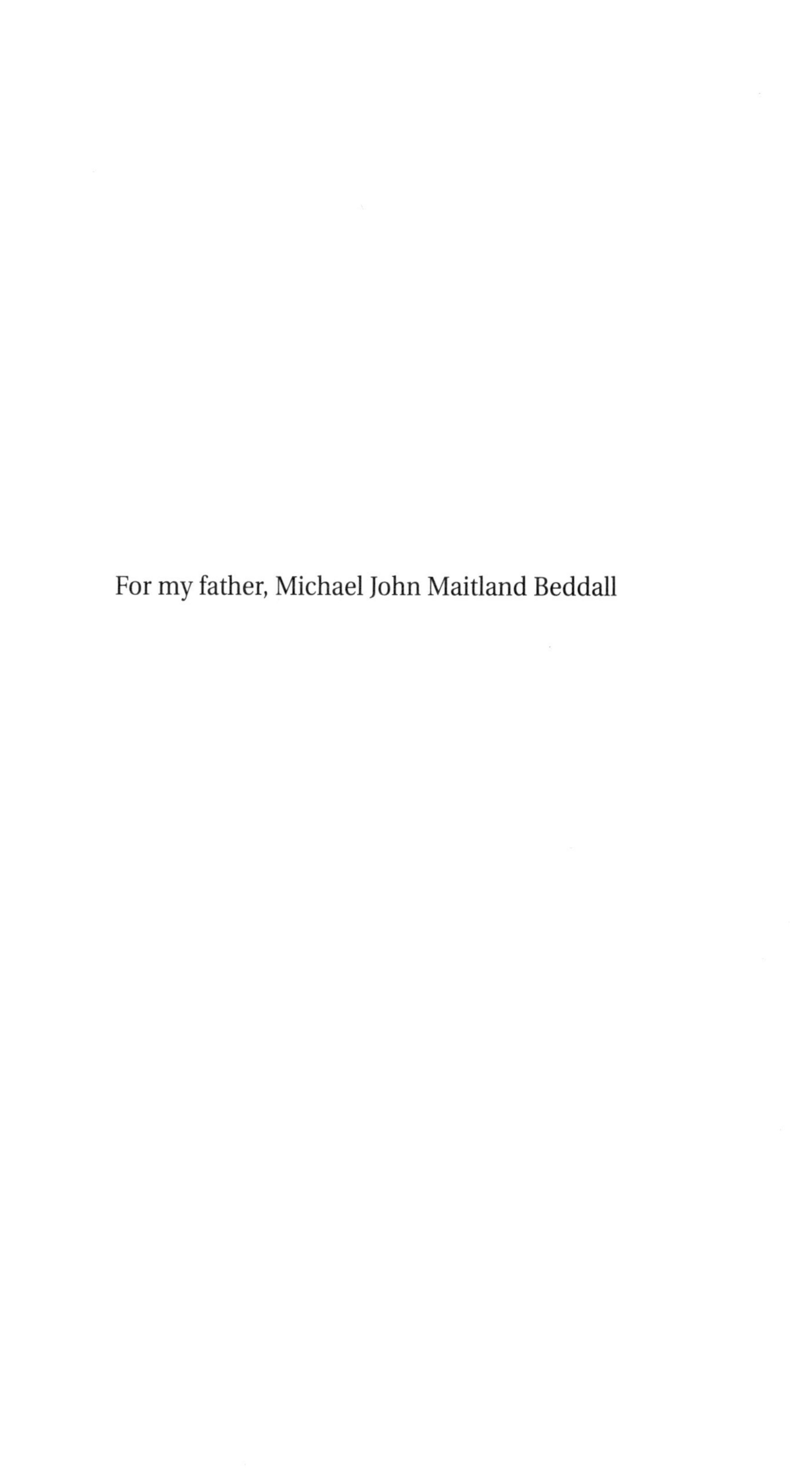

For my father, Michael John Maitland Beddall

Contents

Prologue

Canucks left-winger Geoff Courtnall knew the scouting report on Calgary Flames goaltender Mike Vernon. High, glove side.

The Canucks filed into the visitors' dressing room at the Calgary Saddledome after the third period of game five of the 1994 Stanley Cup playoffs. The players knew if they didn't score a goal in overtime, their season was finished. Courtnall took a few seconds to visualize a goal his former teammate, Wayne Gretzky, had scored against Vernon during the 1988 Stanley Cup playoffs. Shorthanded, Gretzky had skated down the left wing. With Vernon high in the crease to challenge him, he had blasted a slapshot high over the goaltender's glove-hand shoulder.

During the intermission, Courtnall walked out of the dressing room into the corridor where he could light a propane torch to doctor his stick. He put a massive — maybe even illegal — curve on his Easton. If he could get a shot during the overtime period, he was going to shoot high on Vernon.

Eight minutes into the first overtime period, Courtnall got the opportunity he had prepared his stick for. As he hopped over the boards to replace Greg Adams on a line change, Courtnall skated opportunistically down the left wing. A Canucks defenceman broke up a play at the Canucks blueline.

Vancouver Canucks

The puck bounced fortuitously between a Calgary defenceman's legs and onto the streaking Courtnall's stick. Courtnall cruised down towards the Calgary net and wired a slapshot from the top of the face-off circle...

Chapter 1
The Early Years

he spin of a lottery wheel was about to determine the fortunes of the NHL's newest expansion teams — the Vancouver Canucks and the Buffalo Sabres. General manager Bud Poile and the rest of the Canucks' brain trust sat impatiently at a draft table in the Grand Salon room of the swank Queen Elizabeth Hotel in downtown Montreal. Dressed in a dapper black suit, NHL president Clarence Campbell explained the rules of the Amateur and Expansion Drafts. As part of the US$6 million fee to join the National Hockey League for the 1970-71 season, the Canucks and Sabres could each select 18 skaters and 2 goaltenders from the unprotected lists of existing NHL rosters. Perhaps more importantly, one of the teams would also get the opportunity to select the first overall pick at the NHL's 1970 Amateur Draft.

The lottery wheel was numbered 1 through 13. Campbell flipped a coin to see which general manager would have their first choice of numbers. For each draft, one team would get numbers under seven, the other team, numbers over seven. Buffalo general manager Punch Imlach won the toss and chose the higher numbers for both spins. The white-haired Campbell then stepped up to the red-and-white wheel and gave it a whirl. The room — packed with NHL club officials, newspaper reporters, and fans — fell silent as the wheel made several revolutions before finally stopping. Number eight. The Sabres had won first choice at the NHL Expansion Draft for players that would take place the next day.

The stakes were much higher as Campbell prepared to spin the campy-looking wheel a second time. The top prize: a French-Canadian hockey prodigy named Gilbert Perreault. NHL hockey scouts unanimously agreed that the No. 1 draft choice could provide a successful underpinning for an expansion team for seasons to come.

Like a group of casino gamblers praying for their luck to change, the Vancouver Canucks contingent of management, coaches, and scouts craned their necks with nervous anticipation as Campbell spun the wheel again. Having first choice for the Expansion Draft was good, but first choice in the Amateur Draft would be even better. A hush swept across the noisy room as the wheel began to slow down. "Number 1! Vancouver wins the first choice in the Amateur

Draft!" Campbell announced.

Shouts of victory erupted from the Vancouver Canucks' draft table. They would get the slick forward from the Montreal Junior Canadiens. "We had a great celebration at our table. We were going to get Gilbert Perreault," recalled Canucks public relations director Greg Douglas. "We were all ready to go and dress him up in our jersey. As far as we were concerned, we had him."

But, before the celebratory Canucks brass had a chance to sit down, the destiny of the organization would change dramatically. "Time, Mr. Campbell," Buffalo GM Punch Imlach said calmly. "That's not a one, Mr. Campbell, that's an 11."

"The whole room went quiet," remembered Douglas, who was seated at the Canucks' draft table along with GM Bud Poile, coach Hal Laycoe, and the team's scouting staff. "Everybody looked and realized it was an 11 and our table just went quiet."

Imlach was right. A red-faced Campbell, who had called the number, corrected himself. "Gentlemen, there has been a mistake. The number is 11." Buffalo would win Perreault.

The Canucks would have to settle for the next best player available at the draft: Dale Tallon, a 19-year-old smooth-skating defenceman who could also play forward. Vancouver scout John "Peanuts" O'Flaherty attempted to put a positive spin on the draft-day game of roulette: "Maybe it's just as well, Tallon is a lot tougher than Perreault. Stronger defensively too."

Bud Poile was more candid about the day, which was later dubbed "Black Tuesday" in Canucks hockey lore. "I'm not going to call home tonight. The way things are going, my wife is likely to tell me the house has burned down," he joked half-heartedly.

Before Poile officially made Tallon the first-ever Canucks draft pick, he set about building his team through the Expansion Draft. He'd had much success doing this as the general manager of the expansion Philadelphia Flyers in 1967. After the Sabres selected Tom Webster from the Boston Bruins with the first pick, Poile countered by drafting Boston Bruins defenceman Gary Doak, considered to be the best blueliner left unprotected.

Next, Poile selected Orland Kurtenbach from the New York Rangers. Kurtenbach turned out to be the first gamble that paid off for Vancouver. A 34-year-old Alberta native with a wonky back, Kurtenbach admitted he wasn't surprised to hear his name called out during the Expansion Draft. "I knew I was either going to go to Buffalo or Vancouver. I knew that ahead of time and my preference was Vancouver," he recalled. "I had played for Bud Poile in San Francisco and I played for Punch in Toronto — I guess my only concern was whether my back was going to be OK, which it was. Having played for the old Western League Canucks and then coming back to play for expansion-era Canucks was wonderful." He became the Canucks' first captain.

Poile then selected tough forward Rosaire Paiement,

a player he'd gotten to know while he was general manager of the Flyers. He dipped back into the Flyers' talent pool for a long-haired, 22-year-old goaltender named Dunc Wilson. Like Paiement, Wilson had spent most of his pro career with the Flyers' farm team, the Quebec Aces.

Drafted fourth at the Expansion Draft for his toughness was Pat Quinn, a hardrock 26-year-old defenceman from the Toronto Maple Leafs. Quinn had gained notoriety in the 1968-69 playoffs when he had leveled Boston superstar Bobby Orr. Poile continued to stock his expansion team with character players. He purchased Andre Boudrias from the St. Louis Blues. He also added 37-year-old goaltender Charlie Hodge from the Oakland Seals for some experience between the pipes.

Two months later, on August 5, 1970, the Canucks' No.1 draft pick, Dale Tallon, walked into a press conference inside Vancouver's Devonshire Hotel. Dark-haired, with movie-star good looks, he was decked out in a red jacket, orange floral print shirt, and white slacks. He had just signed the richest deal ever given to an NHL rookie. Scoring 39 goals for the Toronto Marlboros in his last year of junior hockey, Tallon was expected to make an immediate impact on the Canucks blueline. But the Canucks' Douglas wisely observed, "He was a talent but he was young, he wasn't ready. But when you're an expansion team, you make them ready."

Despite losing out on the Gilbert Perreault sweepstakes, Vancouver fans were more than ready for the puck to drop at the Pacific Coliseum. The Vancouver Canucks had finally been granted the right to join the league in 1970-71, after being passed over for an expansion franchise in 1967. While Vancouver hockey fans rejoiced at the news, no local businessmen had come forward to put up the franchise fee necessary to secure a team. The search for an owner eventually led to Minnesota businessman Thomas Scallen and his partner Lyman Walters. In 1969, Scallen purchased the Western Hockey League (WHL) Vancouver Canucks to bring into the NHL. As owners of the Medical Investment Corporation, Scallen and Walters knew a lot about running a multimillion-dollar business, but they knew very little about hockey.

Following a cocktail reception at the swanky Bayshore Inn, Walters admitted he wasn't even crazy about the team's moniker. In *The Vancouver Canucks Story,* author Denny Boyd reported him saying, "The word Canuck strikes me as a slang expression that I don't particularly like. If there are no serious objections from the fans, we are going to consider a name change." Fortunately, when Walters and Scallen learned that the team name was in homage to Johnny Canuck — the Canadian fighting man — they reconsidered their position.

Although Vancouver had been snubbed for the six-team expansion in the first go-round, the city had already experienced a rich hockey history — and a Stanley Cup. In 1915, the Vancouver Millionaires finished in first place in the fledgling Pacific Coast Hockey Association, an upstart league formed by future Hall-of-Famers Lester and Frank Patrick. The team's first-place finish meant they would face the Ottawa Senators, the champion of the more established NHL, in a best-of-five championship. The Millionaires were considered one of the best hockey teams ever assembled. Led by Fred "Cyclone" Taylor, they swept the Sens before packed crowds in the 10,500-seat Denman Arena on the shores of Coal Harbour. They outscored their eastern foes 26-8.

More than half a century later, Vancouver hockey fans were eager for a return visit from Lord Stanley's cup. While the rookie American owners of the Canucks had a dearth of hockey experience, they had the common sense to hire a veteran hockey man to run the franchise. Poile had played six seasons in the NHL before becoming a player-coach in 1950-51 for Tulsa in the United States Hockey League. Two years later, he became coach of the WHL's Edmonton Flyers. When Vancouverite Coley Hall purchased San Francisco's team in the WHL, he hired Poile as coach and general manager. Poile won WHL titles in 1964 and 1965. When Philadelphia was granted an expansion NHL franchise in 1967, Poile was named general manager. Poile's hockey smarts became even more evident when the Flyers captured the Western Division in just their first season on Broad Street.

The 45-year-old Poile's search for the Canucks' first coach landed on Hal Laycoe, who had been the coach for the Los Angeles Kings the season prior, compiling a 5-18-1 record. His NHL coaching resume only included 24 games, but he had an impressive record as coach of the WHL's

Portland Buckaroos, winning seven titles in nine seasons, including a pair of Lester Patrick championships.

As Poile continued to cobble together his fledgling hockey organization, Vancouver's chief nemesis, Punch Imlach, would strike again. Not only had the Buffalo GM largely determined which players would play in Vancouver, he also influenced the uniforms they played in. Poile wanted his team colours to be blue and gold, but Punch had filed his selection for the same combination with NHL headquarters before Poile. As a result, the team had to settle on royal blue, kelly green, and white — symbolic of the ocean, forest, and snow-capped mountains in British Columbia. Local artist Joe Borovich designed the first uniform logo: a stylized "C" in the shape of a hockey rink with a white stick in the middle.

The uniform, name, and management structure in place, the expansion Canucks walked out of the tunnel from the dressing room on October 9, 1970. Their first-ever game at the Pacific Coliseum against the Los Angeles Kings was not sold out only because of a glitch in the team's ticket system. An epic pre-game ceremony included such dignitaries as NHL president Clarence Campbell, Premier W.A.C. Bennett, Native Chief Dan George, and Cyclone Taylor. In a full-length fur coat, Vancouver mayor Tom Campbell waved to the crowd.

After the Kings got out to a 2-0 lead, defenceman Barry Wilkins doubled his career goal totals with a backhander that got past the Kings goalie. He instantly made himself a piece of Canucks hockey history. Still, despite all the hype, the first game was less than memorable.

"There was a very long pre-game ceremony, and they introduced everyone in the building. And when the game finally started it was not a good hockey game, it was dull ... much more memorable was the next game," long-time Canucks broadcaster Jim Robson recalled. Two nights later, thanks to a pair of goals from left-winger Wayne Maki, the Canucks defeated the Toronto Maple Leafs 5-3. This time, in front of a sell-out crowd of 15,542, they recorded their first NHL win against one of the most storied franchises in hockey.

The Canucks went on to win more games that year than any of the 653,898 fans who bought tickets could have ever imagined. They finished with a record of 24-46-8, which slotted them in sixth spot in the East Division. "That first-year team was not a bad team," said Robson. Had it not been for a season-ending knee injury to captain Kurtenbach, the team might have even challenged for a playoff berth.

Despite the pressure heaped on his shoulders by the press and local hockey fandom, Dale Tallon had an impressive rookie season. He scored 14 goals and added 42 assists, breaking Bobby Orr's rookie record. Andre "Super Pest" Boudrias led the team with 25 goals and 41 assists. Paiement surprised NHL onlookers with 34 goals and 62 points, along with 152 penalty minutes. Indeed, it was a breakthrough year for "Crackling Rosie" Paiement, who had scored just four goals and five assists in his previous 43 NHL games. In all, four Canucks forwards finished with more than 20 goals each, for the first time in their careers.

Kurtenbach, the team's MVP, recalled the year with pleasure: "It was wonderful for a lot of other players that had been with other NHL clubs and now had the opportunity to play a lot of hockey ... One of the fusing points was we had some vets and they were good people ... Gary Doak, Pat Quinn, Charlie Hodge ... There were a lot of colourful guys."

And there were several colourful moments in that first season. As Boyd related in his book, Buffalo's Imlach had hurled another bomb at his expansion cousin before their first encounter. He referred to the Canucks as the "The 4-F club — Feeble, Folding, Fumbling, and Frustrated." General manager Bud Poile could only bite all his pencils in half while trying to think of an appropriate comeback. In "the closest thing to a religious experience that Poile ever had in hockey," Paiement scored four goals as the Canucks defeated the Sabres 6-3.

On November 5, the Canucks won their first road game against Buffalo. The night witnessed Vancouver netminder Dunc Wilson stopping the team's first penalty shot against Sabres forward Paul Andrea.

Broadcaster Jim Robson, who called all 78 games that season, has a particular favourite moment: "The highlight without question was the February 16 game when they beat the Boston Bruins. Boston were the Stanley Cup champions and they had Cheevers in goal and they had Orr ... and Esposito, Hodge and Cashman, Sanderson ... they had a powerhouse and the Canucks beat them 5-4. Rosaire Paiement scored his third goal of the night with something like 56 seconds left...breaking a 4-4 tie. It was a fantastic game and the place went nuts. That was the most memorable game in the first season."

The first season also provided some follies. George Gardner, nicknamed the "Roly-poly Goalie" because of his steadfast lack of conditioning, let in a soft goal during a Sunday game at Madison Square Garden. Ranger Vic Hatfield had golfed a shot and scored from centre ice. Nobody could figure out how it happened. As it turned out, Gardner, an avid gambler, was busy concentrating on something else. He was squinting at the read-o-graph that displayed updated NFL games results at the opposite end of the arena. Douglas explained, "He had a ton of money on the game and he was watching to see how San Diego was doing and didn't even see the puck go in."

The Canucks had a difficult time living up to the high standards set in their inaugural season. Despite continued goal production from Boudrias and Kurtenbach, the Canucks finished the next season with 48 points. Paiement, meanwhile, struggled, scoring just 10 goals. The big forward's 37-game slump prompted the team to invite world-famous hypnotist "The Amazing Raveen" to help end the goal drought. Raveen attended the Canucks' weekly Tuesday luncheon and hypnotized Paiement, telling him, "You will score tonight."

"It didn't work," Douglas recalled. The team's record was a harbinger of things to come. The next season (1972-73), the Vancouver Canucks' losing ways continued. They finished with a record of 22-47-9, seventh in the East Division. Shortly afterwards, Bud Poile suffered a heart attack and was forced to resign. Hal Laycoe, who had been kicked upstairs as vice-president, was brought on as interim GM. Behind the scenes, a power struggle for the team continued between minority shareholder Coley Hall and owner Tom Scallen. Hall usurped control of the team. He was largely responsible for the hiring of new coach Bill McCreary. He also orchestrated the May 14 trade that sent Dale Tallon to the Chicago Blackhawks.

In addition to scoring 44 goals and 93 assists in 222 games as an original Canuck, Tallon also provided some dubious highlights off the ice. Boyd recalled one: "Dale Tallon, the glamour-dripping super-rookie of the first NHL season, is a young man of many means, a potentially great defenceman, a top golfer, a member of the NHL's best-dressed team and a two-country lady killer. He is also a totally unpredictable radio interviewee. Once a radioman asked Tallon what his relaxing plans were for a brief Canuck layoff and Tallon answered, 'Wall to wall broads.'"

In exchange for their star draft pick, Vancouver received defenceman Jerry Korab and flamboyant goaltender Gary Smith. "Suitcase" Smith was a curly-haired free spirit who had shared the Vezina trophy with Tony Esposito in 1971-72.

Suitcase, with his penchant for full-length fur coats and all-star quips, would become an immediate hit in Vancouver. "Everything you've heard about me is absolutely true ... I am a tremendous goalie," he told reporters after arriving in Vancouver. "He was a character ... Smitty one night let in an overtime goal and stormed off the ice and down the chute and went straight to his car and drove home in his equipment," recalled Douglas.

During the 1973-74 season, Suitcase carried the team. He played in 65 games, compiling a 20-33-8 record and a 3.44 goals-against average. But not even the six-foot-four Smith could stop the team's struggles on and off the ice.

"You could not get a ticket at the Pacific Coliseum for the first two and a half years. The fans were satisfied with what they were seeing except our team was not winning," recalled Douglas. "Midway through the third year, the novelty had worn off and that's when the players began to feel the pressure. That's when management felt the pressure."

In January, Phil Maloney replaced Bill McCreary behind the bench and the team finished with a pitiable 59 points. That summer, Scallen was forced to sell the team after being found guilty in a B.C. provincial court. He had illegally converted $3 million of the money raised from investors in the hockey team to pay off his own personal business debt and created a false stock prospectus. Television and radio magnate Frank Griffiths's Western Broadcasting Company bought the team for $9 million. In 1974-75, Griffiths's Canucks won the Smythe Division championship. Fans at the Pacific Coliseum finally had something to cheer about.

Chapter 2
Tiger and the Cup

ave "Tiger" Williams arrived at the Vancouver International Airport sporting a white cowboy hat, a hunting vest, and jeans. He brought with him a penalty-minute rap sheet a mile long — and a fierce determination to win. "He typifies what we're looking for, the guy who will do anything to win. Maybe the guys we are getting aren't as talented as the two we gave up but their work habits are a lot better," said coach Harry Neale.

The February 18, 1980, trade that made the 26-year-old Williams a Canuck was a risky move. Vancouver Canucks general manager Jake Milford traded talented but under-achieving first-round draft picks Rick Vaive and Bill Derlago for Williams and checking forward Jerry Butler. On paper, the trade tilted heavily in favour of the Leafs. As Williams later proved, hockey isn't played on a sheet of loose-leaf.

Williams had spent the first five and a half seasons of his NHL career in Toronto. Mostly he rode shotgun on the Leafs' top line with Darryl Sittler and Lanny McDonald. Milford believed Williams's fierce competitiveness would rub off on the bottom-dwelling Canucks franchise. In his first full season with the Canucks (1980-81), the 180-pound left-winger earned 343 penalty minutes but scored a career-high 35 goals. It earned him a trip to the NHL all-star game. His penchant for gooning it up and his flamboyant goal-scoring celebration — "the Tiger Shuffle" — immediately endeared him to Canucks fans. But more importantly, the arrival of the gritty Saskatchewan native shook up the country-club atmosphere that had infected the Canucks' dressing room. "Any good athlete always thinks that you're a day away from making the difference," Williams said. "If you don't think that, you should probably be a welder."

Although Williams's offense tailed off in 1981-82 when he scored just 17 times, No. 22 was the instigator of an incident that would launch the Canucks on their improbable 1982 Stanley Cup run. The cinematic moment was reminiscent of the 1970s cult classic *Slap Shot.* At Le Colisée in Quebec City on March 20, Williams took a run at the Nordiques' star centre, Peter Stastny. During an ensuing melee, a fan reached over the boards and took a swing at Williams. Coach Harry Neale and several of Williams's teammates vaulted

Tiger Williams

themselves into the stands in pursuit of the overzealous fan.

Defending the most penalized player in the NHL cost Neale a 10-game suspension: the final five games in the regular season, along with the first five in the playoffs. Defenceman Doug Halward received a seven-game suspension for his part in the altercation. Still, as Williams later recounted in his book, *Tiger: A Hockey Story,* "An incident like that unifies a team dramatically."

With Neale's banishment to the press box, Roger Neilson stepped behind the bench. The 47-year-old had been hired as Neale's associate coach by Jake Milford the previous summer. Williams had played for Neilson in Toronto where Neilson had established a reputation as a tireless tactician and a pioneer in the use of video analysis. "Because I'd worked with Roger Neilson before, it was no great surprise to me that he could organize so well, hand down game plans that were like a set of military instructions. For the other guys, it was a revelation," Williams said, "and they responded tremendously."

For some players on the team, like high-scoring winger Darcy Rota, Neilson brought a fresh approach to the rink. "He always made practices very interesting. He was a great innovator."

As the rookie head coach of the Toronto Maple Leafs in 1977-78, Neilson had proven himself a master strategist and motivator. He led the Leafs past the Los Angeles Kings and the highly favoured New York Islanders in the playoffs. Could he have similar success in Vancouver? During the final five games of the regular season under Neilson, the Canucks went undefeated, forging a 4-0-1 record. They hammered the Los Angeles Kings 7-4 in the final game of the regular season to finish with 77 points, second in the Smythe Division.

For the first time in franchise history, the Canucks had

home-ice advantage for the opening round of the Stanley Cup playoffs. More importantly, the team was on a roll, having finished the season with six wins and three ties. "The incident in Quebec was part of it, but when I look at the last nine games, we went into the playoffs on a real high even though we finished the year under .500," Rota recalled. "For me that was a real key factor: we went into the playoffs believing we could beat anybody."

The Canucks had every reason to feel confident. During the regular season, the team was fifth best in the league in goals-against. Leading the team from the blueline was captain Kevin McCarthy, Lars Lindgren, Colin Campbell, and a big, stay-at-home defenceman, Harold Snepsts. In goal was an unheralded French Canadian, Richard Brodeur, acquired from the Islanders in 1980. He played in 52 regular-season games with the Canucks, compiling a regular-season record of 20-18-2 and 3.35 goals-against average.

At the same time, the team scored a franchise-high 290 goals. Gritty wingers Stan Smyl, Curt Fraser, and Darcy Rota combined for 82 goals. They complemented a talented centre-ice corps that included Thomas Gradin, Ivan Hlinka, and Ivan Boldirev. "We had some skill guys, particularly down the middle but mostly there were a lot of gritty, hardworking competitive guys that were willing to pay the price," recalled Rota. "We were a very focused team that played very hard."

The Canucks lineup at this time included five Swedes: Gradin, Lars Molin, Lars Lindgren, Per-Olov Brasar, and

Anders Elderbrink. Some questioned if they could handle the rigors of the second season, but Tiger Williams wasn't about to let his teammates be intimidated. "He would have little meetings with [the] Swedes and he was telling them that he would look after them and not to worry about anything, just go in and play hard and they would be looked after," *Province* reporter Tony Gallagher recalled.

Unfortunately, two days before hosting its first-ever series opener against the Calgary Flames, a pall fell over the club. As the team scrimmaged during an optional skate at East Van's Britannia Ice Rink, Kevin McCarthy got tangled up with forward Curt Fraser. The team's captain fell awkwardly, breaking his ankle. "That was really quite devastating. Kevin was a great team guy, a great leader," said Rota. Not only had the Canucks lost a valuable member of their power play, they were already threadbare on the blueline. Doug Halward was still serving the last two games of his suspension for the famous brawl in Quebec. So the Canucks were left with Snepsts, Campbell, and Lindgren as the only veterans on a defense corps that included little-known rookies Neil Belland and Andy Schliebener.

Tiger Williams seemed unfazed by the loss of McCarthy. "We'll beat them," Williams predicted prior to the series opener. Williams's blunt comments were prophetic — literally and figuratively. Game one at the Pacific Coliseum was only eight seconds old when acting captain Stan Smyl gave the Canucks a 1-0 lead on a pass from linemate Thomas Gradin.

On the ensuing face-off, Calgary penalty-minute leader Willi Plett tried to shift the momentum of the game by picking a fight with Curt Fraser. Fraser was considered by many to be the best pound-for-pound scrapper on the Canucks team. He knocked Plett to the ice with an overhand right — to the delight of 11,701 Pacific Coliseum fans. "That set the series," Williams said. The Canucks won the game 5-3.

In order to douse the Flames, Roger Neilson had devised a game plan to shut down Lanny McDonald. McDonald had scored 34 goals for Calgary in 55 games after being acquired from the Colorado Rockies earlier in the season. Every time the mustached sniper set foot on the ice, Neilson countered with Williams, who stuck to his old linemate like an offensive-sucking leach. "It's a job," said Williams about his checking assignment at the time. "We knew how important Lanny is to the team and we have to contain him." Later, Williams admitted that the series strained the pair's off-ice friendship. Williams elbowed, kneed, slashed, and agitated McDonald, oftentimes goading him into the penalty box. McDonald didn't register a goal in the series.

In game two in overtime, Williams was the one being cross-checked to the ice by Flames defenceman Bob Murdoch. Parking himself in front of the net, Tiger nevertheless backhanded a pass from Lars Molin past Calgary goalie Pat Riggin. The goal gave the Canucks a 2-1 win. "It wasn't pretty but it went in," Williams told reporters. In game three, Williams also scored the game-winner at 8:17 of the third period.

Vancouver went on to a 3-1 win, sweeping the Flames. When they beat Calgary, as Tiger had predicted, they started to believe in themselves even more.

Tiger tales began making the front pages of the sports sections. "I've long suspected that The Tiger ultimately was destined for heroics — sometime, some place, and with some previously unsung team which needed only the inspirational spark of one man's performance to lift that team from mediocrity to success," wrote columnist Jim Coleman.

Vancouver players knew there was more to their win than Tiger. Their stubby beer-bottle-shaped goaltender had almost single-handedly limited the high-scoring Flames to just five goals in three games. He stopped 103 of the 108 shots he faced. Following the series victory, King Richard's teammates were already comparing him to the Great One. "You talk about Richard the same way you talk about Gretzky," Thomas Gradin said.

The team's unofficial theme song, "Freeze Frame" by the J. Giels Band, blared in the Canucks locker room, in celebration of the franchise's first-ever playoff series victory. Meanwhile, the Los Angeles Kings were also celebrating. They had finished the regular season a whopping 48 points behind Wayne Gretzky's Oilers. The underdog Kings came back from a 5-1 deficit in the third period to defeat Edmonton 6-5 in overtime in what was called "the Miracle on Manchester." They took a 2-1 series lead over the Oilers. The Oilers won game four 3-2. In a fifth, and deciding, game in Edmonton,

Los Angeles completed the improbable upset with a 7-4 win.

Instead of starting on the road against the Oilers, the Canucks were able to pull out the welcome mat at the Pacific Coliseum for the Kings. Gallagher commented, "Let's be reasonable here; they probably wouldn't have beaten the Oilers. That was the biggest break."

The Kings boasted the potent "Triple Crown" line of 50-goal scorer Marcel Dionne and wingmen Dave Taylor and Charlie Simmer. But the Canucks had a new ice-field battle plan prepared by their hot general behind the bench. In game one, Czech import Ivan Hlinka scored a pair of goals. Centre Gary Lupul, a native of Powell River, added the game-winner at the five-minute mark of the third period, giving the Canucks a 3-2 victory. The victory extended the Canucks' unbeaten streak under Neilson to nine games.

But the Triple Crown line, held in check in the first game, got on the score sheet during game two. After Rota opened the scoring with his first of the series, Taylor and Dionne replied. B.C.-born Kings sniper Steve Bozek scored in 4:33 of overtime to give the Kings a 3-2 victory.

Although his suspension had expired, Neale wisely left Neilson in command of the team. The Canucks took a series lead two nights later at the Great Western Forum — thanks to an unlikely goal outburst from Colin Campbell. He netted the game's first goal at 18:09 of the first, and the game-winner 1:23 into overtime. "We usually tell Collie to shoot the puck into the corner," Neilson joked after the game. "He doesn't even score in practice." Brodeur, meanwhile, earned himself another game-star selection, stopping 41 of 44 shots.

In game four, the Canucks scored a 5-4 win. A three-goal outburst from Fraser, Williams, and Rota in the second period chased Kings goaltender Mario Lessard from the net. The Canucks had a 3-1 series lead — despite being outshot 116-67. The diminutive Brodeur cast a very large shadow from his goal crease. "Every time they're down, he comes up with a big save and gives them a lift," Kings sniper Marcel Dionne complained prior to game five.

After rookie Kings centre Bernie Nicholls hushed another sellout crowd just 90 seconds into game five, the Canucks came back for a 5-2 victory. They won the Smythe Division championship, thanks to a pair of second-period goals by Prince George native Rota. In the dying seconds of the game, jubilant fans serenaded the Kings home, with "Na Na Hey Hey Goodbye." The song became a playoff tradition at the Pacific Coliseum that spring.

The Campbell Conference final was against the Chicago Blackhawks, a team led by 119-point centre Denis Savard and Norris Trophy-candidate defenceman Doug Wilson. Game one turned out to be a long night for the upstart Vancouver Canucks. Tied 1-1 after three periods, forward Jim Nill finally scored at 8:58 of the second overtime period. It was the longest playoff game in Canucks history: 88 minutes and 58 seconds. The Canucks again stole the game, thanks to the puck-stopping magic of goaltender Brodeur. "Preceding the winner was the most incredible goaltending one can hope to see from a stubby French-Canadian who remains almost insanely cool under duress," wrote Gallagher. "Brodeur stopped at least eight scoring chances in overtime alone and heaven knows how many before that."

NHL teams scouting the Canucks seemed confounded by Brodeur's style. Gallagher recalled a conversation with Neil Smith, who was, at the time, a scout with the New York Islanders. "He would say they couldn't get a book on Brodeur at all because they would watch him during the warm-up and he would never stop a single puck. And then during the game he never gave up anything, so they never really knew how he was beaten or where his weaknesses were, because the puck was always stopped."

The 18,610 fans who packed noisy Chicago Stadium for game two would witness one of the most memorable moments in Vancouver Canucks history. The Hawks led 2-0 after two periods, but Stan Smyl scored just over a minute into the third to spark the Canucks bench. The lift, however, was short-lived. Denis Savard restored Chicago's two-goal lead at 4:42. When an apparent Canucks goal by Curt Fraser was disallowed, Roger Neilson began to seethe with anger over the inconsistent officiating that seemed to favour the home team. Savard scored again on Chicago's ninth power-play advantage, making the score 4-1 in a fight-marred game. By the third period, Neilson couldn't hide his contempt towards referee Bob Meyers. Standing beside him, Tiger Williams suggested, "Let's throw the sticks on the ice."

"No," Neilson responded, "we're going to surrender."

Neilson put a white towel on the end of a hockey stick in mock surrender. At 16:23 of the third period, Neilson was ejected from the game. Williams and Gerry Minor, both of whom followed their coach with the towel-waving gesture, received 10-minute misconduct penalties. Referee Meyers had penalized Vancouver 23 times for 101 minutes — 19 more PIMs than the Hawks.

With his actions, Neilson had turned a disheartening loss into an emotional rallying point for the Canucks. After the game, defenceman Colin Campbell said, "Roger didn't lose his head. When he does something like that, there's a useful purpose to it."

Darcy Rota agreed. "We weren't going to win the game ... we came back to Vancouver and even ... the truck to meet us had white towels, it was unbelievable. And we came out to a sea of towels in game three; that to me was a real pivotal point of the playoff run."

Before game three, entrepreneurs ringed the Pacific Coliseum with towels the size of face cloths. They were now emblazoned with the slogan "Take no prisoners" and sold for five bucks. Canucks fans quickly adopted the new rallying cry.

The NHL head office was far less amused by Neilson's ref-baiting antics, and fined the team $10,000. Neilson himself received a $1000 penalty for his indiscretion behind the bench. NHL official Brian O'Neill said it "disgraced the championship series. Actions that demean our officials will not be tolerated."

Neilson's towel-waving tactic, however, may have affected the officiating. During game three, the Canucks' checking line of Williams, Gerry Minor, and Lars Molin manhandled Savard all night. They frustrated both the NHL's sixth-leading scorer and Chicago coach Bob Pulford. "It's pretty hard to play hockey when you're carrying them on your back all night," a disgusted Pulford seethed. "How they let all that go on Savard is beyond me. Maybe those white flags worked." Fans had plenty of reasons to wave the towels. Stan Smyl scored the game-winner at 2:05 of the third.

Meanwhile, Conn Smythe trophy candidate Richard Brodeur was gaining a regal following in Vancouver, inspiring bumper stickers, towels, and buttons. A group called King Richard's Army even recorded a single in his honour, called "King Richard." Teammate Williams seemed to be equally impressed with Brodeur: "He's a cool little frog. He is a professional right through. I haven't met anybody in the game I respect more."

Brodeur frustrated the Hawks again in game four. Boldirev scored a pair in a 5-3 victory that sent the Canucks back to Chicago. They were on the verge of clinching their first-ever trip to the Stanley Cup final.

Game one's double-overtime hero, Jim Nill, opened the scoring just 2:40 into game five. Stan Smyl added his sixth goal of the playoffs just over a minute later, giving the Canucks an early 2-0 lead over Tony Esposito and the Hawks. The fight-filled first period included Ron Delorme's drubbing of Grant Mulvey. Then, after Mulvey scored early in the third period to make it 3-2, the Canucks answered with three goals to make the final score 6-2. For Rota, who had suited up with the Hawks for six seasons, the victory tasted especially sweet. "To win game five in Chicago Stadium and I scored the fifth goal, that was the biggest game ever. For the first time in our team history we went to the Stanley Cup final."

Not even Canucks management had planned for a trip to the Stanley Cup final.

"That team had a lot of hurdles," recalled broadcaster Jim Robson. "They had to go right from Chicago to New York and the Canucks, not planning to get to the final, hadn't made any hotel arrangements and we stayed at a hotel that was miles away from the rink in Long Island."

The Canucks now faced the two-time defending Stanley Cup champions, the New York Islanders. Led by Mike Bossy, Brian Trottier, John Tonelli, Bill Nystrom, Denis Potvin, and goalie Billy Smith, the Islanders had finished the season atop the Patrick Division with an enviable 54-16-10 record.

And despite the Vancouver Canucks' miraculous playoff run, the New York press showed little respect for the team from the West Coast. They ridiculed the Canucks' road jerseys, calling them "Darth Vadar costumes, with jagged, garish, orange and yellow stripes — probably the ugliest uniforms in professional sports." They also accused the Canucks of playing a vapid brand of hockey. *New York Times* reporter George Vecsey wrote, "Neilson's Canucks have exploited the gap in the rules." The Islanders' general manager, Bill Torrey, told the same reporter, "It's like a rugby match, anything is possible. It's the way Roger teaches. You know that when you play his team, the game is going to be dragged down."

The Canucks weren't about to be dragged down by the New York press. In game one, centreman Thomas Gradin opened the scoring just 1:29 into the first period. The Canucks found themselves tied 5-5 with the mighty Isles heading into yet another sudden-death overtime. Unfortunately, with just two seconds remaining in the first overtime period, defenceman Harold Snepsts's errant pass deep in the Vancouver end was picked off by Mike Bossy. He wristed a 20-footer into the top left corner of the net, past a helpless and surprised Richard Brodeur.

After the game, the quixotic Williams — his body bruised and battered from the playoff run — remained upbeat about the Canucks' chances: "We'll win our three home games. That means we'll just have to win one here." At home, Canucks fandom remained optimistic too. Some waited more than 40 hours in line for tickets to Thursday's game three in Vancouver. Nearly 50 fans couldn't wait to see the Canucks' on-ice debut in the Stanley Cup final and paid $870 to fly to Uniondale with a tour group. In game two, they watched their Canucks play valiantly again, leading 3-2 heading into the third period. But the Islander machine kicked into high gear, scoring four third-period tallies for a 6-4 win.

Williams was right, the Canucks would need to win all their home games. By the time the Canucks had touched down at Vancouver International Airport, "Towel Power" had officially captivated the province. Tourism British Columbia officials culled signatures from the premier and members of the legislature on a 300-metre long towel to hang inside the Coliseum for game three. The towels, however, would be used to mop up the tears of the suddenly downcast Canucks fans when the Islanders scored a convincing 3-0 victory. On paper, and on the ice, the Islanders proved to be a much better hockey team. "I don't think anybody in the world would have beaten them tonight," Williams said after the game.

In game four, after Butch Goring opened the scoring at 11:38 of the first period, Vancouver fans finally had something to cheer about. Stan Smyl scored his ninth goal of the playoffs to even the score at 1-1. However, Mike Bossy scored his 16th and 17th goals of the playoffs on power plays in the second. The Islanders skated off with the Stanley Cup. Williams, who had clashed with the stick-swinging Isles goaltender throughout the four-game series, still just shrugged his shoulders after the game. "I would have bet my house that they wouldn't have beaten us four straight." He had tried his hardest, finishing the playoffs with 10 points and a Canuck-record 116 penalty minutes.

Williams suited up in two more playoff series for the

Canucks, in 1982-83 and 1983-84, but the team didn't advance past the first round. "They called it a bad trade after Vaive scored 50," said Robson. But Harry Neale had no regrets about the deal. "He would always say 'What do you mean? We got to the final with Tiger Williams, [Toronto] never got to the final.'"

Chapter 3 Pavel Bure: Rocket Launch

The covert Moscow hockey insider who tipped off the Vancouver Canucks about Pavel Bure remains a shadowy figure to this day. "Only three people know his name," Brian Burke (at the time Canucks VP) confided to the *New York Times*. "Pat Quinn, [scout] Mike Penny and myself." The information the Muscovite passed along to the Canucks sparked a cold war at the 1989 NHL Entry Draft in Minnesota.

Had Communism fallen a couple years earlier, Pavel Bure would have been an obvious first-round pick at the draft. The 18-year-old rookie of the year had scored 17 goals in just 32 games in the Soviet elite league in 1988-89. He was arguably the most talented player available in the draft but the climate in the Soviet Union at the time made it difficult to bring players to North America unless they defected. All 21 NHL teams were unwilling to gamble an early round pick on the talented Russian. And after the third round, European players who hadn't played at least 11 games at their country's elite level for two seasons were not eligible for the draft.

According to information circulated to NHL teams, Bure had only suited up for five games with the Central Red Army during the 1987-88 season, meaning he wasn't eligible after the third round. The Canucks had better information, said Burke. "Our man in Moscow kept telling us Pasha, which is what everyone in Russia there called him, had played 11 league games and two scheduled international exhibition games." Vancouver was going to take him in the eighth round until they found out Edmonton had the same plan, so they took him in the sixth.

After NHL vice-president Brian O'Neill announced that the Canucks had selected Pavel Bure of the Soviet Union with the 113th pick, a storm of disapproval erupted. The general managers and hockey scouts huddled at draft tables inside the Metropolitan Sports Center in Bloomington. Several clubs protested the pick. "They were tossing expletives at me and everybody else on the Canucks," Burke said. "Because of the controversy, the NHL had to conduct an investigation."

The Canucks were delighted to have stolen Bure at the draft, but the nagging question remained: Would the pick hold up? They awaited NHL president John Ziegler's ruling on Bure's draft eligibility. With Bure, the Canucks could ice a legitimate game breaker in the lineup — for the first time in the franchise's dismal history.

Playing on a line with Alexander Mogilny and Sergei Fedorov at the 1989 World Junior Championship (WJC), Bure had scored seven goals and three assists in seven games. He earned honours as the best forward at the tournament. But Bure's future in Vancouver seemed unlikely. Nearly a year after the draft, Ziegler ruled against the Canucks, making Bure eligible for selection in the 1990 Entry Draft. Not easily dissuaded, the Canucks enlisted the help of veteran superstar Igor Larionov, who had signed with the Canucks in 1989. Using his Moscow connections, he was able to cull Central Red Army game summary sheets that proved Bure had played the required number of games to be eligible for the draft — just as the Moscow informant had said. After reviewing the information obtained by the Canucks, Ziegler reversed his decision on the eve of the 1990 draft. Burke said the Canucks had been confident their pick would stand. "This informant in Russia got copies of the game sheets that he played in and there were two exhibition games that Bure played in against league opponents that counted. I think Mr. Ziegler made the right decision based on the evidence."

Vancouver still had to get Bure into a Canucks uniform. His linemates at the WJC — left-winger Alexander Mogilny and centre Sergei Fedorov — had already defected from the USSR to start their NHL careers. Red Army officials weren't keen on seeing the final third depart. The three youngsters had been expected to replace the famous, but aging, KLM line — Vladimir Krutov, Igor Larionov, and Sergei Makarov. But Bure, who'd already completed his mandatory two-year military service, balked at re-signing with the Red Army. Many believe he was left off the Soviet roster for the 1991 Canada Cup as a punishment for this perceived insubordination. The snub likely hastened Bure's decision. With help from a Russian living in California, he flew to the U.S. in September 1991, with father Vladimir, a former Olympic swimmer, and brother Valeri.

In his first interview through a translator, Pavel predicted he would score a lot in the NHL. "He was confident he would score 50 goals ... and that's one of the reasons there was this enormous build up to him," recalled sportswriter Tony Gallagher. Canucks players had the chance to meet their potential new teammate after an early season game in California. Few of them could believe Bure would have an immediate impact. "After the [San Jose] game he came into the room and shakes everyone's hand and I remember we were all thinking, 'This is the guy everyone keeps talking about and he looks like a little school boy. This kid can't weigh more than 50 pounds soaking wet,'" recalled defenceman Jyrki Lumme.

Nonetheless, in October 1991, 20-year-old Bure signed a four-year deal worth US$2.7 million. The Central Red Army protested that Bure was still under contract until after the 1992 Olympic Games in Albertville, France. The two clubs faced off in a U.S. courtroom. The Canucks offered to pay the Russian team $200,000 compensation. The Soviets balked at the offer, demanding $250,000. Anxious to start his NHL career, Bure broke the stalemate himself. He stood up and said he'd pay the difference. Out of the side of his mouth, Burke told him to sit down and shut up. "But he's like, 'No, I want to play in the NHL. If I have to, I'll pay.' He was willing to take $50,000 out of his signing bonus to play," recalled Burke.

The next day, Burke met Bure at the Canadian embassy in Seattle to get his work visa. Wanting to avoid a media crush at the Vancouver airport, Burke made alternate travel plans to get Bure from Washington State to the Pacific Coliseum. "I rented a car and drove him across. He was working on his English the whole drive up, 'What's that?'[he would ask] ... That's a river ..."

Bure's much-anticipated debut with the Canucks was against the Winnipeg Jets less than a week later. On his first shift, wearing No. 10, he accelerated into a whitish blur over the Jets' blueline and gave long-suffering Canucks fans their first real out-of-seat hockey experience. "That might be the most memorable night in the history of the Canucks, his first game," recalled Gallagher. "I would say that really stands out to me as maybe the most fun evening of all time with the Canucks ... from that time forward, every time [Bure] touched the puck, everyone was just incredibly excited."

Although the balletic Russian was kept off the score

sheet, he managed three scoring chances, including a third-period breakaway. He gave every one of the 16,123 at the sold-out Pacific Coliseum reason to believe they had witnessed the debut of a superstar-in-the-making.

Sportswriters struggled to find the superlatives to describe the awesome speed and puck-handling ability of the young Soviet star. "Like a football player taking receipt of a punt at his own goal line, Pavel Bure, the Red Rocket, took off like a lightning bolt, side-stepped a couple of defenders, zoomed past another who mistook him for an X-ray, then darted for the opposing goal," wrote *Vancouver Sun* sports reporter Mike Beamish.

Even Bure's teammates stood up at the bench and watched with amazement as Bure rushed the puck. "In his first game, even guys on the bench, we're going, 'Wow! What a great player!' He's definitely one of the most exciting players I've ever played with. Sometimes you see some guys that can skate like the wind but they can't carry a puck in their pocket but Pavel could handle the puck pretty good and he was a great passer too," recalled Lumme.

Vancouver Sun hockey beat reporter Iain MacIntyre would be largely responsible for creating an appropriate sobriquet for the young Russian. He wrote, "If Winnipeg are the Jets, then what do you call Pavel Bure? How about the Russian Rocket? OK, so maybe some football player named Raghib calls himself that, but it fits Bure perfectly. He is the fastest Soviet creation since Sputnik." The moniker stuck.

Pavel Bure

After the game, the angelic-faced Bure said through an interpreter, "I will remember everything about this night for the rest of my life. Thank you to everybody, the fans, my teammates, and coaches. It was my fault I didn't score." For a reporter like Gallagher, who had been forced to sit in the press box through successive seasons of Canucks hockey mediocrity, Bure was a salvation. "Hip, hip, Bure," he gushed, following the Jets game.

Bure wouldn't need to do much apologizing about his inability to score that season. Vancouver's gift from the hockey gods managed to score 34 goals and 60 points. He earned a Calder Trophy as the NHL's top rookie, appearing in only 65 games.

Igor Larinov, who had joined the Canucks along with Valdimir Krutov in 1989, helped his comrade adapt to the rigors of the NHL and acclimatize to North American culture. New best friend Gino Odjick helped Bure to learn English and to play cards. Bure also proved as a rookie that his rocket-fuelled rushes wouldn't be aborted during the tighter-checking playoffs. In his first post-season, Bure registered six goals and four assists in 13 games, including his first NHL hat trick against the Winnipeg Jets in game six of the opening round.

In his first full season with the Canucks, Bure bettered his own predictions. He notched 60 goals and 50 assists, setting new Vancouver records for goals and points. The sale of No. 10 jerseys began to surpass even those of Trevor Linden's. Pavel-mania had gripped the city of Vancouver. Bure matched his own Canucks scoring record the next season, in 1993-94. His most memorable goal in a Canucks uniform, however, was one scored in the playoffs that season. In game seven versus the Calgary Flames, Bure adeptly took a breakaway pass from defenceman Jeff Brown in double overtime and accelerated past a Calgary defender. He deked Calgary netminder Mike Vernon with a move that put an exclamation mark beside one of the most memorable comebacks in NHL history.

Heading into the championship series, the Russian Rocket was leading the post-season with 13 goals. "He's the most talented player I've ever seen," Canucks captain Trevor Linden proclaimed. Although the Canucks lost in the thrilling finals, Bure finished with MVP numbers: 16 goals and 15 assists in 24 games.

During the lockout-shortened 1994-95 season, Bure still managed 20 goals and 23 assists. The next season, 1995-96, a pall of darkness descended over the Canucks. Bure was checked behind the net by Blackhawks defenceman Steve Smith. He tore the anterior cruciate ligament in his right knee, ending his season after just 15 games.

As he stepped onto the ice for the 1996-97 campaign, Bure didn't appear to possess the same game-breaking speed that haunted the dreams of NHL defencemen. He finished the season with 23 goals and 32 assists, playing in just 63 games. He suffered the lingering effects of a whiplash injury sustained in the first game of the season when Calgary Flames defenceman Todd Simpson had checked him headfirst into the boards. But Bure's injury woes wouldn't be the hot topic of conversation among Vancouver hockey fans for long.

In August of 1997, *Province* columnist Gallagher broke

the biggest story in team history. He reported that Bure had met with Pat Quinn to ask for a trade. Bure didn't deny the story. His mysterious life away from the rink included a rumoured marriage of convenience to an American upon his arrival in the U.S. There were also allegations that he had blackmailed the team for a new contract by threatening to sit out during the 1994 playoffs. Kerry Banks, the Vancouver author of *Pavel Bure: The Riddle of The Russian Rocket,* spent a year researching the enigmatic star, hitting roadblocks on the way. "When he heard I was doing a book on Bure, one hockey writer said to me, 'If Bure finds out, he'll probably have somebody break your legs.' He wasn't smiling when he said it. Whether or not his belief has any basis in truth, it does indicate one unsettling aspect of the way Bure is regarded."

Perhaps most intriguing of the rumours are those of Bure's ties with the Russian mafia. In 1996, the U.S. sports television network ESPN broadcast a report alleging that Bure's business partner in his family's watch-making business, Anzor Kikalichvili, was a Russian mob kingpin. Bure acknowledged hearing the allegations about Kikalichvili but denied the validity of the reports. Canucks general manager Pat Quinn responded, "We're fact-finding right now. Everyone here was kind of surprised."

The allegations resurfaced in 1999 during an investigative report by the CBC's *The Fifth Estate.* Bure denied having a position with 21st Century, a business owned by Kikalichvili. The program later showed the company's Moscow billboards that featured Bure and Kikalichvili together. Bure disavowed any association with organized crime, saying, "Trying to clear your name after such false information was like trying to wash yourself from so much dirt."

But Vancouver hockey fans seemed more shocked to learn of Pavel Bure's trade request than they were to learn of any association he might have with the Russian mafia. Apparently, Quinn had told Bure he would be traded after his first request in 1997. The Vancouver general manager was unable to keep his word after being fired.

Playing for coach Mike Keenan, Bure reiterated his request for a trade. Their dealings grew cold. During a road game against the Ottawa Senators on March 20, 1998, Keenan called Bure a "selfish little suck" after a listless first-period effort. When Bure scored a goal and returned to the bench, he was congratulated by the coach. Bure swore at him.

Despite his volatile relationship with Keenan, Bure appeared to fans as his same old game-breaking self. On April 17, he scored his 50th goal of the season against the Calgary Flames in a 4-2 loss. Two nights later, Bure scored the Canucks' lone goal against the Toronto Maple Leafs in a 2-1 loss. It was his final game as a Vancouver Canuck at General Motors Place.

During the summer of 1998, Bure announced publicly that he wanted out of Vancouver. The Russian star didn't deign to say why exactly as he returned to Russia. He said only that he wouldn't fulfil the final year of his contract with the Canucks. The arrival of a man who was part of the management team that originally brought Bure to Vancouver — new GM Brian Burke — didn't diffuse the situation. Bure refused to return to Vancouver, instead working out with his old Red Army team.

"The question everybody wondered about was why he wanted to leave," said his biographer, Banks. "Bure didn't help because he would never articulate. It was pretty obvious it was the dickering over the contract that bugged him and he didn't like Vancouver. He preferred to live in a bigger city that had a Russian community, like New York or Los Angeles. I think it was pretty simple. He also knew the team was getting worse. It's just the Russian way of trying to force the team to do what they want."

Burke, however, refused to be forced into action, saying he would trade Bure when it suited him. That day was January 17, 1999, when Burke sent the Rocket to Florida in a seven-player deal that brought blue-chip defenceman Ed Jovanovski from Florida. Bure's inexplicable trade demand vexed Vancouver Canucks fans. The superstar who had made Pavel a fashionable name for B.C. newborns became a hockey villain.

Bure made his Panther debut on January 21. Sporting borrowed equipment, the travel-weary Bure nevertheless displayed his usual flair, scoring a pair of goals in just 12:09 minutes of ice time. The first goal was vintage Bure, splitting the defense and deking Islander netminder Felix Potvin.

"It was just like Calgary, wasn't it," Bure said to Vancouver reporter Gallagher after the game. He was referring to his first goal, which looked much like his double OT winner in 1994. "I didn't think about it at the time. I just saw space and went for the breakaway." A knee injury limited Bure to just 11 games with Florida. He made the most of each shift, though, scoring 13 goals and adding three assists. During the 1999-00 campaign, Bure played in 74 games, notching 58 goals and 36 points.

Bure's return to General Motors Place came nearly two years after the trade, on October 16, 2001. The 16,859 fans in attendance booed loudly each time Bure touched the puck. Unfazed, Bure scored at 1:36 of the second period. He gave Florida a 1-0 lead after putting a backhander behind Vancouver goaltender Dan Cloutier. Scorned Vancouver fans got the last cheer, however. Cloutier stoned Bure on an overtime breakaway to preserve a 2-2 tie.

Chapter 4
Gino Odjick: The Algonquin Assassin

t the 1990 NHL Entry Draft held at B.C. Place Stadium in Vancouver, even Gino Odjick was surprised when the Canucks called his name. It happened in the fifth round and drew a smattering of cheers from the 19,127 in attendance. One round earlier, the Canucks had selected left-winger Darin Bader with their 65th pick of the draft. Odjick, figuring he'd have to sit through several more rounds on an empty stomach before hearing his name, left the stadium to grab a quick bite. "I was having a hot dog when I got drafted," Odjick laughed. "They usually have a break after the fourth round so I went across the street. I was ranked in the ninth round so I thought I had a lot of time. Somebody said, 'Hey you were just drafted.' Everybody was looking for me."

When Odjick finally made it down to the Canucks' draft table, he extended a big, scarred mitt to shake hands with his NHL employers. All his new coach, Bob McCammon, could say was, "Geez, we had to draft you. Ron Delorme was pouting ever since the second round every time we picked someone else, we finally had to draft you. You better do a good job in camp, kid."

Odjick made his NHL debut with No. 66 stitched on the back of his jersey, but nobody expected him to play like Mario Lemieux. That's not why Canucks amateur scout Ron Delorme persuaded general manager Pat Quinn to select Odjick with the 86th pick. Odjick had racked up 558 penalty minutes in two seasons with the Laval Titans of the Quebec Major Junior Hockey League, earning himself the nickname, "the Algonquin Assassin."

Delorme convinced the Canucks' management to invest in the brave forward that NHL Central Scouting had projected only as a ninth-round prospect. Delorme, himself a veteran of 524 NHL games and a recipient of 667 PIMs, knew what it took to stick in the league as a tough guy. Perhaps he saw a bit of himself in Odjick. Or maybe he saw other qualities in Odjick that other scouts missed. "Odjick had a real strong Memorial Cup and Ronny was really pushing for him," recalled Brian Burke. "He was emphatic that this kid was more than just a tough guy, that he was going to be a player."

Although the scout had no doubt about Odjick, some

in the organization had reservations. Odjick erased them. "During the Memorial Cup, we saw that he had an excellent shot which none of us had appreciated before, other than Ronnie. And he actually played his position fairly well up and down the wing. It was apparent that he was a better player than we thought," Burke said.

At his first training camp with the Vancouver Canucks, the 6-foot-3, 215-pound full-blooded Algonquin Native turned some heads. He was eager to drop the gloves. During a pre-season, all-rookie game in Calgary, Burke realized that the Canucks hadn't squandered their fifth-round draft pick: "He fought Terry Clark, Wendel Clark's brother, he fought Paul Kruse, he fought everybody."

The Canucks still decided to send him to the minors, although he could have played as an overage player for Laval. Burke admitted he was a little apprehensive about giving Odjick the news. "I remember saying to Mike Penny, 'Look if he comes off that chair and starts a fight with me, you've got to jump in here and give me a hand.' Then I told Gino, 'You've had an excellent camp but we're sending you to Milwaukee.' I'm wondering how he's going to take this news and he looks at me and says, 'I don't have to go back to Laval?' I said nope and he pumped his arm in the air like after you score a goal, he was so excited to get a shot at pro hockey."

Dispatched to the Canucks' International Hockey League farm club, the Milwaukee Admirals, the young heavyweight was told to work on his hockey skills and let his injured right hand heal. Odjick took Burke's advice and learned to throw punches as a southpaw. He got into 20 fights in just 17 games with the Admirals. After scoring a career-high 12 goals as a junior in 1989-90, Odjick continued to score on the farm. He netted seven goals and three assists to go along with his 102 penalty minutes. The Canucks kept a close tab on Odjick's progress in the minors. They were without a natural heavyweight in their lineup.

When Pat Quinn arrived to take over the Canucks in 1987, the big Irishman had inherited a last-place team that lacked toughness. Quinn was a former hardrock defenceman who started his coaching career piloting the brawling Philadelphia Flyers. He found the situation as difficult to stomach as a cheap cigar. Although the Canucks had rugged defenceman Garth Butcher, that was all. Quinn bristled as he watched the Canucks' diminutive forwards Dan Quinn, Robert Kron, Steve Bozek, and Brian Bradley get pushed around. After watching the Flames bully the Canucks during a November 19 tilt, Quinn had had enough.

Two days later, Odjick's phone woke him at five a.m. Milwaukee general manager Phil Whittliff told the sleepy winger that the Canucks had recalled him. Driving to the airport, the rookie asked the GM how long he'd be in Vancouver. Whittliff, a former player who'd been with the Admirals organization since 1972, said: "It's up to you. They called Babe Ruth up on an emergency basis for one game and he stayed in the majors his whole career."

If Odjick was going to stay with the team, he knew he'd need some rest. "I just remember thinking, I better sleep on the flight because I won't get a chance to sleep when I get to Vancouver. I slept the whole way." His flight landed in Vancouver just hours prior to the Canucks' face-off against the Chicago Blackhawks. Veteran Canuck Stan Smyl picked him up at the airport. If he was nervous, the Algonquin Assassin didn't show it. "I knew it would be a whole lot easier in the NHL than it was in the minors," Odjick said. He'd been squaring off against some pretty tough customers — mostly using his left hand. "There was Tony Twist, Link Gaetz, Wendel Clark's brother. I think the guys were tougher in the minors than in the NHL at that time."

When they arrived at the Pacific Coliseum, Odjick realized his stay in Vancouver might be short-lived. "I went into the dressing room and looked at my jersey and it was number 66. That was my training camp number," remembered Odjick. High-digit training camp numbers usually meant the player wasn't expected to make the team. "I thought I better not say anything about this, my first game."

Before the seven o'clock face-off, Canucks trainer Pat O'Neill gave him some gloves that matched his new uniform. Odjick took the opportunity to ask if he'd been called up because the team had injuries. "He told me they got pushed around pretty good against Calgary the game before and Pat Quinn got mad and told Ron Delorme, 'We're bringing up your boy.' So I figured they weren't bringing me up for my goal scoring."

Like most Canadian boys, Odjick had dreamed of playing pro hockey. Growing up on the Kitigan Zizi reserve in Maniwaki, Quebec, Odjick always remembered a visit from Montreal Canadiens forward John Chabot. Chabot, from Summerside, P.E.I., was also a Native who'd played in the Quebec Major Junior Hockey League (QMJHL). "It was inspiring to see someone with the same background. I remember Ted Nolan coming too. They achieved their dreams. When you're from an isolated community like we were, it's not until you actually see them or talk to them that you tend to believe it's possible."

If he didn't play professional hockey, Odjick would have probably joined his father, Joe, as a highrise steelworker. "If it's 15 storeys or more, they hire Indians to do the steel work because we're not afraid of heights," he explained. His father toiled for years above Manhattan. "He left Sunday at 7 p.m. to get working Monday at 8 in New York. He left work on Friday at 4 p.m. and got home at 2 or 3 in the morning." When Odjick Sr. came home from work on the weekends, the firewood still had to be done and the hay had to be brought in. "He taught us how to work, that's for sure. If I wouldn't have been a hockey player, I would have done it."

After playing mostly for his reserve hockey team as a youngster, Odjick had been ignored by junior teams at the Bantam Draft. He was preparing to take welding classes at Ottawa's Algonquin College so he could join his father when the phone rang. "One of my school teachers had moved to the city and his son was playing for a tier two team in Ontario. They were short on players so he asked Bob Hartley, who was coaching the Hawkesbury Hawks, to give me a tryout."

Odjick made the cut and suited up for 40 games, scoring two goals and four assists and piling up 167 penalty minutes. Odjick's toughness caught the attention of Pierre Creamer, coach of the QMJHL's Laval Titans. Visits from Chabot and Nolan may have prompted Odjick to dream about a career in pro hockey, but it wasn't until his second season at Laval that he began to believe he could make it as an NHL heavyweight. "People around me told me I had a chance to be an enforcer at the NHL level if I wanted to. I started doing a lot of push-ups and sit-ups."

Like his boyhood idol, Stan Jonathan, Odjick knew he'd have to fight his way into the league. "I knew my role. The first thing a team asks you when you're an enforcer before you're drafted is, are you willing to do the enforcer role at the pro level?" This is because sometimes players play the role in junior and then try to change their game when they get to the pro level. Odjick told the team, "Well, I'd rather be an enforcer than go to work on the highrises with my dad. I'll have no problem doing this role."

As he stepped onto the freshly cleaned sheet of ice at the Pacific Coliseum for the pre-game skate on November 21, Odjick was quickly reminded of why he was there. He felt the hardened stares of a trio of Chicago Blackhawks enforcers sizing him up. "I was really nervous when I went out on the ice and took warm-up, I was shooting pucks around and I could just tell I had Mike Peluso, [Stu] Grimson and [Dave] Manson looking at me thinking 'Who is this kid? Let's fight him tonight and see what he's got.'"

On his first shift in the NHL, Odjick skated in front of the Chicago net and was cross-checked by smashmouth defenceman Dave Manson. Welcome to the NHL. "So right away I got into that first fight. I wasn't really pleased with that one," Odjick recalled. He wanted a more decisive victory. Early in the third period, Odjick nailed Chicago enforcer Stu "The Grim Reaper" Grimson with a good, clean bodycheck. "Then we squared off and got going. I hit him with a couple of good punches and kind of buckled him a few times and as I was walking off the ice, I could hear the 'Gino-Gino' chant." Bob McCammon said to him, "Well kid, I guess you're going to be here for a while."

Odjick was fearless, answering the bell against all the NHL's heavyweight contenders during his first season. He was even prepared to square off against Saddam Hussein.

Ojdick's triumphant heavyweight debut against the Hawks had come during the first Gulf War. An inspired Canucks fan had scrawled a sign that read: "Gino is tougher than Saddam." Seeing the sign during the warm-up, Odjick asked McCammon to point out Saddam Hussein. "I was just coming out of the reserve and we didn't have cable," explained Odjick, smiling. "I was looking around the ice and saying, where the hell is this Saddam Hussein guy?"

Later, when the Canucks played the Los Angeles Kings, Burke needlessly worried about his young pugilist being ready to take on one of the NHL's top enforcers. "He'd fought everyone in the IHL but you don't know if he's ready for a guy like Marty [McSorley]," said Burke. "As soon as they got on the ice, Gino charged the point and fought him. And then we went into Edmonton and he fought Dave Brown three times. This guy was legitimate heavyweight tough."

A cult hockey hero was born. Fans began chanting "Gino-Gino-Gino" from their seats inside the Pacific Coliseum every time Odjick stepped onto the ice. On November 27, Odjick scored his first NHL goal in a 1-1 tie against the Minnesota North Stars. The moment was especially gratifying for Odjick. As he dug the puck out of the net, he acknowledged his parents, who had been flown in for the game by the Canucks organization. "My dad still has the puck. I pointed up to him," he recalled proudly. Odjick, who grew up with five sisters, said his father used to travel everywhere with him. "I remember going to tournaments and we'd pick him up on the side of the road because he'd be coming back from New York to go to the tournaments."

By the end of the 1990-91 season, Odjick had been unofficially inducted into the Canucks' tough-guy hall of fame, alongside other all-time fan favourites like Dave "Tiger" Williams and Ron "The Chief" Delorme. In 45 games, the Algonquin Assassin had scored seven goals. Perhaps more importantly, he had racked up 296 penalty minutes, most of them fighting majors. Odjick won many of the decisions, developing a rep as one of the toughest heavyweights in the league.

Ron Delorme, Odjick's biggest champion at the draft table, had become a mentor for Odjick when he arrived in the NHL. The pair shared a common heritage and NHL job description. Delorme, a Cree from North Battleford, Saskatchewan, had played nine seasons in the NHL and was known more for his fists than his goal-scoring ability. His fierce scrap with Chicago Blackhawks tough guy Grant Mulvey in game five of the 1982 Clarence Campbell final had been a highlight for fans. He constantly shared his tips with his young acolyte. "Ron Delorme showed me this trick with five-pound weights where you punch 100 times as fast as you can. So when you get in a fight, you can punch really fast," recalled Odjick.

Adjusting to the role of NHL enforcer wasn't the only hurdle Odjick faced. He was, after all, from an isolated reserve where he knew his neighbours. His pastimes included hunting for moose or riding snowmobiles. "Living in a very tight-knit reservation, we had our own way of life and own way of thinking and we're very traditional to our Algonquin culture," Odjick said. In the big city of Vancouver, by contrast, he said, "You don't know where you're going. You don't know where you are."

Once he was in the NHL, though, Pat Quinn taught him

"how to be a professional and how to be the best human being possible." Brian Burke also helped. Odjick arrived in Vancouver sporting his best sweater and slacks. He didn't own a suit or tie. "When we went on the road to play our preseason games, he had no clothes," Burke recalled. "Someone went out and bought him a sports coat and he wore that sports coat every day on the road."

After Odjick was called up from the farm, Burke gave Stan Smyl a couple thousand dollars to take Odjick shopping. "You can't come to NHL games without suits and ties and I didn't have any," Odjick recalled. "He knew if he only bought me one, I'd be wearing the same suit every day." Burke's help extended beyond expanding Odjick's wardrobe. "He really took care of his players. He was like a dad, nobody touched his players."

Odjick recalled one particular night at the Calgary Saddledome after he'd broken his right hand during a fight with a Calgary Flames rookie. In the concourse area of the rink, he was met by Flames general manager Doug Risebrough. The former NHL agitator challenged him to a fight. Brian Burke arrived from the press box shortly afterwards. "Burke told him, 'If you're going to go with anybody, you're going to go with me.' Doug changed his mind and went back up the stairs."

During his second season in Vancouver, Odjick became more comfortable with his West Coast surroundings. He moved to the Musqueam Reserve near the University of

British Columbia. He struck up a friendship with new teammate Pavel Bure, who was also finding it difficult to fit in. Nobody could have predicted a more unlikely friendship. The players were as different on the ice as they were off it. But they were disparate souls drawn together by a shared feeling of culture shock and alienation. "He came over from Russia and he was a Red Russian, very proud of his heritage, and when he came I knew the feeling he had. I started teaching him how to speak English. We were two people who came from completely different cultures than what we were put into."

The friendship blossomed on the ice, too. Both players excelled at the roles they were being paid for. It wasn't long, though, before they learned from each other through osmosis. Odjick scored a career-high 16 goals and 29 points, including five game-winners. Many of them were assisted by Bure during the 1993-94 season. Bure learned how to protect himself when Odjick wasn't in the lineup. During game two of the second-round playoff match-up against the Dallas Stars in 1994, Bure retaliated against the constant abuse he was getting from the Stars. He viciously elbowed tough guy Shane Churla to the ice in the first period. Afterward, Bure was fined $500 by the NHL for his hit. "It's not my style, but I had no choice. They're trying to kill me. I'm lucky I didn't get hurt."

Odjick dressed in only 10 games during the 1994 Stanley Cup playoff run. In those days, the enforcers didn't play in too many playoff games. His most memorable moments in a Canucks uniform often preceded a trip to the sin bin. The Maniwaki Mauler recorded more than 100 penalty minutes in each of his eight seasons with the Canucks. He rewrote the team record book as the most penalized player in club history. His 2127 minutes — the equivalent of more than 35 games — eclipsed Garth Butcher's previous record of 1668 minutes. Odjick also holds the Canucks' record for single-game and single-period penalty minutes. He amassed 47 minutes during an on-ice meltdown against the Los Angeles Kings on November 12, 1992.

Odjick racked up the majority of his career penalty minutes against regular Smythe Division foes like Edmonton Oilers tough guy Dave Brown and Los Angeles Kings policeman Marty McSorley. Interestingly, it was New York Ranger and Toronto Maple Leaf enforcer Tie Domi whom Odjick least liked to take on. "I didn't like fighting Tie Domi because you had to punch down and he had such good balance. Plus you couldn't hurt him. He's probably one of the guys as enforcer you have the most respect for. He's only five-foot-nine and he's taken all comers his entire career. Believe me he's taken a lot of punches. He's turned out to be a pretty good player."

Odjick turned out to be a pretty good player, too, just as his mentor Delorme had predicted. Towards the end of his career, he was playing 10 to 12 minutes per game and scoring 8 to 10 times a year. "That was the goal. I never wanted to fight just to see if I was tougher than one guy. I never wanted to be known as the toughest guy in the NHL. I just wanted to be known as a guy that took care of his teammates."

During his tenure in Vancouver, Odjick won the respect of his teammates, coaches, and the fans. But after the firing of Pat Quinn, Odjick found himself in a scrap that he couldn't possibly win. "I was devastated," Odjick recalled, hearing the news. "Me and Pavel were both so mad and disappointed and we knew we wouldn't be around for much longer. We didn't want to be part of it. Although there were times that Pavel and Pat butted heads, Pavel always knew Pat brought the best out of him. He played his best hockey for Pat Quinn, same with myself."

Mike Keenan's arrival in Vancouver was a harbinger of change for the Canucks. The Algonquin Assassin made the mistake of defending his old pal, Trevor Linden, against Keenan's verbal abuse. While others stared at their skates, Odjick just did what he'd been programmed to do his entire career — stand up for his teammates. "There is no use in slandering Trevor Linden or embarrassing a guy who has devoted his heart and soul to this team," Gino Odjick said later. "I know for a fact that Trevor goes all out every time he laces on the skates. In the eight years I've been here, there's no player I respect more than Trevor Linden."

Odjick's staunch public support of Linden succeeded in showing up Keenan in much the same way the coach had ridiculed the former captain. Keenan wasn't amused. On March 23, 1998, Odjick was traded to the New York Islanders in exchange for defenceman Jason Strudwick. Predictably,

Pavel Bure was upset. "He's my best friend and I'm really disappointed," Bure told Vancouver reporters. "Some people say he's not a great hockey player, but he's one of the toughest players in the NHL and he got 15 goals when he played with me. He's part of Canucks history."

One day later, Odjick came out at General Motors Place wearing an unfamiliar Islanders jersey. In the first period, he dropped the gloves with Strudwick, the player who replaced him in the Vancouver lineup. He won the fight easily. A familiar chant erupted from the stands, "Gino-Gino."

Chapter 5
Captains Canuck: Linden and Smyl

During a pre-game ceremony on November 3, 1991, Stan Smyl's No. 12 jersey slowly inched toward the rafters of the Pacific Coliseum. Newly appointed Canucks captain Trevor Linden slapped his Bauer hockey stick against the boards. He joined the sell-out standing crowd to pay homage to "the Steamer" one last time.

For the long-suffering Canucks fans, it was an emotional moment. Smyl, the longest-serving captain in team history, had played his entire 13-year NHL career with the Canucks. He retired as the team's all-time leader in games played (896), goals (262), assists (411), and points (673). Unofficially, Smyl was also the team's all-time leader in hits, heart, and hustle. During an era of on-ice mediocrity, his hard-nosed play had given Vancouver fans at least one thing to cheer about every time he was on the ice. "He was really all there was, oftentimes he was the only reason to go and see a game," recalled *Province* sportswriter Tony Gallagher. "He played so hard every night. He took so many of the losses to heart, as though it was his fault as captain."

Standing at centre ice with his wife Jennifer and his three children, Smyl was also choking back tears. He told the fans, "You made me a better player and a better person. The faith that you had in the Steamer made the game worthwhile to me."

Smyl had been selected 40th overall by the Canucks at the 1978 NHL Amateur Draft. Not even Canucks general manager Jake Milford could have predicted that Smyl's jersey would one day be retired by the team. In fact, when Smyl arrived at training camp, few believed that the five-foot-eight winger with the awkward skating style had a shot at making the team, let alone become the team's captain and leading scorer.

The NHL scouts who doubted him probably hadn't seen Smyl play night after night for the New Westminster Bruins. The feisty winger developed a redoubtable reputation as a fierce bodychecker with a booming slap shot. He'd led the Bruins to three Memorial Cup appearances. In 1978, after his team won its second straight junior championship, he took home the Stafford Smythe Memorial Trophy as the tournament's MVP. Fixated on measuring height and weight, goals and assists, the scouts had overlooked the fact that there wasn't a caliper device for measuring a player's heart.

Smyl left his home in Glendon, Alberta, as a young teenager to play for the B.C. Junior Hockey League's Bellingham Blazers, a feeder team to the Western Canada Hockey League's New West Bruins. By the time he was 15, Stan had told his mom, "I don't want to go to school. I want to be a hockey player." Legendary Bruins coach Ernie "Punch" McLean recognized Smyl's potential the moment he pulled a Blazers jersey over his head. "I said he would make it to the National Hockey League, not on his skill level at that time, but on his heart."

At his first NHL training camp, Smyl ran over Harold Snepsts. He dropped the Canucks' big blueliner with a thud, grabbing the attention of his teammates and first-year head coach Harry Neale. "Here was this rookie coming in and starting to bang people in training camp, this really got everybody's attention and pissed off a few people. But he didn't back down and he kept running around and he did it from the first day he was there and played himself onto the team," recalled Gallagher. "He was a third-round pick, I don't think he was expected to make the team. We knew who he was and what he brought to the table but no one expected him to make the team. Nobody knew the offensive skills he had with the big shot."

Chris Oddleifson, who captained the Canucks in 1976-77, was among the veterans who took notice. Smyl's jarring hit on the team's undisputed physical leader was "the precursor of his career," he said. "He was going to play the game hard."

At the beginning of the 1978-79 season, the Vancouver Canucks stepped onto the ice sporting garish new uniforms. Behind the bench stood an unknown coach named Harry Neale. A new all-rookie line featured Smyl, Swedish import Thomas Gradin, and left-winger Curt Fraser. The new line received better opening-night reviews than the untraditional yellow "V" uniforms. They combined for six points in an 8-2 shellacking of the Colorado Rockies.

Thirteen years later, as Smyl was being feted at centre ice with a brand new van, a Harley Davidson, and a portrait by North Vancouver artist Glen Green, despairing fans rewound the highlight reel of the Steamer's career. During the 1979-80 season, Smyl had led Vancouver with 31 goals, 47 assists, 78 points, and 204 penalty minutes — the last time any NHLer topped his club in these four categories. Smyl's career included three 30-plus goal seasons. In a memorable trip to the Stanley Cup championship in 1982, he scored nine goals and nine assists in 17 games.

Smyl scored just 10 goals in his final three seasons with the Canucks. But he knew the crash course in leadership that he had given to a callow rookie named Trevor Linden was more important for the organization. "From the first day I met him, I could always tell there was something special about Trevor as a player, but even more so as a person," Smyl said.

Stan Smyl

Outwardly, the two had little in common. Stan Smyl was short and stocky. Trevor Linden was tall and lean. Smyl served his junior apprenticeship over 900 kilometres from his Alberta birthplace, Linden played for his hometown junior squad. Linden had the boy-next-door good looks; Smyl's nose looked like a door had hit it. Smyl was a steam engine fuelled by coal, Linden a V-12 running on premium gasoline. One was picked 40th and hoped to make the team; the other was picked second overall and expected to make the team better.

Linden was a prototype power forward with a 6-foot-4, 220-pound frame. He was the building-block player that Canucks general manager Pat Quinn dreamed about selecting with the second-overall pick at the 1988 NHL Entry Draft. NHL Central Scouting had ranked Mike Modano, a high-scoring centreman from the Prince Albert Raiders, the top pick at the draft. But, according to Brian Burke, "With Pat being in charge, we probably would have taken Trevor anyway. We all respected Mike Modano as a player and saw the offensive gifts that Trevor didn't have. We knew Trevor would be a solid two-way player."

Prior to the draft, the Canucks had brought in all of the top picks, subjecting them to a battery of physical and psychological tests. Modano's interviews with the team were almost flawless. "A great kid," Burke recalled, noting that an assistant coach had doubts only about Modano's choirboy mug. "Jack McIlhargey interviewed him and said, 'We can't take him. He doesn't have one scar on his face.'"

Linden's pre-draft interview didn't go as well. Burke remembered him calling the night before to say, "'My dad said I have to call you because I can't come in for the testing tomorrow.' So right away I thought OK, Lou Nanne [GM of the North Stars] is screwing around here. He's going to take him because Minnesota had the first pick." But the young prospect went on to explain that he had to help with the young bulls on his uncle's ranch. Burke asked him, "What's your job? He says, 'Well, I grab these young bulls by the neck, wrestle them to the ground, and hold them while they brand them and cut their nuts off.'" What could Burke say but, "That's no problem Trevor."

Linden's team-first mentality wasn't the only character trait the Canucks coveted.

When the Canucks drafted Linden, his junior coach at Medicine Hat, Barry Melrose, figured that the Canucks had acquired a future leader. "I expect him to become the captain in Vancouver in about three years," Melrose said at the time. "He's had that [leadership quality] his whole life. He's a character kid. I think you'll see Vancouver got the best player in the draft."

Melrose's bold prediction made sense. As a swizzle-stick-thin teenager with the Medicine Hat Tigers in the Western Hockey League, Linden had carried the team to back-to-back Memorial Cups. In his final season in Medicine Hat, Linden showed scouts that he could also score, netting 46 goals and 64 assists in 67 games. And, as Vancouver Canucks fans would soon find out, Linden's favourite season was the spring. In 16 playoff games with the Tigers that season, Linden scored 13 goals and 12 assists.

A teammate of Linden's in Medicine Hat, Dallas Stars forward Rob DiMaio, also recognized the leadership potential of his teammate early on. "Even when he was 16, 17, when I was with him, he carried himself so much older. He was a mature kid. That's why he was a captain at such a young age and he's continued to be a leader throughout his career. He's first class. Guys look up to him."

During Linden's first training camp with the Canucks in Parksville, B.C., the battle-tested veteran Smyl took him under his wing. Linden acknowledged the influence of Smyl's professionalism on and off the ice. Smyl was a good example for him, Gallagher agreed. He would look out onto the ice and see how hard Smyl played. In terms of skill, however, Gallagher said, "Trevor was thought to have a lot more than Stan and a lot more potential."

Trevor had greater expectations placed on him, too. The team had been so unsuccessful that they had received the second overall pick the preceding year. That showed what kind of shape they were in. They were looking for a lift, and Linden provided it. The 18-year-old finished the 1988-89 season tied for the team lead in goals (30) and second in points (59). He became the first rookie in club history to score 30 goals and be named the team's MVP. The *Hockey News* selected Linden as their rookie of the year. He finished second behind New York Rangers Brian Leetch for the NHL's Calder Trophy, awarded to the league's top rookie.

And like Bobby Clarke, the former gap-toothed Flyers

captain with whom he was compared, Linden played hard when it mattered the most — the Stanley Cup playoffs. In his rookie season, Linden appeared in all seven games of the first-round matchup against the heavily favoured Calgary Flames. Although Calgary won the dramatic series on a controversial overtime goal (scored by crease-crashing centre Joel Otto, just after Smyl's breakaway had been stopped by Calgary goaltender Mike Vernon), Linden proved his playoff mettle. The gangly rookie counted three goals and four assists against the eventual 1989 Stanley Cup champions.

Despite struggling through a minor "sophomore jinx" in 1989-90, Linden finished fifth in team scoring with 51 points and 21 goals. The next season, he became the youngest player to make an appearance at the mid-season NHL all-star game and he led the Canucks team in points.

Before the start of the 1991-92 season, Pat Quinn decided it was time for Stan Smyl's heir-apparent to be named officially. After alternating with teammates Doug Lidster and Dan Quinn the year before, Trevor Linden became the full-time captain of the Canucks. In just his fourth season in the NHL, at 21 years of age, Linden was the youngest captain in the league at the time. The Medicine Hat native thrived under the new pressure and the 'C' over his heart. For the second consecutive year, he led the team in scoring, this time with 75 points. His 31 goals ranked him second on the team.

With Linden's leadership and the arrival of Soviet superstar Pavel Bure in Vancouver in 1991-92, Pat Quinn had assembled the underpinnings of a playoff contender in Vancouver. The Canucks closed out the regular season with a 4-4 draw against arch-rival Calgary on April 16. Setting franchise records with 42 wins and 96 points, the team finished first overall in the Smythe.

After defeating the Winnipeg Jets 4-3 in the first round, the Canucks faced the Mark Messier-led Edmonton Oilers. They lost this series 4-2. The next season, the Canucks' Stanley Cup playoff education continued with a second-round loss to the Los Angeles Kings. Eventually, the Canucks would put the playoff lessons to good use, with Trevor Linden standing at the front of the class.

Linden's definitive moment as captain Canuck came during a miraculous springtime of 1994. Exactly 12 years earlier, Stan Smyl had led the Canucks to an improbable trip to New York in the Stanley Cup final against the Islanders. During the 1994 playoffs, Linden was finally able to grow a playoff beard. He also displayed an enviable combination of leadership, grit, and clutch goal-scoring. If Stan Smyl had been "Captain Crunch," Trevor Linden was "Captain Clutch." Linden finished the 1994 Stanley Cup playoffs with 12 goals and 13 assists in 24 playoff games. His overtime winner against Calgary goalie Mike Vernon forced a seventh and deciding game against the Flames. Against the high-powered New York Rangers, Linden's game seven performance was perhaps the grittiest and most determined of the team's 34-year history. With the Canucks trailing 2-0 after the first

Trevor Linden

period, Linden scored a short-handed goal at 5:21. Mark Messier scored on the power play to make it 3-1. Then Linden scored again on a tremendous individual effort, with 15:10 remaining in the third, to make the score 3-2.

"Trevor is one of those players who rises to all occasions," said defenceman Dave Babych. "Those playoffs were one of them. In game seven, he had guys crawling all over his back and he's still scoring goals. When you can still perform like that, it says a lot for the person. There's a lot of guys who do a lot of talking but a large percentage of them don't follow up in the ice, and he certainly did that, he's done it tenfold over the years."

Although he lost out that time, Linden probably figured he'd get another chance to have his name engraved on Lord Stanley's Cup. Especially after the Canucks signed coveted free agent Mark Messier on July 28, 1997. Messier, after all, had willed the Rangers to the 1994 NHL championship, breaking New York's 54-year Stanley Cup drought. Could he do it for the Canucks?

In 1997, the Canucks travelled to Tokyo, Japan, to face the Anaheim Mighty Ducks in the first-ever NHL game to be played outside North America. Linden chose this "Game One '97" to pass over the team captaincy to Messier with his fistful of Stanley Cup rings. Linden's team-first gesture would later be rewarded with a check-from-behind. Less than a month later, on November 4, 1997, Orca Bay officials fired the man who had drafted Linden and made him the team's ninth team captain.

Predictably, Linden took the news about Quinn as hard as anyone on the team. "In a sense, I kind of grew up with Pat Quinn," Linden said. "I was just 18 when I came here. I was a boy. I've always looked up to him, definitely. From the day I got here, he was someone I respected and valued his trust."

Almost immediately, new coach Mike Keenan clashed with Trevor Linden. Just two games into the Keenan era, Linden injured his groin in practice and missed the next eight games. He returned to the lineup for a December 8 game against Keenan's former team, the St. Louis Blues. Linden made a point of congratulating the third and fourth liners for their efforts. But Keenan, upset about his team's performance, purportedly berated Linden in an expletive-peppered tirade between periods. A month later, Keenan benched Linden for the third period of a 4-2 loss to Montreal. He later questioned Linden's effort to the media: "Trevor has the ability to be a front-line player and he certainly has to demonstrate to his teammates that he's a lot more committed that he is. Trevor can step up his game unless he's not the hockey player everybody in the country, including Team Canada, thinks he is. He's probably playing at a 50 percent level."

Keenan appeared intent on purging the club of players who made up the nucleus of the 1994 Stanley Cup final team, players he referred to as "Quinn's boys." When his responsibilities were expanded to include the authority to make trades, he started to disband the team. In January 1998, Kirk McLean and Martin Gelinas — two of Linden's closest friends on the team — were sent to Carolina in exchange for Sean Burke, Geoff Sanderson, and Enrico Ciccone. In February, Linden learned from equipment manager Pat O'Neill that Keenan had traded him to the New York Islanders in exchange for Todd Bertuzzi, Bryan McCabe, and a third-round draft pick.

Rather than firing verbal shots at Keenan, Linden handled the difficult situation with the same character and class that had made him such a fan favourite throughout his career. "I have to say things weren't going really well here, the team was struggling and I was as well," Linden told reporters. "I was given a lot of opportunity here and things weren't happening for me. So I think it became a situation that was going to happen and it wasn't the biggest surprise."

Keenan appeared more diplomatic at the news conference announcing the Linden trade than he had been behind closed doors. "We are certainly very appreciative of the efforts he has made in this community and we wish him particularly well in the next two weeks representing Canada at the Olympics," said Keenan. "We also wish him a great career in New York. I told him change is difficult but that the change would be good for him. He's still a young man and he has a bright future ahead of him."

Local fans and sportswriters alike lamented the trade. "This was the ultimate team guy, a player who had switched from right wing to centre and turned over his captaincy for the good of the club, being blamed for all of Vancouver Canucks problems by a coach who had a two-month history with the organization," seethed *Province* columnist Kent Gilchrist. "Besides being one of the best players to ever pull a Canucks jersey over his head, Linden did the community work because he wanted to, not out of a sense of duty to those paying his salary."

Linden's contributions in Vancouver extended beyond the rink. Away from the cameras, Linden regularly visited the B.C. Children's Hospital. He also created the Trevor Linden Foundation. He made contributions to the development of Canuck Place, a hospice for terminally ill kids, and created the Captain's Corner suite to host underprivileged kids at GM Place during home games.

Linden's trade began a mini NHL tour of duty for him. A month after being traded to the Islanders, Linden was named the team captain. Two seasons later, he was dealt to the Montreal Canadiens for a first-round pick in the 1999 draft. In Montreal, he was a leader both on and off the ice for two seasons before being moved to the Washington Capitals in a 2001 deadline deal.

On November 10, 2001, new Vancouver general manger Brian Burke re-acquired the former captain. Burke had been the Canucks' director of hockey operations when Linden was drafted in 1988. "We're very pleased to have Trevor back in Vancouver," Burke enthused. "Our expectation is that Trevor will add versatility, leadership, and experience to our forwards."

Burke wasn't concerned about bringing the former Canucks captain back in a new role: "I talked to him before he got on the plane, after we made the trade and said, 'You know we have a captain [Markus Naslund]. I'm not bringing you back as a captain, I'm bringing you back as a player and a teammate.' He said 'I understand that.' I think Trevor is one of those guys that could make any team situation work. I think he has no ego when it comes to winning hockey games."

Who says you can't come home again? "Any time you are traded, there is some anxiety," Linden said, almost a year after the trade back to Vancouver. "Certainly coming back here was a special situation for obvious reasons. I was a little anxious about ...being able to find a home here and fit in and all those things because it was a completely different team from the one I left."

Linden notched his first goal as a renewed Canuck on November 23 at Boston. He finished the season with 12 goals and 22 assists in 64 games. He'd played his best hockey in years and was still the same leader in the dressing room. "He's one of the big leaders on this team," confirmed coach Marc Crawford, a former teammate of Stan Smyl. "He's a very big part of our identity, both past and present, and that can't be understated."

Linden would later say that the trade back to Vancouver had rejuvenated his career. "Last year was the most fun I had playing hockey in four or five years. It was a pretty neat experience." On November 25, 2002, in his first full season back with the Canucks, Linden scored his 263rd goal as a Canuck against Minnesota. He had surpassed his one-time mentor, Stan Smyl, for the team's all-time lead in goals. Linden finished the season with 19 goals — his highest output since his

1995-96 season with the Canucks. Perhaps more importantly, he helped the Canucks reach the second round of the playoffs for the first time since 1995-96.

On March 8, 2004, during the infamous game against the Colorado Avalanche in which Todd Bertuzzi sucker-punched Steve Moore, it was Stan Smyl's turn to applaud his former protégé. Linden's pair of assists in the second period against the Avs gave him 674 regular-season career points. As synonymous with the franchise as No. 12, Linden had finally surpassed his mentor as the top point-getter in Canucks history. Although he wasn't on the ice, Smyl deserved an assist on the play.

Chapter 6
The 1994 Stanley Cup Run

Even a decade later, when asked about the seminal moment of the Canucks' trip to the 1994 Stanley Cup championship series, Vancouver fans offer an almost unanimous response: "The Save."

The Save is Vancouver sporting vernacular shorthand for the overtime stop Kirk McLean made in game seven against the Calgary Flames. It's one of the most memorable, most replayed highlights in the team's 34-year history: McLean flying across the crease, his pads stacked, to save a one-timer off the stick of Flames winger Robert Reichel and preserve a 3-3 tie in overtime. The trigger-happy goal judge had already pressed the red-light button, but McLean's skate toe kicked the puck out at the last second. A video review of the save confirmed the puck had not crossed the line.

The sellout crowd inside the Olympic Saddledome — along with a coast-to-coast *Hockey Night in Canada* audience — watched in disbelief. Breaking down the right wing, Theo Fleury had led the three-on-one rush over the Canucks blueline. As he cruised past the face-off dot, he made a deft cross-ice pass to Reichel, a 40-goal scorer. McLean anticipated the pass. "It's tough not to play the man with the puck [Fleury] and I was able to read him a little, then lay over to the man [Reichel] with the puck," McLean said after the game. "Did I know the red light came on behind me? No. I didn't."

The Save would "rank as one of the all-time saves in playoff history," declared one Calgary reporter. But McLean's game-saving heroics set up another event that Canucks fans consider the other seminal moment in the 1994 Stanley Cup playoffs: The Goal. At 2:20 of the second overtime period in the same game, Pavel Bure received a pinpoint pass from defenceman Jeff Brown that sent him blurring past Flames defenceman Zarley Zalapski. Breaking in alone on Mike Vernon, Bure deked the Flames' netminder and slid the puck in the net. The Canucks' memorable come-from-behind series victory was thus concluded in dramatic fashion. "Most people would pick that as the most dramatic goal that the Canucks have ever had," said the team's legendary play-by-play man Jim Robson.

But before The Save, before The Goal, there was The Curve.

Rewind to game five. After the Canucks had shocked the Flames 5-0 in game one, Calgary easily won the next three contests. Game five at the Olympic Saddledome, most agreed, would likely be the last 60 minutes of hockey for the Vancouver Canucks that spring. "There hardly was a soul who didn't think the series was over, and that would probably include the players," said Robson. At the end of regulation time, the game was tied 1-1, with Pavel Bure recording his first goal of the series. That's when the pivotal moment of the Canucks' Stanley Cup playoffs took place. It didn't happen on the ice, but rather outside the Canucks dressing room, between the third period and the start of overtime.

Canucks left-winger Geoff Courtnall, a 26 goal-scorer during the regular season, stood in a small corridor outside the dressing room working on the blade of his Easton. He used a propane blowtorch to give it a wicked bend. "I stepped on it and put a big curve on it. Pavel was out there with me and he said, 'What are you doin'?' and I said 'If I get one shot, it's going high,'" Courtnall recalled. "The places to shoot on Vernon were high glove and five hole. I just thought that if I got a chance, I'd shoot high."

Courtnall got an opportunity eight minutes into overtime. As he cruised down the boards the puck bounced between Calgary defenceman Kevin Dahl's legs and onto his Easton. Courtnall accelerated towards the Flames goal and wired a slapshot from the face-off circle, past Vernon's outstretched glove hand. "Somebody was cutting me off, so I just

Geoff Courtnall

shot it, over his shoulder," Courtnall recalled.

The dramatic overtime winner was a carbon copy of the goal scored by his former Oilers teammate Wayne Gretzky on Vernon during the 1988 Stanley Cup playoffs. "Wayne scored over Vernon's shoulder. On the same exact shot. On the same play down the wing. I just thought: 'If I get a chance today down the wing, I was going to try him over his shoulder because he comes way out,'" Courtnall told Eric Duhatschek of the *Calgary Herald* after the game. "It's just exciting to go home with life. We were up against the wall."

Jim Robson agreed that Courtnall's goal changed the Canucks' playoff trajectory that year. "His goal made it an overtime win and now the series is three games to two ... it's another series. The Courtnall goal really seemed to bring the team together and gave them new life. That got them going."

The goal extended the series, and the confidence, of the Canucks. "When we started the playoffs, I didn't think we had a chance against Calgary. They were the team favoured to win. We struggled all year for consistency. We had great players but we never seemed to find our stride. In the playoffs, Pat [Quinn] tried some different line combinations to balance things out and it seemed to work," Courtnall recalled.

For Courtnall, the OT winner offered a redemption. Prior to game five, the winger's penchant for the marathon shifts had been singled out during an impassioned speech by the Canucks' coach. "Pat Quinn thought Geoff Courtnall was staying on the ice too long and at the end he'd take a penalty and then take another long shift," recalled teammate Gino Odjick, who played 10 games in the 1994 playoffs. "Pat said in the old days if a soldier disobeyed the general, it would be considered mutiny and they'd put his head on the log, 'I'd cut your head off if we were in those days.' He punched a Gatorade cooler and it went flying. Nobody moved or said a word. And boy, that changed the whole team around. We won the next three games and there was nobody staying out there for long shifts," Odjick laughed. "In my view that's what changed the whole thing around right there. Pat Quinn let us know there was no room for individuals."

And when the big Irishman spoke, players listened. He was an intimidating presence, but he'd also won the respect of his players for his loyalty and the manner in which he treated them. Each player in the dressing room had been brought to the Canucks' organization by Quinn. Many had been offered a second chance in Vancouver, like talented defenceman Jyrki Lumme, whose career had stalled in Montreal. "He liked to teach. He didn't play any head games. When he was pissed off, he would put his fist down. He had respect for the guys. He was the best man for the job by far," said Lumme.

Quinn also had history with Vancouver. He had played for the 1970 expansion Canucks for two seasons before being selected by the Atlanta Flames in the Expansion Draft and later becoming their team captain. He then stepped behind the bench as the coach of the Philadelphia Flyers in 1978-79. He earned the Jack Adams award as the top coach in the NHL one season later, after his team finished with 116 points. After four successful seasons on Broad Street, Quinn left hockey to attend law school. He returned to the NHL as the coach of the Los Angeles Kings in 1984-85. The Griffiths family hired Quinn as GM and VP in 1987. Canuck faithful had, by then, sat through 11 consecutive losing seasons. Before the arrival of Quinn, they'd had little to cheer about except for a surprise trip to the Stanley Cup final in 1982.

The Canucks finally had a hockey czar, but the hiring was mired in controversy. Because Quinn had signed with the Canucks while still under contract with the Kings, the NHL fined the organization $310,000 and suspended Quinn. A British Columbia Supreme Court ruling later reduced the fine to $10,000 and allowed Quinn to assume his role as the team's new president.

The big Irishman set out to rebuild the franchise and change the hockey culture in the Vancouver dressing room. Quinn immediately began adding depth to the talent-thin franchise by swapping one talented player for two or more prospects. He made his most important swap on September 15, 1987, when he traded the team's most talented offensive player, Swede Patrik Sundstrom, to the New Jersey Devils in exchange for Greg Adams and Kirk McLean. Quinn's next underpinning was a lanky winger from the Medicine Hat Tigers named Trevor Linden.

In 1989, under the Quinn regime, the Vancouver Canucks qualified for the Stanley Cup finals for the first time in three seasons. In the opening-round against the first-place Calgary Flames, the Canucks surprised hockey pundits by stretching the series to game seven, losing in a heartbreaking OT.

Quinn's knack for acquiring castoffs from other NHL clubs and turning them into valuable contributors became evident in the playoffs that season. Earlier in the year, he had acquired a talented but fragile defenceman, Paul Reinhart, and a useful but undersized forward, Steve Bozek, from Calgary for a third-round draft pick. Both players played prominent roles in the playoffs against Calgary, with Reinhart registering five points in seven games.

Quinn continued to cobble together a Stanley Cup contender at the 1989 NHL Entry Draft in Bloomington, Minnesota. He gambled a sixth-round draft pick on a young Soviet named Pavel Bure. Quinn's "five-year plan" for rebuilding the Canucks franchise began to manifest itself on the ice. During the 1991-92 season, the Canucks finished first in the Smythe Division, setting a franchise record with 96 points. The Canucks continued to improve on the ice in 1992-93, finishing with 101 points, again atop the Smythe. Quinn kept on giving up his proven players in return for packages of lesser stars. No trade was more important than the deadline deal on March 5, 1991. It packaged longtime Canucks blueliner Garth Butcher and forward Dan Quinn in exchange for Cliff Ronning, Sergio Momesso, Geoff Courtnall, and Robert Dirk from St. Louis. Ronning gave the team a deft, play-making centre. Momesso was a robust winger. Courtnall had a knack for scoring key goals, and Dirk was a crease-clearing, stay-at-home defenceman. On that same day, Quinn also acquired defenceman Dana Murzyn from the

Calgary Flames. Expendable in Calgary, Murzyn patrolled the Canucks blueline for years.

Despite the continual upgrade of talent and size, the Canucks had yet to grow a full playoff beard. In 1992, the team rallied from a 3-1 series deficit to defeat the Winnipeg Jets in the Smythe Division semi-final. In the division final, the playoff-tested Edmonton Oilers defeated the Canucks 4-2. A year later, the Canucks again defeated the Jets in the opening round but lost to the Los Angeles Kings in the second round 4-2.

Heading into the 1993-94 season, expectations were rising for the first time among Canuck faithful. Incredibly, Quinn had turned the sad-sack team into a playoff contender. The Canucks started the campaign as the hottest team in the NHL, compiling a 7-1 record. But as the season went sideways, the hoped-for Stanley Cup parade route down Robson Street was cancelled. The team stumbled, finishing the season only one game above .500, and second in the Smythe division. During the season, Quinn was widely criticized for not re-signing Petr Nedved, the Canucks' first pick at the 1991 draft. As the contract stalemate continued, the highly skilled Czech signed with the Blues. On March 14, the Canucks received their compensation: centreman Craig Janney and a second-round pick. Most agreed Quinn had swung a good deal until Janney balked at playing for Vancouver. Quinn was then forced to make a trade for defencemen Jeff Brown and Bret Hedican and rookie forward Nathan La Fayette. The fans decried the trade at the time, but Pat Quinn would later be feted as a hockey genius. His patience and faith in players he had brought to Vancouver was starting to pay off.

After Geoff Courtnall's OT winner against the Flames in game five, it was young captain Trevor Linden's turn to be the hero in game six. Linden moved to centre ice for the Calgary series to help mitigate the Flames' size down the middle. He scored a power-play goal at 16:43 of the first overtime period. The Canucks' 3-2 victory set up Pavel Bure's heroic breakaway deke in game seven. The Canucks had won three straight overtime games.

The Canucks wouldn't have long to savour the victory. Next stop, Dallas. The Stars had finished the regular season seventh overall, seven spots ahead of Vancouver. But Pat Quinn had the team believing. In game one, Martin Gelinas scored the game-winning goal at 15:21 of the third. Kirk McLean stopped 35 pucks as the Canucks won 6-4. McLean posted his second shutout of the playoffs in game two as the Canucks returned to Vancouver leading 2-0. Dallas won game three of the series, 4-3, in Vancouver. The Canucks' overtime streak continued in game four. Sergio Momesso scored at 11:01 of overtime, giving the Canucks an opportunity to advance to the conference semifinals for only the second time in the club's history. Pavel Bure scored twice in game five as the Canucks cruised to a 4-2 victory. After the game, defenceman Jeff Brown said, "When Pavel Bure scored that overtime goal to beat Calgary last series, we pulled together, looked at each other, and realized we had a rare opportunity."

The Canucks faced the Toronto Maple Leafs in the conference final, again opening the series on the road. In game one, the Canucks found themselves in an unusual position, losers of an OT game. The Canucks rebounded in game two with a 4-3 victory. Defenceman Jyrki Lumme scored the game-winner at 4:14 of the third period, breaking the Leafs' home ice advantage. Back at the Pacific Coliseum, games three and four belonged to Kirk McLean. The table-hockey-style goaltender stopped each of the 29 shots the Leafs fired at him in both games. The back-to-back shutouts gave McLean four for the playoffs, equaling an NHL record.

Desperate not to go golfing, the Leafs played a strong game five. They staked themselves to a 3-0 lead after the first period on goals by Wendel Clark, Doug Gilmour, and Mike Eastwood. The Canucks responded with three goals in the second period. Pavel Bure extended his playoff-scoring streak to a Canuck-record 15 games on a goal by Greg Adams. Murray Craven and Nathan La Fayette also scored for the Canucks. Overtime took just 14 seconds to determine the winner. B.C. native Greg Adams scored on Felix Potvin to earn the Canucks their first trip to the Stanley Cup since 1982.

"This is unbelievable, this is what you work for, this is what you dream about," an ecstatic Quinn told reporters after the game.

Just as it had been 12 years before, the Canucks had made the Stanley Cup championship against a team from

New York. And once again, their team was the heavy underdog. Led by their captain, Mark Messier, the New York Rangers had won the President's Trophy as the first-place team in the NHL, finishing with 112 points — 27 more than Vancouver. In their only other Stanley Cup final appearance in 1982, the Canucks had lost four straight to the New York Islanders. Many believed a similar fate awaited the team this time.

But in hockey, a hot goalie can steal a series. In game one, Kirk McLean faced 54 Rangers' shots. Blueliner Bret Hedican, one of Quinn's late season acquisitions, scored the Canucks' first goal. Martin Gelinas, a player plucked off the waiver wire from Quebec in January, scored on a deflection with just 60 seconds remaining in the third period. The game went to sudden-death overtime. Then Greg Adams scored at 19:26 of overtime. It was the Canucks' sixth overtime victory in the playoffs that season.

The Rangers won the next three games, taking a 3-1 series lead, thanks to defenceman Brian Leetch, who scored four goals in 180 minutes of hockey. In game five, with the Stanley Cup inside Madison Square Garden, the never-say-die Canucks looked to spoil a Broadway-sized celebration. Defenceman Jeff Brown's goal gave the Canucks a 1-0 lead after two periods. They built up an insurmountable-looking 3-0 lead early in the third before the Rangers tied the game at 3-3. Dave Babych scored the game-winner at 9:31 of the third. "It looked like the Rangers were going to the Cup and then Babych scored and the Canucks win it 4-3 so coming home, everybody's all pumped up," recalled a relieved Robson.

Game six turned out to be the most exciting game ever played at the Pacific Coliseum. Facing elimination for the fifth time in the 1994 playoffs, Geoff Courtnall provided the Canucks with another pivotal playoff moment. With less than two minutes remaining in the third period, the Victoria native scored what appeared to be his second goal of the night, making the score 4-1. But the red light failed to come on and the play continued. The Rangers went back down the ice and captain Mark Messier scored on a confused-looking McLean with 58 seconds remaining. The referee believed Courtnall's shot had hit the crossbar, so he hadn't blown the whistle. "We were high on the east side doing radio and Tom Larscheid and I could see the puck definitely went in and out and the official didn't stop the play. Everybody knew it was in and then the Rangers score," recalled Robson. Fortunately for the Canucks, the 1994 playoffs marked the first year the NHL used video review. After Messier's tap-in had apparently made it a one-goal game, NHL officials replayed Courtnall's phantom goal. It counted, and as Robson described, "The place goes crazy. From a Canucks' standpoint, certainly the game six of '94 was the best ever."

Jeff Brown added two goals during the game. At one point in the game, *Hockey Night in Canada* TV cameras zoomed in on Petr Nedved, who was in the stands at the Pacific Coliseum. Seeing this, fans chanted, "Thank you,

Petr," in reference to the fact that Brown, along with Hedican and La Fayette, had come to Vancouver in exchange for the Czech. After the game, Pat Quinn told Eric Duhatschek that those three players Nedved fetched had helped put the Canucks in contention for the Cup. "We like Petr. I didn't want to ever lose him. But those things happen and we were fortunate to get the three kids we did. They really filled out our roster and gave us depth. I don't think it's any secret — without that depth we wouldn't be here today."

It was back to Gotham City for game seven. The Rangers got off to a 2-0 lead and the Canucks' chances of a Stanley Cup victory looked bleak. At 5:21 of the second period, though, Trevor Linden scored a shorthanded goal. New York restored their two-goal advantage when Mark Messier scored on the power play. Linden, playing his most dominant game in a Canucks jersey, scored again at 4:30 of the third period. But the closest the Canucks came to tie the game pinged off the crossbar. Nathan La Fayette took a pass from Courtnall and backhanded the puck past goalie Mike Richter only to hit the iron.

Geoff Courtnall, although he had won a Stanley Cup with Edmonton, said the 1994 run in his native British Columbia remains a career highlight. He had scored a Canucks record of three game-winning goals. Did the stick with which he scored the game five winner against Calgary have a legal curve? During a *Hockey Night in Canada* interview that never aired, Robson asked Courtnall about the curve on his Easton.

"I said, 'You mean that you won that game with an illegal stick?' He said, 'But nobody checked in overtime.'"

Chapter 7
Markus Naslund: Dizzy Heights

The swap of disappointing draft choices hardly made newspaper headlines in Vancouver. Markus Naslund came to the Canucks on March 20, 1996, when general manager Pat Quinn sent his team's 1991 first-round pick, Alex Stojanov, to the Penguins. Naslund had asked for a trade from Pittsburgh after being moved off the club's top unit. "I really want out of here and I'm happy to be in Vancouver," Naslund said after the deadline deal. "It took a while. I'm looking forward to getting more chances to play and a fresh, new start."

He had been drafted to score goals. The Pittsburgh Penguins used their first choice, 16th overall, at the 1991 NHL Entry Draft to select Naslund. General manager Craig Patrick had every reason to believe he'd added another sniper to a

Stanley Cup dynasty-in-the-making. That May, the Penguins had hoisted the Stanley Cup and the team looked poised for another set of diamond-encrusted championship rings. Naslund was supposed to add more firepower to a team that already boasted the likes of Mario Lemieux and Czech rookie sensation Jaromir Jagr.

Patrick liked Naslund's strong hockey pedigree. The talented left-winger grew up in Ornskoldsvik, a small pulp and paper town on the east coast of Sweden famous for exporting talented players to the NHL. As a young boy, Naslund dreamed about playing in the NHL, just like his idol Hakan Loob, who won a Stanley Cup with the Calgary Flames in 1989. During his peewee years, Naslund played against another future NHLer, Peter Forsberg. "It was basically me against Peter," Naslund said, recalling the first time playing against Forsberg. "I think we won 9-8 and we both scored seven goals."

The two players would be arch-rivals until Naslund turned 16 and both began playing for the same junior hockey club. Born just 10 days apart, the pair have been friends, teammates, or competitors ever since. At the 1993 World Junior Championship in Gavle, Sweden, Naslund played on a line with Forsberg and Niklas Sundstrom. He led the competition with goals and finished second in assists and points. His 13 goals still stand as a tournament record.

But the NHL would have to wait. Before joining the Penguins, Naslund — like many Swedish players — decided to hone his skills at home. Playing for the powerful club MoDo with old pal Forsberg, he scored 22 goals and 39 points during the 1992-93 season. Having proven himself in the Swedish Elite League, the 5-foot-11, 195-pounder figured he was then ready for the NHL.

Joining the Pittsburgh Penguins prior to the 1993-94 season, the highly touted Swede struggled to acclimatize himself in the NHL. The players were bigger, the ice surface was smaller, and the intensity much greater than in the Swedish game. He made his rookie debut on October 5, 1993 against the Philadelphia Flyers. It took more than a month for the young winger to score his first NHL goal during a 3-3 tie on the road against the St. Louis Blues. Naslund dressed for 71 games in his rookie season and recorded only four goals and 11 assists. His sophomore campaign didn't prove to be any more satisfying. During the lockout-shortened 1994-95 campaign, he dressed for 14 games with the Pens, registering two goals and two assists.

As Naslund would later admit, his inauspicious start in the NHL forced him to face a type of on-ice adversity he wasn't prepared for. "It was the first time in my whole career that I didn't have any success. I was used to being the star or at least one of the better players. All of the sudden, I was on the fourth line and they didn't even care if I dressed."

Naslund seriously contemplated zipping up his hockey bag and returning to the more familiar Swedish Elite League. But, wanting to prove he belonged in the NHL alongside other elite players like Forsberg, he returned for another season. The start of the 1995-96 season looked like it might be a breakthrough campaign for the forward. Playing on a line with superstar Lemieux, Naslund showed flashes of the brilliance he'd shown as a youngster. In 66 games, he'd netted 19 goals and 33 assists. But after being demoted from the Lemieux line in December, the 22-year-old winger was again questioning his future with the Pens.

While Naslund struggled to find his NHL scoring touch, countryman and friend Forsberg seemed born to play in the NHL. In the lockout-shortened 1994-95 season, Forsberg scored 15 goals and 35 assists and won the Calder Trophy as the league's top rookie. Forsberg finished the 1995-96 season with 30 goals and 86 assists in 82 games. He was fifth overall in NHL scoring. Naslund, meanwhile, hoped a change of locale to Vancouver would jumpstart his floundering NHL career.

In 10 regular-season games with the Canucks, Naslund managed only three goals — a hat trick versus the Calgary Flames on April 13. In the first round of the Stanley Cup playoffs, Naslund would then face-off against Forsberg and the Colorado Avalanche. The Avs beat the Canucks in six games. In his first-ever playoff appearance, Naslund scored a goal and two assists. Forsberg, meanwhile, scored 10 goals and 11 assists as the Avs went on to sip bubbly from Lord Stanley's Cup.

During the 1996-97 season, Naslund fired a career-high

21 goals, finishing fifth among the Canucks with 41 points. He tied for second on the team with four game-winners. That summer, he looked forward to returning to the rink. But, after the team's pitiable start to the 1997-98 season, GM Quinn and coach Tom Renney were both replaced.

Mike Keenan, an intolerant coach with a short fuse, scrutinized Naslund's play and found it wanting. He almost immediately benched the winger. On January 5, Naslund returned to the ice after three straight games as a healthy scratch. He scored a goal and an assist in a 3-2 victory over the Los Angles Kings. Although he was back in the lineup, he still had a lot to prove to Keenan, who'd publicly questioned the Swede's intensity. Naslund voiced his own displeasure over his lack of playing time to local reporters. He'd started the season on the first line but he was dropping fast. A headline in the *Vancouver Sun* read: "Naslund asks to play — anywhere: The Vancouver Canucks forward informed the team he'd like a trade if he cannot get regular ice time."

It was a difficult time for Naslund who, at times, appeared lost on the ice. He finished the season with 14 goals and 20 assists. His future in Vancouver was far from certain. During the off-season, he and close friend Adrian Aucoin, a Canucks defenceman also suffering from Keenan's wrath, went on a fishing trip in Sweden. Naslund confided to the blueliner that he was considering another trade request.

Naslund started the 1998-99 season on the fourth line with Brandon Convery and converted defenceman Bert

Robertsson — hardly the type of creative linemates that would allow Naslund to display his offensive skills. Again Naslund searched for answers. "My first year here, he was very frustrated," recalled Brian Burke. "We had a slow start and Mike Keenan was here and he wasn't getting the proper ice time and he was very frustrated. I sat down with him and said, 'Look Markus, it's a new situation and you have to be patient.' He did not ask for a trade or bitch about his ice time or bitch about anything. He was just very frustrated because the puck wasn't going in. I got several trade offers for Markus my first year so I sat down with him and said, 'I'm not trading you Markus. If things don't improve for you here, there might be a coaching change in the future but you're not going anywhere.'"

Then fate intervened: Alexander Mogilny suffered a knee sprain. It moved Naslund to the Canucks' top line with Mark Messier and rugged right winger Brad May. "Keenan had no alternative but to play Markus, he didn't have anyone else so he had to play him, he kept throwing him out and Markus just thrived," Gallagher recalled. Naslund made the most of the opportunity, scoring 19 points in the next 13 games. His game was finally reflecting the offensive potential scouts had projected years earlier. "Mike pushed him and goaded him, and to some degree Naslund believes that a lot of that pushing and goading helped," said Gallagher. Keenan's tough-love approach had, after all, jumpstarted the flat-lining careers of future all-stars Chris Pronger and Joe Thornton. "At the same time, in the back of Markus's mind, he always felt that all he needed was a chance to get on the ice. And it took injuries for that to happen," Gallagher added.

Naslund finished the season with a career-high 36 goals and 66 points. Playing with Messier most of the season, he averaged 20 minutes of ice time and took 205 shots on net. His play earned him a spot on the World Team for the 1999 NHL all-star game in Tampa. Naslund's confidence and ice time grew exponentially. He was having fun again, and with it came points. In 1999-00, he led the Canucks in scoring with 27 goals and 38 assists. Naslund surfaced as one of the team's brightest offensive talents and as a leader in the locker room.

With so many top Swedes on their roster, the Canucks held their 2000-01 pre-season training camp in Stockholm, Sweden. The return of Mark Messier to the Rangers had left the Canucks without a captain. Burke told Coach Crawford he had to come back to him with a recommendation for team captain. The coaching staff went around and around, never coming up with a different name. "They talked about Todd [Bertuzzi] they talked about Jovo [Ed Jovanovski], but it kept coming back to Markus. So we met in my hotel suite and Crow said, 'We're naming Markus captain,' and I said, 'Good for you, I think it's a great choice.'" On September 15, 2000, Markus Naslund became the first Swedish captain of the Canucks.

Naslund appeared comfortable shouldering the burden

of the "C" stitched on his jersey. He scored a career-high 41 goals — the most ever scored by a Canucks captain — despite suffering a season-ending broken leg on March 16. Naslund's remarkable season helped the Canucks to their first playoff encounter in five seasons. Unfortunately, without Naslund in the lineup, the Colorado Avalanche swept the plucky but undermanned Canucks.

Naslund's on-ice ascendancy earned him a new contract in the summer of 2001. Vancouver Canucks president and general manager Brian Burke announced that the team had extended their star captain's contract through the 2004-05 season. Naslund, who had one year remaining on his previous deal, had agreed to a three-year extension. "We're very pleased to reach this long term agreement with Markus," Burke said. "He has demonstrated the class, integrity, and leadership required to be a great captain in this league, and we couldn't ask for a better person to lead the Canucks into the future."

After signing his name on a contract that paid him more than US$5 million per season, Naslund registered another career-best campaign in 2001-02. He finished second in the NHL's Art Ross race with 90 points in 81 games. He also became the only player in franchise history to lead the league in scoring after January 1 and was named to the NHL's first all-star team by fan balloting. He didn't disappoint, netting a hat trick and an assist, while being named the game's second star.

"Nazzy," as he's known to his teammates, was also making the players on his line better. In 2002-03, Todd Bertuzzi scored a career-high 97 points and 46 goals. The line's centre, Brendan Morrison, was also flourishing, establishing career highs with 25 goals and 46 assists. "I'm in a situation in which I can accomplish things — Markus has made me a more patient player," linemate Bertuzzi told *Sports Illustrated.* "Before, I'd want to get the puck off my stick as soon as possible. Markus saw me differently, as a guy with skill. Now I'm holding onto the puck, using the extra second to do something creative."

Besides raising the level of his teammate's play, Naslund was also earning recognition as one of the NHL's elite players. At the 2003 NHL Players Association (NHLPA) awards luncheon held in the Hockey Hall of Fame, Naslund made hockey history. A 10-year NHL veteran at 29, he had enjoyed another career season with the Vancouver Canucks. Blessed with one of the league's best wrist shots, the flashy left-winger had scored 48 times and added 56 assists for a career-high 104 points. Naslund had also established a new single-game career high when he scored a goal and added five assists against the Atlanta Thrashers on February 25. He led all NHL sharpshooters with 12 game-winning goals and 56 power-play points. Had it not been for boyhood friend Peter Forsberg, who scored a hat trick on the final day of the NHL regular season, Naslund would have captured the league's scoring derby. Instead, he finished two points behind

Forsberg, who netted 29 goals and 77 assists. Naslund finished runner-up for the Art Ross Trophy — awarded to the top point-producer in the NHL during the regular season — for the second straight season.

Still, none of that mattered. Senator Frank Mahovlich, a member of the Hockey Hall of Fame, presented Naslund with the 2003 Lester B. Pearson Award as the most outstanding player during the NHL regular season. Named after the former prime minister, the award had been handed out since 1970-71. Boston Bruins forward Phil Esposito is the first name on a list of winners that includes the game's greatest stars. Wayne Gretzky won the award five times. Mario Lemieux's name is engraved on the trophy four times. As the other two nominees, Forsberg and Joe Thornton of the Boston Bruins, applauded him, Naslund collected the hardware dressed in a dapper beige suit, blue shirt, and matching tie. He became the first Vancouver Canuck and the first Swedish-born player to win the prestigious award.

For Naslund, like the recipients before him, receiving recognition from his opponents was the highlight of collecting the award. "I can honestly say this one is special, even though it doesn't get the publicity the Hart Trophy gets," Naslund said earnestly. "It's still a neat thing when your peers vote for you." One of the players who voted for Naslund was Forsberg, who told reporters, "I think he had a great year. He deserved it."

Naslund talked to reporters about the indelible imprint

Marcus Naslund

that playing on a line with former Canucks captain Mark Messier, a two-time winner of the Pearson award, made on his career. "Anytime you're around greatness, which I look at him [Messier] being, I think you try to pick up things. Just trying to see how he tried to keep the team tight, not only on the ice but off the ice, that's the stuff that you try to remember," Naslund said.

The dizzy heights of glory Naslund experienced that muggy June afternoon in Toronto stood in stark contrast to the high-altitude sickness he had once suffered as a healthy scratch — watching his teammates from the GM Place press box. After several disappointing seasons, Naslund had at last fulfilled the potential that ranked him among the elite prospects prior to the 1991 Draft.

Along with the recognition from his peers, Naslund had also become one of the league's most marketable superstars. In 2003, Nike Canada selected Naslund as one of the stars of the company's "Light It Up" campaign. The television commercials were designed to inspire young players to embrace a more offensive style of play and to foster excitement about the beauty of the game of hockey. In one 60-second spot, the talented left-winger chases a puck out of the hockey arena onto a busy street, down an alleyway, and into a hotel restaurant kitchen. He crashes through a plate-glass window of a hotel lobby and then grabs a cab back to the hockey rink. Nike Canada spokesman Derek Kent said, "We chose Naslund as a Nike athlete because he represents what the Light It Up campaign is all about: bringing creativity and offense back into the game. That is what he does for the Canucks every time he laces his [skates] up."

Naslund also answers the tough questions each time he

unlaces his skates.

Vancouver fans adore Naslund's candor. Vancouver sportswriters throng to No. 19's locker stall — win, lose or draw. Unlike his linemate Bertuzzi's antagonistic rapport with local reporters, or some of his other teammates' penchant for platitudes, Naslund can be counted on for an honest, articulate summation of the game.

On the final day of the 2003 season, the Canucks lost to the Los Angeles Kings, giving the Colorado Avs the division title and Peter Forsberg the Art Ross Trophy. Naslund bluntly told the fans: "As you can see, we're pretty upset. We choked. We'll play a lot better in the playoffs." While many local pundits accused the Canucks of trying to get Naslund the puck in that game so he could win the Art Ross Trophy, Naslund said he wasn't concerned about personal awards. "I would have been perfectly happy had we won the division and that was my goal today."

Following a disappointing loss to the Minnesota Wild in the second round of the 2003 Stanley Cup playoffs, Naslund finally trumped his old friend Peter Forsberg. On the final day of the next (2003-4) season, he scored his 35th goal of the season. The Canucks defeated the Edmonton Oilers 5-2, ending the Avs' nine-year reign as Northwest Division champions. "We're happy about winning the [Northwest Division] title but we all know that's not what we're playing for," Naslund told a crush of reporters around his stall after the game.

Despite suffering a hyper-extended elbow February

16, and losing linemate Todd Bertuzzi on March 8 to a season-ending suspension, Naslund finished the season with 84 points in 78 games. It was his sixth-straight season as the team's top point-producer.

The Canucks' title-clinching victory set up a first-round playoff match-up against the Calgary Flames. The hard-hat team had finished three spots behind the Canucks in the West. Superstitious Canucks fans seemed delighted about the first-round match-up. The last time the teams had met in the playoffs in 1994, the Canucks won a seven-game series and advanced to the Stanley Cup final for the first time in a dozen years.

But after a series-opening 5-3 victory, the Canucks' season again ended in bitter disappointment. The Flames prevailed in a seventh-game overtime thriller on a goal by former Canuck Martin Gelinas.

The dispiriting loss and looming NHL labour dispute led to considerable speculation. Naslund, in his final year of a contract with the team, may have played his final game in a Canucks uniform. Naslund had intimated in the past that he might not sign another NHL contract. Would he return to Sweden to play in the Swedish Elite League and raise his three young children? Naslund admitted that 2003-04 had been the most draining season in his career due to his injury, the Bertuzzi incident, and all the media scrutiny. He told reporters his future in Vancouver depended on the NHL and NHLPA signing a new collective bargaining agreement in the summer. "I've got one more year on my deal and if there's a season, I'm definitely planning on coming back."

If not, Naslund's last assist as a member of the Vancouver Canucks will be replayed for years to come. With the Canucks trailing the Flames 2-1 in the dying seconds of game seven, Naslund rushed the puck from inside his own blueline. With just 5.7 seconds left on the clock and barely any fans in their seats, he deked his way in front of the Calgary net. His shot was banged in by linemate Matt Cooke to tie the game. Burke commented, "For that rush, there's only three or four guys in the National Hockey League that can make that play and he's one of them. It was just electrifying."

Chapter 8

Brian Burke: The GM Back in Place

The news was blunt and jarring, like a two-handed crosscheck. Orca Bay Sports and Entertainment had ended popular Pat Quinn's 10-year stint as hockey boss. "John McCaw and the ownership of the Vancouver Canucks have stated their desire to field a Stanley Cup competitor, but others have expressed concern about where we're at," Orca Bay deputy chairman Stan McCammon announced.

The most successful era in Vancouver Canucks history wound up abruptly as disbelieving Canucks fans heard the news on November 4, 1997. To make matters worse, Orca Bay officials didn't have a replacement candidate for Canucks general manager and president in mind. Instead, interim GM duties were spread between Orca Bay senior vice- president Stephen Bellringer, manager of hockey operations Steve Tambellini, and assistant GM Mike Penny. Nine days later, mercurial coach Mike Keenan was hired to replace Tom Renney. The power structure of the Canucks' organization was confused further.

Just as fans attempted to reconcile the fact that the Griffiths family-run Canucks had morphed into a cold-hearted corporation, they were jolted again. On January 2, the team traded goaltender Kirk McLean and hardworking forward Martin Gelinas — two heroes from the 1994 Stanley Cup final team. Later that month, Keenan continued the ignominious disbanding of the 1994 team by trading Vancouver fan favourites, Trevor Linden and Gino Odjick, to the New York Islanders. The Canucks, for years the laughingstock of the NHL because of inept management, poor records, and dubious uniform choices, had become a joke once more.

A decade after hiring Quinn away from the Los Angles Kings, the Canucks were again in a desperate search for a new hockey boss to lead the team back to the top of the standings. Handicapping the list of candidates for the general manager vacancy, *Vancouver Sun* reporter Mike Beamish included former Canucks vice-president and director of hockey operations Brian Burke with Cliff Fletcher, Mike Keenan, John Muckler, and Mike Gillis. Beside Burke's bio, Beamish wrote: "Anyone familiar with Burke's competitive nature knows he's spinning his wheels at the head office in New York, and he dearly would love another shot a building a team, as he did with middling results in Hartford." But, Beamish continued knowingly, "He might be too much of a loose cannon for those corporate, image-is-everything folks at Orca Bay."

Not long ago, visitors walking through the lobby of Gate 5 at General Motors Place were greeted by a photograph of Brian Burke taken during his playing days in the American Hockey League — bearded and helmet-less, blood rushing down his face. The image epitomized Burke's approach to the game, both as a player and more recently as a hockey executive. "I think belligerence is an asset ... show me a successful person who didn't stubbornly adhere to what they believed in. Successful people believe in themselves and don't back down," Burke said.

Fortunately, reclusive Vancouver Canucks owner John McCaw, who'd made his fortune in the telecommunications industry, had the sense to telephone Brian Burke. Burke seemed eager to return to Vancouver, despite getting advice to the contrary. Although former Canucks GM Pat Quinn had been positive about the Vancouver hockey market, most GMs in the NHL fraternity believed employment in Canada posed a much greater challenge — a weaker Canadian dollar and more critical press. "I was advised by people I really respect not to even think about the Vancouver job, but I knew the city and I knew the market and I knew it was one of the greatest hockey towns in the world and I love Vancouver," Burke said.

The official announcement of Brian Burke's hiring on June 22, 1998, heralded a new sheriff in town. He wasn't shooting blanks. "I want to be crystal clear about this, I have been given authority over the entire hockey operation," Burke said at a press conference held in the bowels of GM Place. He had arrived sporting a pair of Vancouver Canucks cufflinks that had been given to him during his going-away party in 1992. But he knew he'd have to roll up his sleeves in order to turn the fortunes of the floundering club around.

To shape the Canucks into a more competitive team on the ice, Burke also knew he would first have to make the team more competitive off the ice. In 1998, the high-salaried last-place team had lost $36 million while playing in front of rows of empty seats. Their season ticket base was around 7000. "When I got here, this team was bleeding red ink, not just leaking red ink, it was gushing," he recalled. "To me there was no alternative but for somebody to come in here and say, 'We're not going to run this like somebody's hobby; we are going to run this like a business."

Burke's hockey resume made him the perfect man for the job. Born in Rhode Island and raised in Minnesota, Burke didn't start playing hockey until he was 13. Despite what he called "limited ability," he managed to crack the Providence College team as a walk-on. He later earned a full scholarship and the team captaincy. After Providence, Burke signed with the Philadelphia Flyers. He played for the team's American Hockey League farm club, the Maine Mariners, during the

1977-78 season. The Mariners won the Calder Cup and Burke was undefeated in 10 fights, racking up three goals and five assists in 65 games. He knew, however, that his skill level had taken him as far as he could get on the ice. He decided to hit the books instead, gaining acceptance to Harvard Law School. He practiced law for six years in Boston as a player agent. Then he received a call from a man he'd gotten to know in the Philadelphia organization, the same man to whom he'd later loaned his law books — Pat Quinn.

Quinn had been hired in 1987 by Arthur Griffiths to rebuild the perpetually struggling Vancouver franchise that had just finished its 11th season in a row under .500. Quinn's first move was to hire Burke as his vice-president and director of hockey operations. Burke was put in charge of the team's scouting system, its farm team, and negotiating all players contracts. In five seasons, the pair of Irishmen built a 59-point bottom dweller into a 96-point Smythe Division champion. "He gave me my first shot here and I'm forever grateful for that," Burke said of his mentor Quinn.

Burke returned to Vancouver to take over Quinn's job as president and general manager of the Canucks in the summer of 1998. The tough-talking Irishman didn't back down from anyone: the local press, opposing general managers, NHL officials, player agents, and — occasionally — his own players. And while his blunt personality annoyed some people, he was also the most sought-after quote in the NHL. A sample of Burke's most memorable smart bombs:

On rookie goalie Alex Auld becoming starter Dan Cloutier's backup for the 2003-04 season: "There's no way that Alex Auld was going to be on the team this year unless he flew to France during the summer and bathed in the holy waters at Lourdes."

On unrestricted free-agent winger Trent Klatt: "If Trent can get three years at over a million dollars from someone else, God bless him, I'll drive him to the airport."

On the officiating during the Canucks' first-round series against the Detroit Red Wings in the 2002 Western Conference quarter final: "I want to point out that Todd Bertuzzi does not play for Detroit. It just looks like it because he's wearing two or three red sweaters all the time."

On the media: "We never start these fights. Like a general manager never wakes up and says, 'Hey who can I fight with today in the media?' We pick up the newspaper and read some garbage story that should be at the bottom of a bird cage, or wrapping a fish, or in the corner of a kitchen for a puppy ... and if it's something about our hockey team that is untrue or unfair ... we fly off the handle and react."

On Pavel Bure's trade request: "The inmates don't run the asylum. If a player wants to be traded, that's fine but he's got a contract to play here. And the only way a player gets traded in my organization, is if it upgrades my organization."

On Burke himself: "I think fans would agree, whether they like me or hate me, that when I'm talking, I'm telling the truth. It may not be what they want to hear. I don't have media consultants. It's me."

Burke's bombastic quotes marked a welcome departure from the usual formal GM-speak of the NHL. The fact that the tough-talking Burke backed up his words made him one of the most successful general managers in the history of the Vancouver franchise. Burke's return to the West Coast was greeted by both the local hockey fandom and hockey beat reporters much like the triumphant return of a sheriff to a lawless frontier. Even for a hockey franchise rich in misadventure and dubious uniform design, the seven months that preceded Burke's arrival represented the nadir of the modern-era Canucks.

Vancouver was Burke's biggest challenge as a hockey executive. He inherited a last-place team in complete disarray. The Canucks finished the 1997-98 season with a pitiful 64 points — seventh overall in the Pacific Division and second-worst overall in the entire league. Not even the off-season free-agent signing of Mark Messier, a player expected to take the Canucks deep into the Stanley Cup playoffs, helped. To make matters worse, Pavel Bure, the club's first and only 60-goal scorer, desperately wanted to be traded. "It was a tough first month on the job," Burke admitted. "Your superstar says, 'I don't want to play here anymore,' and we lost Jyrki Lumme that summer too. We lost one of our best defencemen and our best forward."

Most troubling to Burke, however, was the prevailing perception of the team as overpaid and underachieving.

"The team had totally lost touch with the community and the business community. To me it was, 'OK we can't fix the product right away, to turn a team around takes time but we can certainly address the other two issues.'" Burke, a tireless worker who only takes time off on St. Patrick's Day, began a hockey blitzkrieg. He met with season ticket holders, held town meetings, attended chamber of commerce meetings, and agreed to speaking engagements. "I was doing three or four of those a day," recalled Burke. Canucks players, meanwhile, stepped off the ice and into the community. They campaigned for literacy, visited hospitals and schools, and showed they cared.

Growing up in a large, Irish Catholic family may have made Burke belligerent, but it also taught him the value of a dollar. Running a Canadian-market team, Burke realized he'd have to fight hard to save money in order to stay economically viable in a Canadian market. The Diet Coke-sipping GM began watching the Canucks' operating budget as closely as the calories in his soft drinks. After arriving in Vancouver, he began trimming player payroll while improving the team in the standings — something believed impossible by most free-spending NHL general managers. That's not to say, however, that Burke the businessman wasn't sometimes at odds with Burke the hockey man. "The way the sports model works is the GM wants to improve the product so he spends more money. We had to improve the product while we spent less money," he explained. The decision not to exercise the option on Mark Messier's $6 million contract was gut-wrenchingly difficult, but Burke felt the team couldn't afford the salary. He also had to unload high-priced Soviet superstar Alex Mogilny in a trade to New Jersey in exchange for Brendan Morrison and Denis Pederson. The decision was again based on the economics of the game.

Paying his players not a penny more than fair market value was a philosophy Burke had adopted when he worked as Pat Quinn's chief contract negotiator. Vancouver player agent Ron Perrick remembered sitting across from Burke at the negotiation table during his first stint with the Canucks. "What you see is what you get with Brian. If he thinks he's right, he's not going to pussy foot around. He does his homework and makes you work for every inch," said Perrick, whose NHL clients include Cliff Ronning and Rod Brind'Amour.

Burke made no apologies for his hardball negotiating tactics. "The players have to fight for the money here. Our philosophy is to pay what is fair, but if you pay players a penny more than market value then you've wasted a penny."

Paying fair market value wasn't the only way he kept the team's payroll manageable. Burke could tell you down to the nickel exactly what it costs to take a cab from GM Place to the airport. He could also tell you that if he's going on an overnight business trip, it's cheaper for him drive to the Vancouver airport and pay for overnight parking. If the trip is longer than three days, it's less expensive to take a cab and leave his SUV parked at the rink. "That's how closely we watch the money here," he said.

To turn the Canucks around a second time, working in a much chillier NHL economic climate for Canadian teams, Burke relied heavily on lessons learned from his two biggest hockey mentors, Quinn and Lou Lamoriello. At Providence, Burke had been coached by the longstanding New Jersey Devils president and general manager Lamoriello. Burke claimed, "In terms of the modern era on how to put a team together, Lamoriello is the architect. If you can't create massive revenues and you have to keep an eye on what you spend, you don't have a choice, you've got to watch those costs and contain them."

As a player's agent, Burke was equally cost conscious, refusing to take on clients who didn't abide by his prescribed budget limit on what players could spend on new cars and clothes with their first NHL contracts. "You hire me, I work hourly, and you agree to these rules in terms of budget, or you get somebody else," Burke explained to prospective clients. One year, when the dollar limit for a new car happened to be $14,000, according to the "Burke Rules," Winnipeg rookie Peter Taglianetti called his agent from a Saab dealership. The young defenceman told Burke he'd talked the car dealer down to $14,400. "Can I buy the car?" he asked. "I said, put the dealer on the phone," Burke recalled. "The car dealer gets on the phone and I said, 'In 30 seconds you're either selling him that car for $14,000 or he's walking out the door. He says 'OK.' Peter gets back on the phone and I say, 'You're OK for the budget this year.'"

However, Burke knew that fiscal responsibility alone wouldn't put fans in the seats at GM Place. Burke's first major move as GM in Vancouver was the January 1999 blockbuster trade that sent petulant Soviet star Pavel Bure to the Florida Panthers for Ed Jovanovski and others. The deal he made one week later may have been the seminal moment in turning around the franchise, though.

On January 24, 1999, Burke hired Marc Crawford, a coach who had won the Stanley Cup as the bench boss of the Colorado Avalanche in 1996. In 1994, "Crow," as he was known, had been named the youngest recipient of the Jack Adams trophy, awarded to the league's top coach. "I think bringing Crow in was a huge step toward bringing the credibility of the franchise back; not only did it get rid of the unpopular Mike Keenan, but people knew Crow as a winner."

Burke and Crawford also could agree on a style of hockey they wanted the team to play. When he interviewed Crawford, Burke reiterated that he didn't want to play the suffocating, defensive brand of hockey that had become in vogue in the NHL. "I wanted to play an entertaining style, no trap, no left-wing lock, none of that crap, I want to skate. I want to trade chances. In Canada, fans don't want to watch the trap. You're not going to get them into the building playing a conservative style. We played a run-and-gun entertaining style," Burke said.

Burke's blueprint for building a strong organization also called for developing a strong nucleus and farm system through the draft. When Burke left the Canucks to take over the floundering Hartford Whalers during the 1992-93 season, he had started the team's rebuilding process with a blockbuster deal on draft day. It landed him Chris Pronger, a defenceman who had matured into a Norris Trophy-calibre blueliner. Burke again made a headline-grabbing deal at the 1999 NHL Entry Draft in Tampa. He acquired the second and third overall picks in order to take Daniel and Henrik Sedin.

In 1999-2000, Burke's team enjoyed a 25-point turnaround. One season later, the Canucks qualified for the Stanley Cup playoffs for the first time in four seasons. In 2001, fellow GMs voted him the *Sporting News* NHL Executive of the Year. By 2002-03, the moves Burke made on and off the ice had managed to improve his club's points for the fourth consecutive season. Finishing with a club-record 104 points, the Canucks also made the playoffs for the third straight year. Burke had managed to cut losses significantly, getting the payroll to a more manageable level. He improved the quality of the game on the ice, which led to an increase in the season ticket base in 2003.

At the start of the 2003-04 season, Burke's playoff-tested Canucks set out for their ultimate goal — the Stanley Cup. Focus shifted away from the team in February, however. Burke made newspaper headlines and lit up the phone boards at local radio call-in shows after he described himself as a "lame-duck GM." Burke, of course, was referring to the fact that his contract with the Canucks would expire on July 1, 2004. Stan McCammon, the CEO of Orca Bay Sports and Entertainment, said the Canucks' ownership would deal with Burke's contract at the end of the season. Such assurances didn't assuage the displeasure of the fans. They feared losing the architect of the dramatic franchise turnaround. One fan started a Web site called signbrianburke.com, imploring fans to sign an online petition for the club to re-sign Burke. An online survey conducted by the *Vancouver Sun* showed that 75.6 of respondents wanted Burke back at the helm.

Burke's Irish bluster would ostensibly cost him his job as the president and general manager of the Vancouver Canucks. After an unexpected first-round exit in the 2004 Stanley Cup finals to the Calgary Flames, Seattle-based billionaire John McCaw decided not to renew Burke's contract. McCammon declined to talk to the media about why Brian Burke's contract had not been renewed. Many speculated that the fractious relationship between the two men led to the Canucks boss's dismissal. "I think I've had a very good relationship with Brian. That has no play in this decision," countered McCammon. "Brian's probably done as masterful a job in taking a franchise that was in the position we're in and turning it [around]. Obviously, in doing so, he's had a great deal of support from a variety of people, but at the end of the day, he's the one, to use his [Burke's] term, who had the hands on the wheel.'"

After the firing of Brian Burke, it was the media's turn to be belligerent. "Either there's a problem between Burke and McCammon or Orca Bay just dumped the best GM in franchise history on a whim. Given this market's investment in this team, it deserved some kind — any kind come to think of it — of explanation on Monday," wrote *Province* columnist Ed Willes.

Vancouver Sun columnist Gary Mason also seethed over the firing of one of the hockey club's most successful and popular general managers with no explanation from ownership: "Well, let me say the whole thing stinks. The decision, the pathetically weak and cowardly response by ownership, the whole thing. It's like the day they fired Pat Quinn, except this time they remembered to thank the guy for his years of service."

Given Burke's record as the GM of the Canucks, it seems unthinkable that he was "trumped." He arrived in Vancouver to inherit a bottom-dwelling 64-point team. Burke quickly turned the team into an 83-point playoff team in two seasons. His team made four straight playoff appearances and had back-to-back seasons of more than 100 points. The Canucks had a season ticket base of 16,600 and 86 straight sellouts. Off the ice, Burke had similar success: the introduction of pay-per-view games and a venture into a lottery partnership. Sure, Burke was often at odds with the media, and he didn't exactly fit the profile of an Orca Bay executive. But the building was sold out and the team had just won its first divisional title in 11 years.

At his final press conference with the Vancouver media, Burke wasn't his usual belligerent self, choosing instead to take the moment to thank all those who had helped him along the way. He named everyone from the Canucks' scouting staff to owner John McCaw for the opportunity to run the organization. Burke didn't mention McCammon, however, intimating that personal relationships had played a role in his demise. "Irishmen are supposed to be good at politics. I guess I'm not because I have not figured out this part of the job."

Three days after the Canucks decided not to renew Burke's contract, the organization hired his former right-hand man, Dave Nonis, as the new general manager. The ninth GM in team history must now attempt to break the curse of Black Tuesday — the day the team lost a lottery wheel spin for future Hall-of-Famer Gilbert Perreault — and bring Lord Stanley back to the West Coast for the first time since 1915.

Further Reading

Banks, Kerry. *Pavel Bure: The Riddle of the Russian Rocket.* Greystone Books, 1999.

Boyd, Denny. *The Vancouver Canucks Story.* McGraw-Hill Ryerson, 1973.

Gallagher, Tony and Gasher, Mike. *Towels, Triumph and Tears: The Vancouver Canucks and their Amazing Drive to the 1982 Stanley Cup Final.* Harbour Publishing, 1982.

Jewison, Norm. *Vancouver Canucks: The First Twenty Years.* Polestar Press Ltd., 1990.

MacIntyre, Iain. *Vancouver Canucks.* Creative Education, 1996.

Rossiter, Sean. *Vancouver Canucks: The Silver Edition.* Opus Productions Inc., 1994.

Acknowledgments

I want to thank all those who took the time to share with me their engaging stories about the Vancouver Canucks: Kerry Banks, Brian Burke, Greg Douglas, Tony Gallagher, Orland Kurtenbach, Chris Oddleifson, Gino Odjick, Jim Robson, Darcy Rota, and Tiger Williams. I would also like to acknowledge the excellent sportswriters of the *Vancouver Sun, Vancouver Province, Calgary Herald, Edmonton Journal,* and *New York Times,* for supplying many of the quotes contained in these stories. Denny Boyd's *The Vancouver Story* and *Tiger: A Hockey Story,* written by James Lawton, were also valuable sources for quotes in this book. Thanks to Michael Harling for his guidance and Trevor Doull for his exhaustive newspaper clipping library from the 1982 Stanley Cup playoffs. Special thanks to Kara Turner of Altitude for the opportunity to write this book and editor Joan Dixon for adding the varnish. Finally, I'd like to thank Heather and Graham MacKenzie for all their support.

Photo Credits

Cover: Jack Murray / Vancouver Canucks Archives; Paul Bereswill / Hockey Hall of Fame: page 29; Doug MacLellan / Hockey Hall of Fame: pages 50, 82, 92; O-Pee-Chee / Hockey Hall of Fame: page 76; Dave Sandford / Hockey Hall of Fame: page 114.

About the Author

Justin Beddall is a National Magazine Award winning writer whose mother bought him a standing-room-only ticket from a scalper to game four of the 1982 Stanley Cup final at Vancouver's Pacific Coliseum when he was 12. He has followed the team ever since. Currently a sports reporter for the *North Shore Outlook* newspaper, he has also written for *Vancouver Magazine*, the *Vancouver Sun*, and *BC Business* magazine.

AMAZING STORIES

also available!

ISBN 1-55153-797-4

AMAZING STORIES

also available!

ISBN 1-55153-794-X

AMAZING STORIES

also available!

ISBN 1-55153-798-2

AMAZING STORIES

also available!

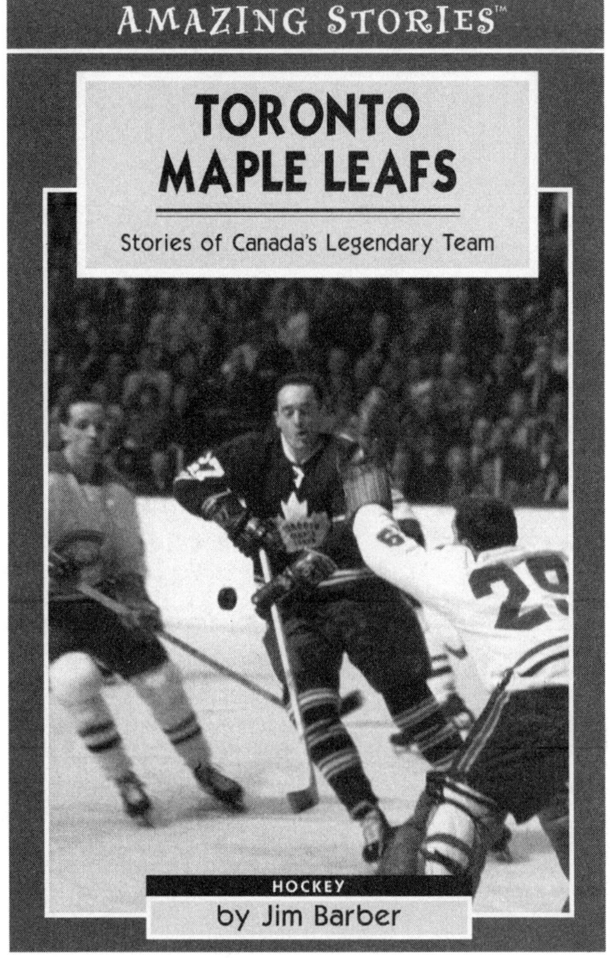

ISBN 1-55153-788-5

AMAZING STORIES

also available!

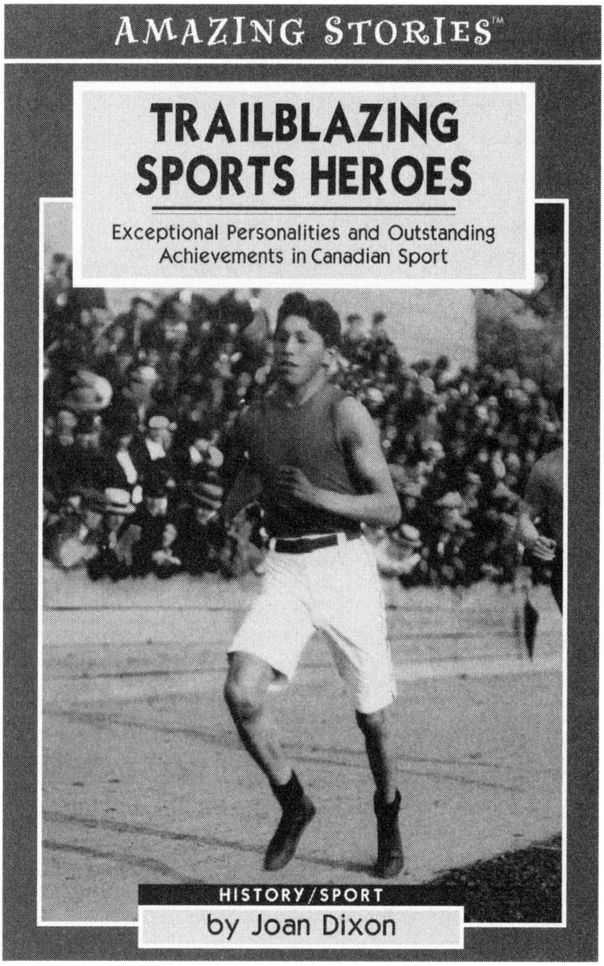

ISBN 1-55153-796-4

OTHER AMAZING STORIES

ISBN	Title	ISBN	Title
1-55153-959-4	A War Bride's Story	1-55153-951-9	Ontario Murders
1-55153-794-X	Calgary Flames	1-55153-790-7	Ottawa Senators
1-55153-947-0	Canada's Rumrunners	1-55153-960-8	Ottawa Titans
1-55153-966-7	Canadian Spies	1-55153-945-4	Pierre Elliot Trudeau
1-55153-795-8	D-Day	1-55153-981-0	Rattenbury
1-55153-972-1	David Thompson	1-55153-991-8	Rebel Women
1-55153-982-9	Dinosaur Hunters	1-55153-995-0	Rescue Dogs
1-55153-970-5	Early Voyageurs	1-55153-985-3	Riding on the Wild Side
1-55153-798-2	Edmonton Oilers	1-55153-974-8	Risk Takers and Innovators
1-55153-968-3	Edwin Alonzo Boyd	1-55153-956-X	Robert Service
1-55153-996-9	Emily Carr	1-55153-799-0	Roberta Bondar
1-55153-961-6	Étienne Brûlé	1-55153-997-7	Sam Steele
1-55153-791-5	Extraordinary Accounts of Native Life on the West Coast	1-55153-954-3	Snowmobile Adventures
		1-55153-971-3	Stolen Horses
		1-55153-952-7	Strange Events
1-55153-993-4	Ghost Town Stories	1-55153-783-4	Strange Events and More
1-55153-992-6	Ghost Town Stories II	1-55153-986-1	Tales from the West Coast
1-55153-984-5	Ghost Town Stories III	1-55153-978-0	The Avro Arrow Story
1-55153-973-X	Great Canadian Love Stories	1-55153-943-8	The Black Donnellys
		1-55153-942-X	The Halifax Explosion
1-55153-777-X	Great Cat Stories	1-55153-994-2	The Heart of a Horse
1-55153-946-2	Great Dog Stories	1-55153-944-6	The Life of a Loyalist
1-55153-773-7	Great Military Leaders	1-55153-787-7	The Mad Trapper
1-55153-785-0	Grey Owl	1-55153-789-3	The Mounties
1-55153-958-6	Hudson's Bay Company Adventures	1-55153-948-9	The War of 1812 Against the States
1-55153-969-1	Klondike Joe Boyle	1-55153-788-5	Toronto Maple Leafs
1-55153-980-2	Legendary Show Jumpers	1-55153-976-4	Trailblazing Sports Heroes
1-55153-775-3	Lucy Maud Montgomery		
1-55153-967-5	Marie Anne Lagimodière	1-55153-977-2	Unsung Heroes of the Royal Canadian Air Force
1-55153-964-0	Marilyn Bell		
1-55153-999-3	Mary Schäffer	1-55153-792-3	Vancouver Canucks
1-55153-953-5	Moe Norman	1-55153-989-6	Vancouver's Old-Time Scoundrels
1-55153-965-9	Native Chiefs and Famous Métis	1-55153-990-X	West Coast Adventures
1-55153-962-4	Niagara Daredevils	1-55153-987-X	Wilderness Tales
1-55153-793-1	Norman Bethune	1-55153-873-3	Women Explorers

These titles are available wherever you buy books. If you have trouble finding the book you want, call the Altitude order desk at **1-800-957-6888**, e-mail your request to: **orderdesk@altitudepublishing.com** or visit our Web site **at www.amazingstories.ca**

New **AMAZING STORIES** titles are published every month.

Comments on other *Amazing Stories* from readers & reviewers

"Tightly written volumes filled with lots of wit and humour about famous and infamous Canadians."
Eric Shackleton, *The Globe and Mail*

"The heightened sense of drama and intrigue, combined with a good dose of human interest is what sets Amazing Stories *apart."*
Pamela Klaffke, *Calgary Herald*

"This is popular history as it should be... For this price, buy two and give one to a friend."
Terry Cook, a reader from Ottawa, on ***Rebel Women***

"Glasner creates the moment of the explosion itself in graphic detail...she builds detail upon gruesome detail to create a convincingly authentic picture."
Peggy McKinnon, *The Sunday Herald,* on ***The Halifax Explosion***

"It was wonderful...I found I could not put it down. I was sorry when it was completed."
Dorothy F. from Manitoba on ***Marie-Anne Lagimodière***

"Stories are rich in description, and bristle with a clever, stylish realness."
Mark Weber, *Central Alberta Advisor,* on ***Ghost Town Stories II***

"A compelling read. Bertin...has selected only the most intriguing tales, which she narrates with a wealth of detail."
Joyce Glasner, *New Brunswick Reader,* on ***Strange Events***

"The resulting book is one readers will want to share with all the women in their lives."
Lynn Martel, *Rocky Mountain Outlook,* on ***Women Explorers***

CALGARY FLAMES

AMAZING STORIES

CALGARY FLAMES

Fire on Ice

HOCKEY

by Monte Stewart

PUBLISHED BY ALTITUDE PUBLISHING CANADA LTD.
1500 Railway Avenue, Canmore, Alberta T1W 1P6
www.altitudepublishing.com
1-800-957-6888

First published 2004

Publisher	Stephen Hutchings
Associate Publisher	Kara Turner
Editors	Stephen Smith, Joan Dixon

We acknowledge the financial support of the Government of Canada through the Book Publishing Industry Development Program (BPIDP) for our publishing activities.

Altitude GreenTree Program 
Altitude Publishing will plant twice as many trees as were used in the manufacturing of this product.

We acknowledge the support of the Canada Council for the Arts which in 2003 invested $21.7 million in writing and publishing throughout Canada.

Canada Council for the Arts   Conseil des Arts du Canada

National Library of Canada Cataloguing in Publication Data

Stewart, Monte, 1962-
Calgary Flames / Monte Stewart.

(Amazing stories)
Includes bibliographical references.
ISBN 1-55153-794-X

1. Calgary Flames (Hockey team)--History.
I. Title. II. Series: Amazing stories (Canmore, Alta.)

GV848.C28S74 2004 796.962'64'09712338 C2004-903745-5

Printed and bound in Canada by Friesens
4 6 8 9 7 5 3

In memory of Ed Whalen

Contents

Prologue

March 9, 1991: Calgary Flames vs. St. Louis Blues
It was supposed to be just another regular season game, but he made it one to remember.

According to the scouts, he was too small to play in the National Hockey League. The Flames had only drafted him — in the eighth round in 1987 — because their Salt Lake City farm club needed someone who could help boost sagging attendance. Calgary's general manager at the time, Cliff Fletcher, thought the fans would love his determination, his speed, and his feisty play. The GM was right.

But the kid from Manitoba surprised almost everyone by making the Flames. Fletcher was so impressed with his progress that he gave up Brett Hull to the Blues. The Golden Brett had become a superstar there and given St. Louis one of the most potent power plays in the league.

Tonight, it was the job of "the Littlest Flame," as he was known, to stop Hull when Calgary was killing penalties. But he didn't just stop Hull, he commandeered the puck and scored a shorthanded goal. And then another. And then another. He scored three shorthanded goals as Calgary doubled the Blues 8-4. No other Flame — no other player in the NHL — had ever done that.

And Theoren Fleury is only one of the amazing parts of the story of the Calgary Flames.

Chapter 1
A New Home in Calgary

Nothing like this had ever happened when Cliff Fletcher was with Montreal. Rising up through the ranks of the Canadiens organization as a scout and executive, he didn't have to worry about how big the crowds were, or who would pay the bills. Tickets to a National Hockey League game at the Forum were as precious as a Rembrandt. Heck, some people might have sold one of the Old Masters' paintings just to see the likes of Jean Beliveau, Yvan Cournoyer, Guy Lafleur, and a young goaltender named Ken Dryden.

But Fletcher, the Flames general manager, was discovering that Atlanta, in the late 1970s, was definitely not like Montreal. Still, he strove to make the Atlanta franchise like the Canadiens, just as he had with the St. Louis Blues, where he trained as a chief scout and assistant general manager before he was hired as the Atlanta Flames' first general manager in the summer of 1972.

Baseball was the big game in Atlanta, thanks to Braves slugger Hank Aaron, who had broken Babe Ruth's all-time home run record. Football and basketball — pro or college, it didn't matter — were also very popular. Hockey was just an afterthought.

The Flames had been in the NHL since 1972-73, when they joined the league at the same time as the New York Islanders. But the crowds were small, the club was struggling, and the owners (a group of Georgia businessmen headed by real estate developer Tom Cousins) were tired of losing money. Unlike Major League Baseball, the National Football League, or the National Basketball Association, the NHL did not have the luxury of millions of dollars worth of television revenue. There was only one way for the club to turn its fortunes around. It would have to sell more tickets.

Fletcher could not count on a rivalry with an opposing team to bring people through the turnstiles. The Flames did not have any nearby opponents in the southwestern U.S. sunbelt. The Islanders were their biggest rivals, but they were way up in New York. The team had to do something else, or get someone else, who would put people in the seats.

The GM decided it was time to take action. He needed to make a move that would generate buzz. In coming years, he would receive the nickname “Trader Cliff” because of his fondness for making big deals. Some reporters believed there was no trade that he didn’t like.

Most of the NHL’s stars at that time hailed from Canada, which produced more NHLers than any other country. The trouble was, most Atlanta hockey fans did not know much about Canada. Like many southerners, they thought it was under snow 12 months of the year. As good as the player might be, a Canadian hockey star might still not appeal to average Americans. European players, like Swedes Borje Salming and Inge Hammerstrom of the Toronto Maple Leafs, were just starting to enter the league. But they would also be a tough sell in the hometown of Coca Cola. Fletcher decided instead to stake the fate of the Atlanta Flames franchise on an all-American hero.

Few people were familiar with the name Jim Craig before the 1980 Winter Olympics. Now, it seemed, almost everyone in America knew him. A college player from Easton, Massachusetts, he had made the U.S. Olympic team — a squad comprised mostly of college players like himself — under coach Herb Brooks. Craig then backstopped the underdog U.S. to the gold medal in Lake Placid by upsetting the favoured Soviet Union.

Their triumph became known as the Miracle On Ice. In a year when America was struggling to deal with the hostage-taking in Iran and another oil crisis, the gold medal victory was a real treat. Craig was lauded as an American hero. His heroics helped spur a rise in hockey's popularity in the U.S. Eventually, the U.S. would become a perennial contender for Olympic, world championship, and World Cup gold. The American victory would also inspire a generation of youngsters to dream of becoming professional hockey players just like Jim Craig.

Fletcher believed that Craig, whom the Flames had drafted in the fourth round in 1977, would be the perfect fit for the struggling team. He signed him to a contract and Craig came out for his first game as a Flame draped in an American flag. Craig's signing would also set the stage for the game's internationalization as Fletcher and other general managers started to look beyond North America for talent. The Flames' expectations of Craig were enormous. Contrary to his Olympic experience, he was expected to win and save a franchise.

Craig joined Atlanta just six days after his stunning gold medal performance. His debut produced a rare sellout at The Omni as he stopped 24 of 25 shots to lead the Flames to a 4-1 win over the Colorado Rockies.

Unfortunately, Craig could not continue his magic. He went winless in three more regular season starts. In the playoffs that year, the New York Rangers quickly extinguished the Flames in four games. As it turned out, America's hero would last only part of one season with the Flames — which was their last in Atlanta.

At the end of the 1979-80 campaign, after not finding the solution to his team's woes within the U.S., Fletcher decided to look outside the country. He turned his attention north to Canada where, following the merger of the NHL and the World Hockey Association (WHA), the game was enjoying a boom. That season, the NHL had welcomed the Winnipeg Jets, Quebec Nordiques, Hartford Whalers, and Edmonton Oilers. Edmonton was fortunate to feature the young superstar Wayne Gretzky.

Edmonton's southerly rival, Calgary, was home to Canada's oil and gas industry and fearless entrepreneurs who liked to work hard and play hard. Calgary pined for an NHL club of its own too, especially after its misadventures with the WHA.

The Calgary Broncos were actually supposed to be one of the WHA's original 10 clubs in 1972. But the Broncos never played a game because owner Bob Brownridge suddenly became ill and didn't pay the $100,000 franchise fee. Three years later, Calgary got another chance to become home to a WHA club. Vancouver businessman Jim Pattison moved the Blazers to Calgary from the west coast and changed the team's name to the Cowboys, in keeping with the city's long association with the Calgary Stampede, the world's richest rodeo. During the Cowboys' two seasons, they were known more for their colourful characters than their on-ice success. Many fans thought goaltender Don "Smokey" McLeod was crazy. He was the only player in pro hockey who used a curved stick to help him shoot the puck out of his team's zone. He also used a first baseman's glove because he could handle the puck better with it. Cowboy forward Rick Jodzio helped maintain the WHA's reputation as a fighters' league. In the first round of the playoffs in their first year, and the only year they made the playoffs, Jodzio jumped Quebec Nordiques superstar defenceman Marc Tardif, prompting one of the largest bench-clearing brawls in pro-hockey history. Tardif suffered brain injuries and lost several teeth. Jodzio pleaded guilty to an assault charge, was fined and suspended. After their second season, the Cowboys folded with the rest of the WHA and were not among the teams that merged into the NHL.

Calgary fans were shocked at the idea that their city could not support a professional hockey franchise. Cowtown had in fact enjoyed a rich hockey history since Alberta became a province in 1905. Calgary's memorable teams included the Calgary Mustangs during World War II, the Calgary Stampeders senior club of the 1960s and 1970s, and the Calgary Centennials of the Western Canada Junior Hockey League in the early 1970s. The Centennials featured a tall lanky goaltender named John Davidson, now a well-known hockey broadcaster. They were coached by the legendary Scotty Munro, whose name graces the league championship trophy. During his half-century in hockey, cigar-chomping Munro had tutored several future NHLers: hall-of-famers Bert Olmstead and Glenn Hall, and Calgary native Mike Rogers, another broadcaster.

While the Flames were struggling in Atlanta, both on the ice and financially, six ambitious oilmen were quietly inquiring about bringing an NHL club to Calgary. The oilmen, including a geologist named Harley Hotchkiss, and a couple of brothers, Doc and Byron (B.J.) Seaman, wanted to do something to help build their community and help amateur hockey. They believed that an NHL franchise could do just that. The group quietly approached the Alberta government about funding a state-of-the-art rink because many people believed that the WHA Cowboys had struggled because they played in the old Calgary Corral. Thanks to a young mayor named Ralph Klein, the city was already putting together a bid to host the 1988 Winter Olympics. The plans called for a new arena. Hotchkiss and the Seamans promised to use the club's proceeds to help fund amateur hockey in the province.

Confident that they could get the money for the arena, the Hotchkiss group offered to purchase the Atlanta Flames from Cousins and his partners for US$14 million. The Cousins real estate consortium wanted to sell the club because land prices had fallen.

But Vancouver real estate tycoon Nelson Skalbania had got wind of the Calgarians' plans. The rogue was notorious for flipping properties, including sports franchises. A few years earlier, as the owner of the WHA Indianapolis Racers, he had sold the playing rights of teenage phenom Wayne Gretzky to Edmonton Oilers' owner Peter Pocklington. Different accounts of the trade had the two owners working out the deal either on a napkin in a restaurant, or over a game of backgammon.

Skalbania snatched the Flames from the willing Atlanta owners, outbidding the Calgary group by a couple of million. He announced that the team would be moving to Calgary. A week after buying the Flames, Skalbania approached the six oilmen and offered them a stake in the franchise. They bought in and eventually took over the franchise from Skalbania, who by then was on the verge of personal bankruptcy — due to other impulsive deals.

So, on May 21, 1980, the Atlanta Flames became the Calgary Flames and Calgary's flaming 'C' logo replaced Atlanta's flaming 'A'. Fletcher moved north with the team and resumed his duties as general manager. However, Jim Craig, the would-be saviour of the Atlanta team, was dealt to the Boston Bruins for draft picks. He spent only part of one season with Boston then was shipped to the minors and the U.S. national program. He did not get another chance with an NHL club until he signed a free-agent contract with Minnesota in 1983-84. He played only three games with the North Stars and wound down his career in the minors with Salt Lake. Just four years after guiding the U.S. to Olympic glory, Jim Craig's pro hockey career was over.

But after a rocky start in Atlanta, the Flames' best years were about to begin.

Chapter 2
Loyal Al and Badger Bob

Al MacNeil became the first coach in Calgary Flames history. He would become the club's longest-serving employee — over a quarter century.

MacNeil first broke into the NHL in the 1950s — a time when few players from his home province of Nova Scotia reached the six-team National Hockey League. Nova Scotia players faced an uphill struggle because there was no major junior league in the Maritimes. With no draft yet in place, NHL clubs protected players from teams in their areas, regardless of where the player was born and raised. The Toronto Maple Leafs, under legendary Conn Smythe, had been given more leeway than other clubs so controlled much of Eastern

Canada. It was quite a coup for a kid from Nova Scotia to get to play for the Toronto Marlboros in the Leafs feeder system. MacNeil earned his crack at the NHL captaining the Toronto Marlboros to the 1955-56 Memorial Cup championship.

Generously listed at 5-foot-10, MacNeil was a short, stocky defenceman in an era when, like today, teams looked for large rear guards. Despite shuffling between the minors and the NHL, he managed to play 524 games over his 15-year career with Toronto, Montreal, Chicago, New York, and the expansion Pittsburgh. As the end of his playing days approached, he became a player-coach. At the start of the 1970-71 season, MacNeil finally retired as a player and devoted his full attention to coaching as an assistant with the Montreal Canadiens. He dreamed of one day becoming a head coach in the NHL.

His chance would come sooner than he, or anyone else, imagined. In 1970, the Canadiens had missed the post-season for the first time since 1948 — an unforgivable calamity in Montreal. Just 23 games into the next regular season, the struggling Canadiens fired coach Claude Ruel. Their general manager Sam Pollock appointed MacNeil to replace Ruel. Despite having no NHL head coaching experience, MacNeil was expected to lead the hallowed Habs back to the playoffs.

As if those expectations were not enough, MacNeil faced additional pressure off the ice. He took the Habs' reins during the most tumultuous time in Quebec's modern history.

Quebec's separatist sentiments had erupted in an

episode of terrorism. On October 16, 1970, for the first time in Canadian history outside of war, Prime Minister Pierre Trudeau invoked the War Measures Act. An extremist group known as the Front de Libération du Québec (FLQ) had kidnapped British diplomat James Cross and Quebec Labour Minister Pierre Laporte, who was later found dead in the trunk of a car. The War Measures Act suspended the Canadian Bill of Rights, and gave the federal government sweeping powers to search and arrest people connected with the FLQ. Army tanks rolled through downtown Montreal. The events left a deep sense of distrust between anglophones and francophones — which extended right into the Canadiens' dressing room. MacNeil, an anglophone from the Maritimes who did not speak French, had inadvertently walked into the middle of the October Crisis. He replaced Ruel only a day after Cross was released.

Despite becoming a beacon of political discontent, MacNeil did guide the Habs back to the playoffs. He took the team all the way to the Stanley Cup finals, when he dared to bench Henri Richard, one of the most popular players in the Habs' history. Richard had called MacNeil the worst coach for whom he had ever played and the controversy intensified the bitter French–English relations prevalent across the province. The Montreal Forum was the subject of numerous bomb threats. MacNeil and his family were placed under police protection. But after losing the first two games of the final in Chicago, the Canadiens came back to win the

Cup — on two goals by Richard. Richard's success spelled MacNeil's demise.

The first Nova Scotia-born Stanley Cup-champion coach also became the first Stanley Cup-champion coach to lose his job following that season. MacNeil said he resigned. Members of Canadiens' management implied that he was fired. Nonetheless, still loyal to the organization, MacNeil became coach and general manager of its farm team, the Nova Scotia Voyageurs. He led the Voyageurs to three Calder Cup championships and was twice named the American Hockey League coach of the year. Even though he was then only a minor-league coach, MacNeil was named as an assistant coach of Team Canada's squad of NHLers for both the 1971 and 1976 Canada Cup tournaments. No other minor-league coach had accomplished that feat.

But MacNeil longed for a chance to return to the NHL. Fletcher and MacNeil had been old friends since their days together with the Montreal organization. When Fletcher offered MacNeil the Atlanta Flames' coaching post in 1978-79, MacNeil jumped at the chance. Despite the turmoil surrounding the team's future, MacNeil put the Flames in the playoffs.

When the Flames moved to Calgary, they instantly became the most popular team in town. They even dethroned the Canadian Football League's beloved Stampeders. But unlike his days in Montreal, MacNeil did not have a bunch of stars at his disposal to work with. However, he did have one player who was clearly more offensively gifted than the rest — Kent Nilsson.

Nilsson, who had toiled under MacNeil in Atlanta, would become the first of many unlikely Calgary Flames heroes. The team drafted him in the fourth round in 1976, when he appeared to be a long shot to make the NHL. The league at the time featured only a handful of Europeans. Instead of joining the Flames right away, he stayed in his native Sweden for one more season and then signed with the WHA Winnipeg Jets. Ironically, Nilsson posted 107 points in each of those two seasons. When the Jets joined the NHL, the Atlanta Flames were able to re-claim him under the terms of the merger.

In his first season in Calgary, Nilsson earned the nickname "Magic Man" because of his deft passing, creative stickhandling, and ability to score consistently — with apparently little effort. He led the Flames with 49 goals and 82 assists and finished third in league scoring behind Wayne Gretzky and Marcel Dionne. In the process, he became the first European-trained player to produce more than 100 points in a single NHL season.

Thanks to Nilsson and hard-working players like veteran centre Don Lever and rookie winger Jim Peplinski, the Calgary Flames finished third in their division. They advanced all the way to the Stanley Cup semi-finals against the upstart Minnesota North Stars. Alas, the slipper did not fit the Cinderella team and the North Stars ousted the

Flames in six games.

The following season, the Flames could not match their first year's success, however Fletcher swung a deal that would help the franchise become a Stanley Cup contender for many years to come. On November 25, 1981, Flames GM "Trader" Cliff acquired Lanny McDonald from Colorado.

McDonald, known even then by his trademark bushy moustache, gave the Flames instant credibility as a team to be reckoned with. His middle name — King — would soon symbolize his status with the Flames.

Although McDonald had grown up on a farm near Hanna, Alberta, he had thrived in Toronto. Drafted fourth overall in 1973, he had become one of the Maple Leafs' dominant players, along with his buddy, linemate and captain, Darryl Sittler. They turned the Leafs back into a legitimate Stanley Cup contender under cantankerous owner Harold Ballard. But McDonald had been caught in the middle of a feud between Ballard, general manager Punch Imlach, and Sittler. McDonald was traded to Colorado as a way to get back at Sittler, who had a no-trade clause in his contract.

Even today, Toronto fans, players, and unusually sentimental reporters grow sad while recalling McDonald's trade. Many years later, they can still recall where they were and what they were doing when they heard their beloved Lanny had been traded. McDonald enjoyed his brief stint in Colorado, under colourful Rockies coach Don Cherry, but the financially struggling franchise was a cellar dweller.

Therefore, in addition to helping the Flames franchise, the trade to Calgary boosted McDonald's briefly stalled career. As he had been with the Toronto Maple Leafs, he became the inspirational leader for the Flames.

In spite of Lanny, Calgary was swept 3-0 in the first round of the 1982 playoffs by the Vancouver Canucks. Featuring former Toronto coach Roger Neilson and McDonald's old pal Tiger Williams, the Canucks later qualified for the Stanley Cup finals for the first time in the franchise's history. At the end of the season, GM Fletcher decided that a coaching change was necessary and fired his friend Al MacNeil. As he had done with Montreal, the former coach remained loyal to the Flames and accepted a management post.

Fletcher found his new coach in an unlikely place. "Badger" Bob Johnson earned his nickname by coaching for 15 seasons at the University of Wisconsin, where he won three National Collegiate Athletic Association hockey titles. While at Wisconsin, Johnson also coached U.S. national teams and the 1976 Olympic team. But the Minneapolis, Minnesota, native had no previous professional experience, either as a player or coach. Many observers wondered how he would handle the brash pros, who were used to playing for ex-NHLers. Although they might not say so publicly, it's widely acknowledged that NHLers prefer to play for coaches who have also played in the league.

Johnson, perhaps because he served as a U.S. Army medic during the Korean War, was not fazed by what others thought about him. His positive attitude, his obvious love for the game, and his genuine concern for people were remarkable. "Some people looked at him and shook their heads, as if he were the Nutty Professor," wrote hockey reporter George Johnson. "He certainly didn't lack for ego or confidence, but there was an ingratiating naivete about his enthusiasm that couldn't help but win you over. He had time for anyone interested in hockey."

Another reporter covering the Flames, Eric Duhatschek, recalled a road trip to Toronto when Bob Johnson's character shone through loud and clear. Johnson and many of the Flames players who were originally from Toronto or other parts of Ontario were eating breakfast with family in the café of the hotel where the team was staying. Badger Bob got up from his table, popped around the restaurant and assured the players' parents that the team was looking after their boys. Duhatschek, a Toronto native, also happened to be dining there with his mother and father. "Don't worry, Mr. and Mrs. Duhatschek, we're taking good care of Eric, too," said Johnson.

Coaches traditionally were not supposed to get along with reporters. Badger was not afraid to be different — in many ways. Rather than kick garbage cans or yell at his players after a loss, as many other coaches would have done, Johnson looked for the positives of any performance, no matter how lopsided the score. He also lived by his favourite expression — "It's a great day for hockey!" — and displayed quirky mannerisms behind the bench. During games, he frequently tugged on his large nose, yanked on his eyebrows, or scribbled his observations on a small notepad. At that time, no other NHL coach took notes during games. Today, because of Johnson, it is hard to find one who does not.

The American-born coach also opened the NHL's eyes to players from his homeland, who despite the 1980 Miracle On Ice, were still often ignored on draft day. "Badger paved the way for Americans to play at [the NHL] level," said American defenceman Gary Suter, who played under him for two seasons in Calgary. "Before guys like him, hockey was a Canadians-only game. People like him had a lot to do with guys like me making it to the NHL. We owe him a lot."

Because of his willingness to employ unusual coaching methods, his attention to detail, and his competitive nature, Johnson managed to get the most out of his players —regardless of where they came from. In 1982-83, Johnson extracted the best results from his superstars — Nilsson and McDonald. Picking up where he had left off the previous season, McDonald tallied 66 goals — more than any Flames player, in Calgary or Atlanta, had ever scored before. Nilsson faced high expectations because of his previous offensive numbers and his obvious brilliance with the puck. He led the team in overall scoring with 104 points, to add to McDonald's 98. As a result of the two stars' exploits, the Flames placed second in the Smythe Division behind their arch rivals, the Edmonton Oilers.

In the post-season, the Flames avenged their previous year's loss to the Canucks by eliminating Vancouver in four games. The Flames, however, were no match for Gretzky, Mark Messier, and company. The Oilers, a predominantly young team, won the best-of-seven Smythe Division finals in five games. It was the first of many great Calgary–Edmonton playoff series to come.

McDonald was named to the NHL's second all-star team and received the Bill Masterton Trophy for sportsmanship, perseverance, and dedication to hockey. He would have preferred to hoist another trophy — the Stanley Cup.

Chapter 3
Unsung Heroes

It was January 1985. Lanny McDonald was starting to wonder whether he would ever get a chance to win the Stanley Cup. He knew that first the Flames would have to beat Edmonton in the playoffs — which they had never done before. After bowing to the Oilers in the 1982-83 playoffs, Calgary had lost to them again — in seven games — in the second round of the following year's post-season. The Oilers went on to claim their first ever Stanley Cup. The message was clear. If the Flames could beat Edmonton, they could contend for the Cup. But in 1984-85, Winnipeg upset the Flames, denying them a rematch with the Oilers, who captured their second straight Stanley Cup. Now midway through the 1985-86 regular season, it looked like Calgary would have a hard time just making the playoffs. The Flames had just suffered their eighth straight loss — against Edmonton.

"Watching the Calgary Flames right now is like watching a pickup game on a pond," said Fletcher. "The effort has been there, but our defence had better get back to the basics." But Badger Bob was more positive than ever. "Yeah, 51 shots on the Oilers, sounds like a pretty good pickup game to me," he retorted.

The loss to Edmonton had been entertaining for another reason. During one altercation, Oilers tough guy Marty McSorley's sweater came off and centre Doug Risebrough snatched it. Sitting in the penalty box, much to the delight of fans, Risebrough shredded McSorley's jersey with his skates. After the game, the Oilers hung McSorley's tattered jersey in their dressing room for the media to see. Edmonton general manager Glen Sather, a former Montreal Canadien, announced that his friendship with Risebrough, also a former Canadien, was over. He vowed to send the Flames a bill for $1,000, although nobody was sure how he came up with that figure.

"Fletcher's so paranoid about our team," said Sather. "He thinks the only way the Flames can beat us is by beating the crap out of us, which is ridiculous." The win actually marked Edmonton's 17th win over the Flames in their last 20 meetings. But at that time, the Flames had been losing to everyone.

Coach Johnson could not explain the team's funk. For the first time in his lengthy career, he did not have an answer for his questioners. "You go to pick up the dry cleaning and they ask you what's wrong with your club, you go to buy a paper and they want to know what's wrong, and you buy gas and the guy wants to know what's wrong," he said. "I can't tell anyone how to solve it, because this has never happened to me before. I can't look back and say what I did in '62 because it just didn't happen. I've always been fortunate to have winners."

The successful coach refused to give up hope. Instead, he decided to get creative on and off the ice. Doing his impression of a batter in baseball, Johnson swung an imaginary bat and told the team that they should not think too much. To help his players relax, he handed out a yoga assignment. He also became more cheerful than ever. Good game, he would say after another loss. Good job, he would say, to a disheartened player, praising him for a goal or a check. Although it did not affect anything in the standings, the positive attitude became an absolute psychological necessary for Johnson and his team. "You need PMA (positive mental attitude)... and all you can do is look in the mirror and come out all fired up," he counselled.

Between December 14 and January 7, the Flames continued to suffer. Eleven straight losses, no ties. The most humiliating moment came when the Flames lost 9-1 at home to Hartford. But Johnson advised his players and reporters not to worry, because the Flames had the other teams exactly where they wanted them. Other clubs would now take the Flames lightly, leaving themselves vulnerable. Reporters and players just shook their heads at the unusual coach.

Amazingly, the coach's words would prove prophetic. The Flames ended the losing streak with a 5-4 overtime victory at home against Vancouver — the same team that had started them on their nosedive. Over the rest of the regular season, Calgary would never again lose two games in a row — thanks to one special newcomer.

On February 1, 1986, Trader Cliff acquired Joey Mullen from the St. Louis Blues. Mullen was a player who knew the meaning of adversity. Always considered small for a hockey player, Mullen grew up in the notorious Hell's Kitchen neighbourhood of New York City. Prostitutes and drug dealers frequented the area, and violence was a way of life, but Joey and his brothers concentrated on sports instead. Their father happened to be the guy who drove the Zamboni between periods of Rangers games at Madison Square Garden. Both Joey and his brother Brian made it to the NHL after learning the game playing roller hockey with a ball of black tape.

Although Mullen excelled with a couple of New York City junior teams, he was not offered a university scholarship, which was then the ticket to the NHL for most American players. So he scraped together $700 to cover his first year at Boston College before earning a scholarship his second year. Mullen averaged better than two points per game during both seasons at BC, but no NHL team chose to draft him.

Someone from the Blues finally noticed him and the club signed him as a free agent. In each of his four-plus seasons with St. Louis, he notched at least a point per game. He was also a consistent playoff performer, although just before he was traded, he had been held pointless in the 1984-85 post-season. Minnesota swept the Blues in three games.

Looking back, Mullen's trade for three journeymen was inexplicable and, undoubtedly, one that St. Louis general manager Ron Caron would regret. The Missouri city's loss was Calgary's gain. As soon as he arrived in Calgary, Mullen started scoring and again produced better than a point per game. He was also a gentleman on the ice, receiving only 11 penalty minutes.

Mullen was just one of many unsung heroes on the Flames roster that season. Like him, they knew all about hardship and some of them were not expected to make the NHL. Winger Colin Patterson had excelled at Canada's other sport — lacrosse — and as a teenager helped the national team to a world championship bronze medal. But he had not been considered much of a prospect at hockey. After playing tier II junior in Ontario, Patterson headed to Clarkson College, a small school in New York. He was intent on getting a degree in business and marketing while playing hockey on the side. Never drafted, he never expected to play in the NHL because as he said, "to be honest, I wasn't that good."

A Flames scout spotted Patterson on a visit to Clarkson to watch one of Patterson's teammates, Jim Laing. Laing, ironically, was drafted by the Flames but never played a game with Calgary. Calgary offered Patterson a free agent contract. He jumped at the chance to play pro, even though he expected to toil in the minors. His father, an engineer, and his mother, a teacher, both valued education more highly, and were not very happy with their son's decision to leave college early. "And they felt, much like I sort of felt at the time, too, was I really going to play in the NHL? But at the time, you know, the money that they were offering ($30,000) for the minor-league salary was very good. I wasn't going to make that anywhere else. I said: 'Well, if I can play four years in the minors, that way I'd be able to make some money and start a career afterwards.' "

Patterson would eventually get his marketing and management degree from Clarkson and become a successful executive with Shaw TV. But he would only play 13 games in the minors while becoming a mainstay with the Flames. Playing every shift like it was his last, he delighted Johnson with his hard-working ways. "He said I was a project for him, he was going to make me better — and he did," recalled Patterson.

While Patterson was becoming a better defensive player, Hakan Loob was displaying offensive prowess in his first NHL season. Although the Flames had drafted him in 1980, Loob chose to stay with Farjestads BK for four seasons in his native Sweden. Fans had wondered how the slight 175-pound winger, generously listed at five-foot-nine, would handle the rough stuff in the NHL. But Loob was on his way to producing 30 goals and 23 assists to earn a spot on the NHL's all-rookie team.

Joel Otto, a hulking six-foot-four and 220-pound centre was another free agent signing from an American college. Many reporters and fans had never heard of Bemidji State, a National Collegiate Athletic Association (NCAA) Division II school in Otto's home state of Minnesota. If it was hard for Division I players to reach the NHL, it was twice as hard for Division II players. Although the NCAA is known for its large schools, like the University of Michigan and the UCLA, it also contains much smaller schools like Bemidji. Few scouts in any sport, let alone hockey, which is considered a regional game in the U.S., ever set foot on campus.

Winger Tim Hunter, a native of Calgary, was known more for his fighting ability than his scoring talent, but he had also worked hard and managed to impress Johnson. After being drafted by Atlanta in 1979, and spending one more year of major junior and two more in the minors, he was finally getting his chance to stick with the Flames.

Defenceman Jamie Macoun was yet another undrafted player from the U.S. college ranks. After joining the Flames midway through his third season with the Ohio State Buckeyes, in 1982-83, the native of Newmarket, Ontario, did not play a single game in the minors.

And then there was Doug Risebrough. As a 20-year-old rookie in 1974, Risebrough had managed to capture one of the two open roster spots on the most talented teams in NHL history, the Montreal Canadiens. With them, he won four straight Stanley Cups. In hockey parlance, Risebrough was a grinder — a player put out specifically to stop the other team's best players. After being traded to the Flames, he also emerged as a leader — by playing through several knee injuries. "I guess I'm a bit accident-prone, but I open myself up to it," said Risebrough, who played with a knee brace. "When you play at a certain level, you get hurt. Being injury-free is an insult . . . When you're not aching, maybe you're not doing the right things out there."

Calgary's goaltending situation was still uncertain. Reggie Lemelin was having an average year and Marc D'Amour, who suffered from severe dehydration during games, had not panned out as a backup. Calgary native Mike Vernon, an up-and-coming pro who had spent most of the season in the minors, appeared to be in the coach's doghouse. He had publicly challenged Johnson, contending the coach was not giving him a fair shot. Johnson said Vernon would have to earn his playing time. Eventually, Vernon would leave Johnson no other choice but to play him, because he played better than Calgary's other masked men. In 18 games, the young goaltender posted a 9-3-3 record.

Thanks to the unheralded young players and the veteran Risebrough, Calgary's 11-game losing streak became a distant memory.

The Flames placed sixth overall in the 1985-86 season,

but still finished 30 points behind the Oilers' juggernaut. Edmonton finished first overall, thanks to Gretzky's 215 points and 48 goals from Paul Coffey, the most by a defenceman in one season. Edmonton also owned the Battle of Alberta. The Flames had only managed to beat their rivals once — late in the season — as they romped to a 9-3 decision. It was an important victory because the Flames knew that if they were going to advance very far in the playoffs they would have to beat the two-time defending Stanley Cup champions.

The all-Alberta series of the second round started on a hilarious note at Northlands Coliseum in Edmonton. In the first period, rookie defenceman Gary Suter's expensive aluminum stick flew into the stands. Al Murray, a Calgary assistant trainer, jumped into the stands to get it. Edmonton fans refused to give it back and he got into a scuffle. From the bench, head medical trainer "Bearcat" Murray saw his son getting punched so he climbed over the glass to help him. Jumping down about eight feet, he landed awkwardly on a step and injured his ankle. As he was rolled out on a stretcher to an ambulance, a TV photographer followed him. Bearcat, easily recognizable by his bald head and bushy moustache, blew kisses at the camera. The Bearcat legend was born. After being fitted with a cast with a special spiked shoe to help him walk on the ice, he went back behind the Calgary bench for the second period.

Fans watching the game on TV in Boston were so impressed by Murray's courageous and successful efforts to retrieve Suter's stick that they launched the Bearcat Murray Fan Club! Whenever Bearcat would visit a rink in Boston, Montreal, or Quebec City, his faithful followers would don skull caps, fake noses, and moustaches. The native of High River, Alberta, who had inherited his nickname from his father, became the only trainer in the NHL with his own groupies.

Back on the ice, the cocky Vernon emerged as the starter ahead of Lemelin as the Flames and Oilers went back and forth until game seven on April 30, 1986 at Northlands Coliseum. With the score tied 2-2 and only about seven minutes to go in the third period, Calgary's Perry Berezan shot the puck along the boards. Edmonton goaltender Grant Fuhr went behind the net to stop it. Rookie Edmonton defenceman Steve Smith raced back to get it. But as Fuhr was returning to his net, Smith tried to fire the puck up ice —through the crease. The disk hit the back of Fuhr's leg — and caromed into the net. Smith fell to the ice and buried his face in shame as the Oilers' faithful went silent. Finally, he got up with tears streaming down his face. The goal was credited to Berezan, who was on the bench by that time. The Flames held on to win the game and the series. For the first time ever, Calgary eliminated Edmonton in the post-season. But the Flames did not just upset their rivals — they derailed an impending dynasty.

In the semi-finals, Calgary faced St. Louis and ex-Flames Eddy Beers, Gino Cavallini, and Charlie Bourgeois. Again the series went to seven games as St. Louis goaltender Rick Wamsley delivered a masterful performance. But Calgary prevailed again — and advanced to the Stanley Cup finals for the first time in its franchise's history. At last, McDonald was going to get a shot at the Cup. For the first time since 1967, the final pitted two Canadian teams against each other: Calgary vs. Montreal.

Like Badger, Montreal Canadiens coach Jean Perron had also elected to go with a rookie goaltender. Patrick Roy, a rakish Quebec City native, had racked up an impressive 11-4 record so far in the playoffs. In front of Roy, the Canadiens had some players from their halcyon days, but whose careers were then coming to a close — Bob Gainey, Larry Robinson, and the injured Mario Tremblay. The Habs also featured several promising young players, such as Guy Carbonneau, Chris Chelios, and rookies Claude Lemieux and Brian Skrudland.

The Flames, aside from the aging McDonald and injury-riddled Risebrough, were a young, inexperienced team. Most players were still in their 20s. By finishing ahead of the Habs in the regular season, Calgary had home-ice advantage in the final. The Flames controlled the first game, winning 5-3 at the Saddledome. Their chances of victory were also looking good in the second game as they remained tied 2-2 heading into overtime.

Then something bizarre happened. On the opening face-off, Skrudland grabbed a loose puck, raced toward Vernon on a breakaway and scored — just nine seconds into

O.T. It was the fastest overtime goal in NHL history.

The Flames never recovered. Montreal took both games at the Forum as future hall-of-famer Roy earned his first NHL playoff shutout. The teams returned to Calgary, and the Canadiens won 4-3 to capture the Cup.

After the game, Lanny McDonald slumped beside his locker in the Flames dressing room. As the cameras clicked and rolled, he did all he could to hold back his tears as he answered reporters' questions. Teammates and fans alike hoped that somehow, some way, the Flames would win the Cup for their beloved Lanny. McDonald just hoped that his team would get back into the finals — and give him one more chance — before he retired.

Chapter 4 A New Era

Calgary's 1987-88 training camp was full of hype. A year had passed since the Flames' improbable run to the final. Unfortunately, Winnipeg had stunned Calgary in the first round of the next season. Coach Bob Johnson had resigned suddenly to head up the governing body of hockey in the U.S. so Terry Crisp, Calgary's former farm club coach, was now running the bench. He had several tough decisions to make because several rookies were vying for jobs. Reporters wondered who would steal the show this year.

Would it be Brett Hull, the son of former Chicago superstar Bobby, whom Crisp had coached in the minors? Or former Cornell University centre Joe Nieuwendyk who had been the draft pick Calgary acquired for Kent Nilsson? Maybe tough-guy Gary Roberts? One of the goaltending prospects? The answer was none of the above. It turned out to be someone they least expected, but someone who also knew all about challenges.

He swaggered into town like he owned the place. The team listed him at five-foot-five and 153 pounds, but he insisted that he was actually five-foot-six and 158 pounds. His name was Theoren Fleury, a 19-year-old who grew up in Russell, Manitoba, just across the provincial border from his birthplace of Oxbow, Saskatchewan.

The previous Christmas, Fleury had been involved in one of the most infamous incidents in international junior hockey history. At Piestany, Czechoslovakia, which became known as the Piestany Punch Up, Canada's junior team squared off against the Soviets. Fleury was Team Canada's captain and — living up to his reputation as an agitator — became involved in a scuffle that erupted into a bench-clearing brawl. The Soviets did not, as a rule, drop their gloves, so this action alone was quite amazing. It got worse. Unable to control the mayhem, the officials left the ice. Tournament organizers finally brought the situation under control — 20 minutes later — by dimming the lights. The game was cancelled, both teams were disqualified, and their records erased from the tournament's official statistics.

At best, Fleury was supposed to be a long shot to make the Flames team that year or any other year. Calgary had selected him in the eighth round of the 1987 draft. Fletcher would claim years later that the farm team had needed an attraction that could help sell tickets. But Fleury quickly gained notice from the big club because of the way he took on much bigger players. “My size gives me more incentive to play hard,” Fleury said. “The quote I always use is, ‘Big guys prove they can’t play. Little guys prove they can.’”

Coach Crisp gave him a chance to prove himself against the Chicago Blackhawks in an exhibition game, assigning him to check top scorer Denis Savard. Afterwards, Fleury acted like a kid who had just been given a lifetime supply of computer games. “It was a big thrill being on the ice with Savard,” he said. “The heart was pumping. I thought, ‘Holy cow, that’s Denis Savard! He’s a very exciting player, like myself.”

That cocky attitude did not endear Fleury to veteran Flames, with whom he sparred in workouts. However Fletcher and the coaches raved about his willingness to get physical and about his offensive talent. Fletcher called him the best player for his size that he had ever seen, based on his ability to combine his antagonistic style with pure offensive skills. “Before camp, I’d have said it was highly unlikely,” said Fletcher, about Fleury’s hopes of ever playing in the NHL. “Now, I’m prepared to say that he has a pretty good chance.”

That comment could be interpreted another way. It also meant that Fletcher was willing, in the future, to make moves that would get Fleury into the lineup. But at the end of the training camp, he was sent back to his junior team in

Moose Jaw for one more season. "I've proven I can play in this league," said Fleury. "I'm going down with the intention of being the best player in the Western Hockey League. I couldn't be happier. I had a great camp."

Although they did not take camp by storm the way Fleury did, two other rookies also impressed Fletcher and the coaching staff. Nieuwendyk stayed with the team after camp ended and started his NHL career on a scoring tear. Not bad considering that he had been ignored as a prospect when he was in midget. The Ontario Hockey Association, now known as the Ontario Hockey League, selected its players in an annual midget draft. Since no teams chose Nieuwendyk, he made his way to Cornell University in Ithaca, New York. There he grew a few inches and put on more weight, making him difficult to move from in front of the net. He was the East Coast Athletic Conference's rookie of the year in 1984-85 and a two-time first all-star. The Flames managed not to miss this prospect: they drafted Nieuwendyk in the second round of the NHL draft in 1985.

The other rookie star of the training camp was Nieuwendyk's best friend from their days growing up in Whitby, Ontario, Gary Roberts. The very physical Roberts soon made up for the absence of Risebrough who had retired and become an assistant coach because of knee and shoulder injuries. While Nieuwendyk had taken the U.S. college route to the NHL, Roberts took the major junior route with the Ottawa 67s and Guelph Platers, winning Memorial Cups with both teams. After leaving Whitby as a teenager, when he was still in high school, Roberts had trouble adjusting to life in Ottawa. Because he was a hockey player, he was often challenged to fight in his new school. But his Ottawa coach Brian Kilrea had invoked a strict no-fighting policy for Roberts, at least off the ice. One day, in a classroom with a teacher present, Roberts did get into a fight. Fearing the worst, he told Kilrea what happened. After getting confirmation from the teacher that the other boy had started the fight, Kilrea allowed Roberts to stay with the team. Roberts learned to control his fiery temper and became one of Ottawa's best players as well as a Calgary first-round draft pick in 1984.

Reunited after a few years of playing apart, Roberts and Nieuwendyk both quickly became comfortable at the NHL level. By December 29, after Calgary stomped Montreal 9-3, Nieuwendyk already had four hat-tricks. "If somebody told me I'd have 26 goals by the halfway mark, I wouldn't have believed it," said Nieuwendyk. "I don't feel any pressure." His new coach joked, "We're going to keep him around for a while. We're not going to send him to the minors. We'll probably take a little longer look at the kid."

Coach Crisp was not nearly as enamoured with his club's backup goaltender. Doug Dadswell, a free agent signing from Cornell, had assumed the job. But Dadswell did not inspire confidence in Crisp — or GM Fletcher. The GM went looking for a veteran backup. He called up St. Louis Blues general manager Ron Caron, with whom he had worked in the Montreal and St. Louis organizations. Fletcher and Caron had worked out the Mullen deal the previous season.

Although Fletcher had appeared to have fleeced him in the Mullen deal, Caron was willing to trade with his old friend again. Caron wanted one player in particular — Brett Hull. The winger was off to a hot start in his first full NHL season with 50 points in 52 games. But, Fletcher reasoned, the Flames had plenty of offence. Nieuwendyk was on a roll — and the promising Theoren Fleury was in a race for the Western Hockey League scoring lead with Joe Sakic of the Swift Current Broncos. So, Fletcher completed the deal.

Hull would become one of the most prolific goal scorers in NHL history and snare at least three Stanley Cups. "We knew he was going to be a scorer, but we didn't know how good a scorer he was going to be," said Crisp. Crisp maintained that the deal made sense at the time because it provided Calgary with what it needed — more goaltending and defence. In return for Hull and utility forward Steve Bozek, Fletcher obtained goaltender Rick Wamsley, who had impressed Calgary the year the Flames advanced to the Stanley Cup final, and Rob Ramage, a solid defenceman who also stood out in that series.

Keeping tabs on his former club's recruiting prowess, Fletcher knew that Wamsley had started his NHL career with the Habs, where one season he shared the William Jennings Trophy with Denis Herron for best team goals-against average. The GM also knew that Wamsley didn't wobble when facing adversity. While he was with Montreal, Wamsley's son Ryan had died of cancer. In his memory, Wamsley helped fund a special room for cancer patients. Whenever he travelled to Montreal, he visited the room and paid tribute to his late son. Wamsley turned out to be steady, although not spectacular, as a backup to Vernon, who enjoyed his finest career year as a pro.

Nieuwendyk finished with a rookie record of 51 goals, surpassing the previous mark of 50 set by Islanders star Mike Bossy, to easily win the league's rookie of the year award. For the first time in franchise history, Calgary finished first overall, even better than the dreaded Oilers.

But after easily eliminating the Los Angeles Kings in four games, the Flames were swept 4-0 by the Oilers, who went on to win their fourth Cup in five years.

Now, as the Flames prepared for the 1988-89 season, fans and media alike started to question the team's character. What would it take to win the Cup?

Chapter 5
Chasing the Stanley Cup

Doug Gilmour joined the Flames at the start of their 1988-89 training camp — but not by choice. The St. Louis Blues shipped Gilmour to Calgary in a package deal mainly because the parents of a 14-year-old girl who babysat his daughter had filed a $1 million lawsuit against him. The babysitter's parents alleged that he had molested her. The lawsuit proceeded, even though a grand jury decided there was insufficient evidence to lay charges. Even St. Louis prosecuting attorney George Westfall suggested the whole affair smacked of extortion.

Blues chairman Mike Shanahan later admitted that trading Gilmour "broke [GM] Ron Caron's heart." But, said

Shanahan, the deal had to be done to get Gilmour out from under intense public scrutiny — and let the team get back to business. "The trade wasn't based on the normal circumstances to improve your team, and that bothered us most of all," said Shanahan. Bullard, the key player going the other way, would play only 20 games with St. Louis. Craig Coxe would play only half a season there. Tim Corkery would stay in college that season.

Fortunately, the controversy did not affect Gilmour's play. He had faced misfortune before. When Gilmour was 16, his cousin Michael Anson, only a year younger, had died of cancer. "In a matter of two years he wasted away until nothing was left of him," Gilmour recalled. "I've never forgotten that. It made me realize how important life is." Gilmour also faced obstacles because of his size while growing up in Kingston, Ontario, a hometown he shared with one of his boosters, broadcaster Don Cherry. Although he was listed in NHL records as 5-foot-11 and 170 pounds, Gilmour always appeared to be shorter and slighter. During each game, he sweated off several pounds and often became dehydrated. As a result, he was not expected to be a star when he played for the Cornwall Royals of the Ontario Hockey League. "He was so small, he would just barely make a lot of teams as he was growing up," said Gordie Wood, a scout for the Royals. "But the people who figured that forgot about his heart. He just never let anything stop him."

Gilmour surprised his critics by being selected the

OHL's player of the year in 1982-83 as he compiled 70 goals and led the league with 107 assists and 177 points. However, he was not drafted into the NHL until the seventh round. Dismayed by the Blues' offer, he fled to West Germany, thinking he might play there. The Blues lured him back with a better deal within days. He made the club right away and did not play a single game in the minors. In his first three seasons in St. Louis, he was perceived as a checker, because he never produced more than 57 points. In 1986-87, his offensive output exploded to 107 points and he followed that up with 86 and 85-point seasons.

As the 1988-89 season began, Gilmour was viewed as a saviour, someone who could help the Flames take their final step to the top of the mountain. The Flames faced intense pressure to make up for their early exit the previous season. Calgary also had an image to live up to.

Since coming to Calgary, the Flames had never missed the playoffs. It was now a given that the Flames would make the playoffs every year. The only question was how far they would advance in the post-season. Flames supporters had come to expect excellence. Calgary had also become known as a good place to play.

Calgary was a "small-market franchise" because the city's population was tiny compared to cities like New York and Boston. Since the Flames had fewer potential fans, the team could not attract as much TV revenue with which to pay huge salaries to superstars. Despite this, players from other teams still welcomed trades to Calgary because they knew that general manager Fletcher would treat them well. But Coach Crisp was wary of his team becoming too comfortable. He knew that his players were making a lot more money than he did when he was playing. Calgary also had an experienced team and veterans on one-way contracts could earn just as much playing in the minors as in the NHL, so there was no financial incentive for them to perform at their best. Crisp was afraid that they would not play as well as they could play.

With Gilmour in the lineup, the Flames started the 1988-89 season slowly with a 4-4 tie at home with the New York Islanders and a 6-5 overtime loss in Los Angeles. Then Calgary racked up five wins and a tie in their next six games. In addition to Gilmour, several other players were starting to shine — including centre Jiri Hrdina and Jamie Macoun.

Hrdina had joined the Flames after the 1988 Winter Olympics in Calgary. Although Czechoslovakia was still a communist nation and residents were not allowed to move to other countries, Fletcher negotiated Hrdina's release from his former team and gained permission for him to come to Canada. At the age of 30, because he had not played more than 25 games the previous season, Hrdina was the NHL's oldest rookie. Politics and age aside, his arrival in the NHL was amazing because the native of Mlada Boleslav had struggled to earn a spot with the Czechoslovakian national squad.

Meanwhile, Macoun was back after missing the entire 1987-88 season following a controversial accident. Losing control of his sports car, he had suffered a broken and nerve-damaged arm, as well as internal injuries and severe cuts. He was initially charged with drinking and driving, but pled guilty to a lesser charge of dangerous driving and paid a $1,000 fine. He had to submit to alcohol counselling and underwent extensive rehabilitation on his injured arm. The damage to his reputation may have been worse. The story splashed across the sports news and many questioned whether he was getting off too lightly. But Macoun showed no signs of any recurring problems and played regularly.

Macoun's return gave Calgary one of the strongest defence corps in the NHL. MacInnis, with his booming shot, and Suter, the NHL's rookie of the year in 1985-86, made Calgary's No. 1 power play unit one of the best in the league. Gilmour was scoring at a steady pace while team scoring leader Joe Mullen was near the top of the league in both goals and assists. Hakan Loob, MacInnis, and Suter were all producing at a healthy clip.

Meanwhile, down south in Salt Lake, Fleury, in his first full pro season, was constantly turning the red light on. After taking Calgary's training camp by storm the previous season, Fleury had gone back to Moose Jaw, captained Canada to a gold medal during a much more peaceful world junior championships, and completed his junior eligibility with Moose Jaw. Tying Joe Sakic of the Swift Current Broncos for the Western League scoring title, Fleury had lived up to his bold prediction that he would be the best player on the junior circuit.

Off the ice, Fleury was learning how to be a teenage father to his infant son, Josh, after girlfriend Shannon Griffin had given birth a few months earlier. It wasn't the first or the last of Fleury's challenges in life. He was in the early stages of a substance abuse problem, which would haunt him years later. Although it wasn't known at the time, his parents had also suffered from addictions. And, as it turned out, his former junior coach, Graham James, had also sexually abused players when Fleury was still in junior. James would be convicted of his crimes years later. If Fleury had been aware of some of the coach's activities, he had not let on.

Fleury signed with the Flames in time to join their farm club in Salt Lake for the American League playoffs. He counted eight goals in only 11 games and helped the Golden Eagles claim the Calder Cup championship, while also earning the playoff MVP honours. After attending his second Calgary training camp, he was sent back to Salt Lake because, unlike the veterans, he was on a two-way deal that paid him less in the minors.

As Fleury began the season in the minors, the Flames got off to a slow start with their new star Gilmour. They quickly rebounded. In their first 16 games, they only lost three times. Later they launched a 13-game undefeated streak, allaying Crisp's earlier fears that they would become complacent and not try their hardest. But, around Christmas time, Calgary went into the doldrums. After losing only four times in their first 46 outings, the Flames had only four wins in their last 10 games. The poor showings posed additional concern because, with the exception of Montreal, they all came against Smythe Division rivals — teams that they would have to beat in the first two rounds, often the toughest, of the playoffs.

The Flames needed someone who could shake them out of their lethargy, someone who could lift the team offensively if necessary and provide the grit that appeared to be lacking. Crisp and Fletcher knew exactly where to find him. On the first day of 1989, the Flames called up Fleury. "We were looking for some kind of spark," recalled Crisp. "We had a lot of good pieces in place. He was playing so well in the minors. He was a bottle of energy. He made things go."

Flames management personnel, said Crisp, wanted to find out whether Fleury was any good or whether they were just wasting their time trying to develop him into an NHLer. "He was a little buzz bomb," said Crisp. "He'd go out and stir up the hornet's nest and he could make things happen." The pesky forward, who could play both centre and wing, continued his high-scoring ways in the NHL. He saw action on the power play and penalty killing units while also taking a regular shift.

The Flames had their answer. Fleury was there to stay. Someone else's job was in jeopardy. "What he did was, he made everybody accountable," said Crisp. The Flames lost a total of only six games in January and February. In addition to Fleury and the other stars, so-called lesser lights such as Otto, Patterson, Peplinski, Tim Hunter, and Mark Hunter were also providing timely goals. But one veteran was struggling. His name was Lanny McDonald.

It was widely believed that this would be McDonald's final season in the NHL, although he was not ready to confirm his retirement plans. His offence had declined steadily in recent years and his nagging injuries were catching up with him. At the beginning of the season, McDonald had appeared to be a shoe-in to garner two milestones — his 500th goal and his 1000th career point. As February turned into March, he still had not attained them.

Coach Crisp was naturally not concerned about a player's personal achievements. He was only concerned about his team's achievements. So, on many nights, McDonald sat in the press box while his younger teammates played. "That's probably the hardest and toughest thing you'll do as a coach, when you have the character of the guys who have earned the right to be there," said Crisp.

Unlike many of his rival coaches, Crisp had a deep and talented lineup. He merely tried to put in the right players at the right time. McDonald kept working hard in practice, and in early March, the coach put him back into games. On March 7, 1989, he collected his 1,000th career point as he scored two goals in a 9-5 win over Winnipeg. On March 21, against the

New York Islanders, he carried the puck behind the net and scored his 500th career goal on a wraparound.

But there was still one prize that McDonald was missing. The Stanley Cup.

Meanwhile, Fletcher and Crisp felt the team was also missing something. Although the Flames had plenty of scorers, and a steady goaltender in Vernon, they did not have enough checkers for the GM's or the coach's liking. With 12 games left in the regular season, while McDonald was chasing his milestones, Fletcher acquired winger Brian MacLellan from the Minnesota North Stars.

Again, Fletcher had plucked a player who had overcome many odds to reach the NHL — and who was playing beyond anyone's expectations of him. Growing up in Guelph, Ontario, MacLellan started playing hockey later than most of his friends. While his buddies were skating, MacLellan was in a leg brace, suffering from Legg-Perthes disease, a condition that attacks the hip joint. Doctors later recommended that he start playing hockey because exercise and the cool, moist arena air might improve the condition. MacLellan joined a house league team in Guelph and worked intensely on his game. The hip never bothered him again. He grew to six-foot-three and earned many offers from U.S. colleges. He opted to attend Ohio's Bowling Green University, where he was named to the All-American team in all four years of his college eligibility. No NHL team drafted him. In 1982, the Kings took a chance and signed him as a free agent.

Over the next two years, on a line with Marcel Dionne, MacLellan scored 25 and 31 goals, respectively. Mid-way through his fourth season in L.A., MacLellan was traded to the Rangers. After he fell out of favour with coach Ted Sator because he refused to play a more physical style, New York sent MacLellan to Minnesota. The North Stars were able to tap MacLellan's potential in 1986-87 and he produced 32 goals and added 31 assists.

Like McDonald, MacLellan knew that his NHL days were numbered. He was already taking college courses off-season to prepare for a business career after his playing days. So far in his seven-year career, MacLellan's teams had only made the playoffs twice. For the previous three seasons, the North Stars had not qualified for the post-season. At last, like McDonald, he was going to get his shot at the Cup.

The Flames finished the regular season with a 54-17-9 record — one of the best in modern NHL history. They were assured of home-ice advantage, meaning they would host the first two games and the seventh game, if necessary, of each series. In other words, Calgary was the obvious favourite to win Lord Stanley's mug. The pressure was on.

Calgary drew the Canucks in the opening round. After finishing fourth in the Smythe Division, Vancouver was not expected to do much in the post-season, but coach Bob McCammon was not nicknamed "Cagey" for nothing. He had earned the moniker for using his brain rather than his brawn while playing and coaching in the tough International

League. Much to the delight of reporters, he was also quick with colourful quotes, which he used as barbs to upset his team's opponents. As a former Oilers assistant, he was a veteran of the Battle of Alberta, so he liked to claim, "Cliff Fletcher built his team to beat Edmonton. Now he's got a big team that plays tough and doesn't know how else to play."

In the first game, former Flame Paul Reinhart scored at 2:47 of overtime to give the Canucks a 4-3 victory at the Saddledome. The Flames countered with a 5-2 decision in game two, tying the series as it shifted to the West Coast. The Flames subdued the Pacific Coliseum crowd by blanking the Canucks 4-0 in the third game, but Vancouver took the fourth game, 5-3. Back in Calgary, Vernon posted his second shutout of the series in the fifth game as the Flames won 4-0 and took a 3-2 lead in games.

Before game six, Cagey again accused the Flames of succeeding because they were goons, rather than talented players who capitalized on their skills. "They're trying to make it like they're the Cinderella of this thing." The Canucks rode the barb and the hot goaltending of Kirk McLean to a 6-3 victory in Vancouver in the sixth game, setting the stage for a dramatic seventh and deciding contest at the Saddledome on April 15, 1989.

The upstart Canucks had forced the Flames to a seventh game. Now, it was Vernon's turn to shine. Among his more memorable saves, he foiled Stan Smyl on a breakaway, picking off his hard wrist shot with his trapper mitt. He also forced Tony Tanti to hit the post on a wraparound and barely got his toe on a Petri Skriko slapshot. Thanks to Vernon, the score was tied 3-3 after regulation time. With less than a minute to go in the first overtime period, Peplinski skated with the puck along the right-wing boards and fired it at the net as Otto tangled with Canucks defenceman Harold Snepsts. Although Otto had his back to Peplinski, the puck hit Otto's skate and somehow went in, giving the Flames 4-3 wins in both the game and the series. "That was a heart-stopper," Crisp recalled in an understatement.

The tension increased as the Flames advanced to meet the Los Angeles Kings and a former foe from the Battle of Alberta — the dreaded Gretzky. In the opening game, Bearcat Murray almost caused a few coronaries himself. When Kings' sniper Bernie Nicholls decked Vernon, Murray hopped over the boards and raced to Vernon. Bearcat wore spiked shoes, which were designed to prevent him from slipping on the ice. They did not let him down and he arrived in Vernon's crease in a few seconds — but the whistle had not blown. "I think we're in trouble here," Bearcat told Vernon, pushing him to the safety of the back of the net and hoping the referee wouldn't see them. The play continued at the other end of the ice. A few moments later, MacInnis scored. The Kings players and coaches howled in protest, but the goal was allowed to stand. The Flames went on to win the game — despite Gretzky — and sweep the series. Except for Bearcat's shenanigans, the battle that many thought would go seven games was surprisingly without drama.

The Flames then advanced to the Clarence Campbell Conference finals against the Mike Keenan-coached Chicago Blackhawks. Calgary disposed of the Blackhawks in relatively easy fashion, taking the series 4-1. As co-captain McDonald held up the Clarence Campbell Trophy, the Saddledome chanted "Lanny! Lanny!" in a deafening roar. As he skated off the ice, sweat pouring from his playoff beard, spectators sensed that McDonald was making one of his last appearances. They were ecstatic that he would get another chance to put his name on the Cup. They still must have wondered, how much ice time would he get?

The Stanley Cup final series opened May 14, 1989. Calgary skated away with a 4-3 win. Montreal doubled Calgary 4-2 in the second game and the series headed to Montreal tied 1-1. Ryan Walter's goal in double overtime gave the hometown Habs a 4-3 decision and the series lead. The Flames rallied to beat Montreal 4-2 in game four at the Forum.

Back in Calgary, the Flames delighted the Saddledome faithful with a 3-2 victory, which also gave Crisp's crew a 3-2 series lead. For the third straight game, McDonald had watched from the press box. The series returned to Montreal, with Calgary on the verge of clinching its first Stanley Cup. Many wondered whether McDonald had already played his final game as a Flame. Would Crisp sit him out again?

In Montreal, Cliff Fletcher, showing a rarely seen superstitious side, had two other people on his mind — radio play-by-play announcer Peter Maher and his sidekick, colour commentator Doug Barkley. Maher had been calling the Flames action — home and away — since their second season in Calgary.

Hockey players, coaches, and managers can be creatures of habit. They will stick to the same routines if they think it brings them luck. On road trips, a team member will choose his seat on the team bus — and sit there every time. Before the bus leaves the hotel for the game, the manager checks to make sure that everyone is aboard simply by looking at their regular seats. Anyone missing is a cause for concern, because his absence could be a bad omen.

Maher and Barkley usually took the team bus to the rink. They also sat in the same seats to satisfy the superstitious. On the bus before game four in Montreal — which the Flames lost — Fletcher had noticed the absence of the broadcasters. Maher and Barkley had taken a cab to the Forum that time because media were staying at a different hotel.

Before game six, Fletcher had ordered Maher and Barkley to be on the bus. He did not want any part of the team's routine to change before such an important game. Although they again had a shorter route to the Forum from their own hotel, Maher and Barkley complied. They took a cab to the Flames' hotel to get on the bus. Earlier in the day, Maher had also snuck out and bought three tiny bottles of champagne — one for himself, one for his brother who would also be in the booth that night, and one for Barkley

— and slipped them into his bag. Would this be the night?

When the Flames came out for the opening face-off, McDonald was among the starters. McDonald even wore the captain's 'C'. Crisp stunned many observers by leaving co-captains Tim Hunter and Jim Peplinski out of the lineup. He did not feel that they were playing as well as they could and thought the Flames needed more offence than physical prowess that night.

At least McDonald was at least in uniform — rather than in the press box — for what was likely to be the final game of his career. But coach Crisp had more surprises — he inserted McDonald on a line with Nieuwendyk and Roberts. McDonald, knowing that each shift could be the last of his career, was flying from the start. It was obvious he wanted to remember this night forever.

The score was tied 1-1 after the first period. Early in the second, as a penalty to McDonald was expiring, Nieuwendyk carried the puck over centre ice towards the Montreal zone. McDonald raced out of the sin bin and joined the action. Nieuwendyk fired a shot on goal, but Roy kicked it out. McDonald zoomed in for the rebound and one-timed it past the startled Montreal netminder to give Calgary a 2-1 lead at 4:24. McDonald ecstatically lifted his arms above his head and danced in celebration. Wasn't it perfect, he mused. What might be his last goal as a Flame had come in the same rink as his first one.

The Habs came back to tie the score 2-2. In the third

Lanny McDonald holding the Stanley Cup.

period, Gilmour knocked in his own rebound and then added an empty-net goal to give the Flames a 4-2 victory — and their first Stanley Cup. And, for the first time ever, a visiting team had captured the Stanley Cup on Forum ice.

As the final horn sounded, Crisp, so relieved at having won, scaled the glass behind the bench into the first row of seats — and planted a kiss firmly on the lips of Al MacNeil's surprised wife Norma, while his own wife Sheila sat amused nearby. Up in the radio booth, Maher borrowed a line from a song by rock star Rod Stewart. "Yeah, baby!" Maher roared into the microphone. After handing out his hidden champagne to his brother and Barkley, Maher decided that "yeah, baby!" would be his signature phrase. He vowed to only use it on very special occasions.

Down on the ice, Hunter and Peplinski, still dressed in their red longjohns from watching the game in the dressing room, hoisted the Stanley Cup together. Owner Harley Hotchkiss looked on from the bench area. "Should I be out there?" Hotchkiss asked MacNeil. "You don't get this chance very often," said MacNeil. "Get out there!"

So the Calgary Flames — players, coaches, managers, trainers, and owners — assembled for a famous team photo, lying, sitting, or kneeling as they crowded into the shot. It was a moment they would remember for the rest of their lives. It was also their last time on ice together.

Chapter 6
Life After Gilmour

fter he and Calgary won the Cup at last, McDonald retired during a gala party on the lawn of his home. Approximately 100 old friends came to say farewell, including the couple who billeted him while he played junior in Lethbridge. McDonald spoke to reporters from a wooden podium that was about a foot off the ground. Oblivious to the significance of the occasion, Lanny's five-year-old son amused himself by jumping on and off the wooden structure. He thumped here, there, and everywhere. Nobody — not even the radio reporters, whose clips were disrupted — seemed to mind.

But fans became perturbed when, in a more surprising move, Hakan Loob also quit the NHL. He returned to play in his homeland, Sweden, where he wanted his young children to attend school.

The Flames held their 1989-90 training camp in Moscow, one of the first NHL teams to do so, reflecting the modernization of communism in the former superpower. In the Flames lineup was Sergei Makarov, one of the first former soviet stars allowed to play in the NHL.

Changes to Calgary's lineup continued as the Flames returned to Calgary and began the regular season. After only six games, captain Jim Peplinski unexpectedly retired — at the age of 29 — because he no longer enjoyed pro hockey.

Despite these blows, Calgary still finished first overall in the 1989-90 season. But after the Los Angeles Kings stunned Calgary in the first-round of the playoffs, coach Crisp lost his job. He was surprised and upset, feeling that the team's top finish had earned him another season.

In 1990-91, under new coach Risebrough, the Flames placed a respectable fourth overall as Fleury potted a career-high 51 goals. But Calgary lost to the Edmonton Oilers in seven games —once again — and in the first round. After 19 years at the helm of the franchise, president and general manager Cliff Fletcher resigned to take on the challenges of the Toronto Maple Leafs. Risebrough became general manager, but kept his coaching duties. The following season brought catastrophe.

With salaries escalating rapidly throughout the league, many Flames — Gilmour in particular — had been complaining about their contracts. On January 1, with the Flames struggling, he walked out on the team, and demanded a trade.

The next day, Risebrough shipped him to the Leafs in the largest trade in NHL history. Ten players were involved. Popular backup goaltender Rick Wamsley and defencemen Macoun and Rick Nattress and prospect Kent Manderville went with Gilmour to Toronto. Journalists and fans alike felt that Fletcher had fleeced his old protégé Risebrough. Calgary received Gary Leeman, a former 50-goal scorer with Toronto, who was supposed to be Calgary's new saviour. He only produced two goals and seven assists in 29 games.

Risebrough was heavily criticized for trading Gilmour so soon after his walkout. Late in the regular season, after a humiliating 11-0 loss to the Canucks in Vancouver, Risebrough resigned as coach. Assistant coach Guy Charron was appointed interim head coach for the balance of the season, which was interrupted by a general players' strike. He managed to light a fire under Calgary's struggling veterans, posting a respectable 6-7-3 record. But, for the first time since coming to Calgary, the Flames missed the playoffs.

What a difference two years made for the Flames.

In the off-season, Risebrough went looking for a new permanent head coach. After taking his time, Risebrough finally hired Dave King, the coach and general manager of Canada's national team. In February, while the Flames had been struggling, King had guided Canada to an Olympic silver medal — Canada's first Games hardware since 1968. The accomplishment was particularly impressive because, in those days, the NHL did not interrupt its season so that its players could participate in the Olympics. Canada's silver medal squad consisted primarily of amateurs, NHL castoffs, and holdouts like centre Eric Lindros and goaltender Sean Burke. After King had developed their castoffs and prospects, NHL clubs routinely plucked the players.

Because his teams were always deficient talent-wise, King became a master strategist, especially against the Soviet Union, whom he regarded as the cat to Canada's pigeon. He taught young Canadian players to believe in themselves — and they thrived. "I've always believed that the most important thing in coaching is never to be critical of anything other than the performance of a person," said King. Unlike most NHL coaches, who had played in the league, King was a career coach. Thanks to King, Canada's national program became a model for the rest of the world.

After nine seasons at the Canadian team's helm, though, King longed to coach in the world's best league — the NHL. "In the NHL there's a danger," said King. "Your job is on the line all the time. Not many people can do it successfully. That draws you to it. It's difficult and a great challenge." His challenge with the Flames was to get them back to the playoffs.

Before King could get his feet wet in the 1992-93 season, bad luck struck the Flames again. In October, Nieuwendyk nailed Vernon with a shot in the head in practice. The goalie suffered a 15-stitch cut to his forehead and had to sit out five games.

In November, defenceman Al MacInnis experienced a Remembrance Day that he would rather forget. In a game at Hartford, MacInnis was racing back to his own end to retrieve the puck with Whalers' rookie Patrick Poulin in hot pursuit. As MacInnis picked up the puck in the corner, Poulin poked him in the back of the legs with his stick. With his legs spread wide, MacInnis lost his balance, wishboned into the boards, and suffered a dislocated hip. The injury threatened to end his career.

Shortly after doctors reinserted the hip bone into its socket, however, MacInnis began his rehabilitation. A few weeks later, he shed his crutches and began off-ice workouts. "I'm surprised to see him walking around," said Dale Tallon, who had also dislocated a hip while playing for Chicago and still walked with a limp. "It was the most painful injury I ever had." Baseball and football star Bo Jackson had suffered a similar injury, forcing him to retire from both sports prematurely. MacInnis managed to avoid poor blood flow, which would have caused the hip to degenerate, by swimming for 30 minutes a day, and completing hip exercises that simulated skating, riding a stationary bike, and lifting weights. He began skating in January — only seven weeks after the injury — and resumed playing a short time later. Was the Flames' luck turning around at last?

Then the Flames suffered another major blow in a game

against the Philadelphia Flyers. Their high-scoring Roberts suffered a broken blood vessel in his thigh from Flyers defenceman Gary Galley's knee. The Flames flew to Toronto after the game; Roberts left the plane on a wheelchair and immediately underwent surgery. This injury also threatened to end Roberts' career.

But something incredible happened while Roberts, MacInnis, and several other players were out with injuries. Calgary kept winning. Living up to his reputation as a master tactician and excellent teacher, King got the most out of several other players — grateful Flames who knew all about overcoming the odds.

Defenceman Frank Musil had defected from Czechoslovakia with his wife, a former tennis star, in time to join the NHL for the 1986-87 season. He was so determined to learn English that he enrolled in kindergarten classes. The six-foot-three and 215-pound Musil had made an interesting contrast to his five-year-old classmates!

Defenceman Jim Kyte, once one of the most feared fighters in the game, was the first legally deaf player to toil in the NHL. As a result of a hereditary nerve condition, the Ottawa native's hearing had declined steadily since he was three years old. Although he could speak, quite eloquently in fact, he learned sign language. During off-seasons, he worked with deaf and hearing-impaired children at special hockey camps.

Winger Ron Stern had been only a teenager when his

father, a Montreal restaurateur, was murdered in a gangland slaying. Stern, still playing junior hockey at the time, managed to overcome his grief and crack the Vancouver Canucks roster after a few seasons in the minors.

As the end of the regular season approached, thanks to the amazing gritty performances of these unsung heroes, Calgary was assured of a playoff berth. With Roberts still out, the Flames were getting most of their goals from Fleury, Robert Reichel, Suter and Nieuwendyk. If Calgary was going do anything in the post-season, more players would have to score.

Defensive defenceman Trent Yawney was hoping he could contribute. With five games to go in the regular season, Yawney was still looking for his first goal. "You know it's getting tough when your wife starts bugging you," said Yawney. He had almost scored in a 4-3 victory over the San Jose Sharks. But Otto got his stick on Yawney's slapshot and got credit for the goal. In the next four games, despite coming close several times, Yawney still could not score. The regular season finale, again against San Jose, was his last chance. With Roberts back in the lineup after missing more than a third of the season, he set up Yawney — and the defenceman finally scored. The Flames beat the Sharks 7-3 to finish ninth overall.

Calgary opened the post-season against Los Angeles — and Yawney scored again, and again, and again. Suddenly, after three games, he was one of the hottest Flames. Most of Calgary's regular top scorers could not turn the red light on.

Vernon had also suffered an ankle injury and only played parts of the last two games. Backup Jeff Reese struggled at times and the Kings took the series in six.

In 1993-94, Calgary captured the new Pacific Division's title. In the first round, they faced Vancouver — for the fifth time in 13 years. The Canucks blanked the Flames 5-0 in the first game. Vernon, heavily criticized for his play in the first game, stoned the Canucks over the next three games. Calgary took a 3-1 series lead back to the Saddledome. At last, Calgary's first-round playoff jinx appeared to be coming to an end. But the Canucks stunned the Flames by taking the next three games — all in overtime — to capture the series in seven games. Pavel Bure's decisive breakaway goal spelled Vernon's departure. In June 1994, 13 years after he joined the Flames as a draft choice, he was traded to the Detroit Red Wings for defenceman Steve Chiasson. A couple of days later, Calgary traded MacInnis to St. Louis for defenceman Phil Housley, while the clubs also swapped draft picks.

As a result of the deals, most of the players from Calgary's Stanley Cup-winning squad were gone. The Flames once dreamed of becoming a dynasty but now they would have to win with a different cast of players.

Chapter 7
Iginla Arrives

It was the fall of 1995 — and Calgary fans were staying away in droves. They were angry. The previous spring, the regular season had been reduced to 48 games because of a lockout. San Jose's goal, in the third overtime period in the seventh game, eliminated the Flames in the first round of the playoffs — once again. Fans were fed up with millionaire hockey players who griped about low salaries, while average players earned more than Lanny McDonald did in his heyday. Bad trades were also coming back to haunt the Flames. Although three years had passed since Gilmour's departure, it still rankled the Flames' faithful followers.

General manager Risebrough responded by firing coach

King in the off-season.

Risebrough became persona non grata. Griping about him in letters to the editor and on radio talk shows, fans wanted him out. One more bad trade, and one more bad season, they thought, and the financially struggling Flames could be forced to move out of Calgary.

The owners did not heed the fans' wishes — but they didn't show much faith in Risebrough either. In a bizarre move, they promoted assistant general manager Al Coates to a vice-president's post. In other words, Risebrough's underling became his boss. It certainly appeared as if Risebrough's job was in jeopardy.

Risebrough had managed to sign Fleury after he held out in training camp, but the troubled GM failed to ink Joe Nieuwendyk to a new agreement. The Calgary captain stayed away from camp, too, and when the regular season began, he demanded a trade or a new contract. Based on his offensive production throughout his career, he was due to earn about $5 million per season. The Flames could not afford to keep him. They could also not afford to surrender him without getting a decent player in return. Fans became even more livid. Nieuwendyk's holdout was reminding them of the Gilmour dispute, and everyone knew what had happened then. Risebrough refused to budge — so Nieuwendyk sat and waited.

The Flames started terribly under new coach Pierre Page, posting only one victory in their first 11 games. When the season — and Nieuwendyk's contract impasse — stretched into November, new vice-president Coates decided it was time to act. He fired his former boss Risebrough and took over as the club's GM. In December, with the Flames still playing terribly, Coates traded Nieuwendyk to the Dallas Stars. In return, Calgary obtained utility forward Corey Millen. They also got a junior prospect who played for the Kamloops Blazers and was preparing to suit up for Canada's junior team for the upcoming world championships in Boston. His name was Jarome Iginla.

In addition to excelling at hockey, Iginla was the starting catcher on Canada's national junior baseball team. One of the few black players in hockey, Iginla had grown up in an Edmonton suburb. Although his Nigerian-born father and Canadian mother divorced when he was a baby, Iginla maintained close relationships with both parents and enjoyed a happy and prosperous childhood in St.Albert.

St. Albert was also the hometown of former Oilers' star Mark Messier. Like Messier, his idol, Iginla could handle the rough going and he was a prolific scorer. Although he was often subject to racist remarks on the ice as opponents tried to throw him off his game, he had made the Kamloops lineup as a 16-year-old and already helped the Blazers win two Memorial Cup titles.

His trade to Calgary during the world juniors in Boston generated considerable buzz, because many journalists were present. Despite the attention surrounding him, Iginla thrived during the tournament. With five goals and seven assists in only seven games, he led Canada to the gold medal. Iginla returned to the Western League following the tournament and continued to score frequently. He finished the season as the Western League's fourth leading scorer with 63 goals and 73 assists and was named the player of the year.

Meanwhile, the Flames were making a late-season surge, thanks to the return of Roberts from an ongoing neck injury. He played only 35 games but still finished as Calgary's fifth top scorer with 20 goals and 22 assists. His courageous comeback would earn him the Masterton Trophy for perseverance and dedication to hockey. More importantly, it helped the Flames secure a playoff berth as they placed 15th overall. (Playoff seedings were now based on overall standings rather than divisional results.)

The Flames faced the Chicago Blackhawks in the playoffs — and promptly lost the first two games. By then the Kamloops' Blazers season was over, so general manager Coates called Iginla. While most of his teammates were sleeping in after a night of partying, 18-year-old Iginla flew to Calgary, signed a contract, and played that same night. Wearing No. 24 rather than his now familiar No. 12, Iginla notched his first NHL goal and an assist in his first two pro games. Rookies were generally considered lucky to start in regular season games, but Iginla played a regular shift in the post-season. Fleury was so impressed that he said the kid could play on his line any time.

In spite of Iginla's help, the Flames were still eliminated in four straight games. They had not advanced beyond the first round of the playoffs since their 1988-89 Stanley Cup championship. The following three seasons came and went in a blur as the Flames reached new levels of futility and missed the playoffs every year. Iginla proved to be a gem among cobblestones as he led all rookies with 50 points in his first full pro season. However, even he slumped through his sophomore campaign.

As for the rest of the team, faces kept changing. Roberts retired for a year and then came out of retirement following neck surgery. He was traded to Hartford where he hoped his travel miles — and the risk of re-injuring his neck — would be reduced.

Fleury was now the only player remaining from Calgary's Stanley Cup-winning team. He was also among the highest-paid players in the NHL and would soon be seeking a new deal. Everyone knew that it was just a matter of time before, he, too, would be traded because the team could not afford to pay him a huge salary. There was more pressure than ever on the organization to find young players who could help the Flames regain their respect — and challenge the league's best for the Cup.

Page lasted one more season and then Brian Sutter took his place as coach. And, in February 1999, Coates traded Fleury to the Colorado Avalanche in a package deal. The key player coming to Calgary had yet to play in the NHL. He was an 18-year-old defenceman who had also played with the Kamloops Blazers — Robyn Regehr.

Although he was a Canadian citizen, Regehr had spent his early childhood in Brazil, where he was born, and Indonesia, as his parents served as international aid workers. As a result, he only started playing hockey when his family returned to their roots in Rosthern, Saskatchewan. Despite the late start, the game came naturally to Robyn. He made the Blazers as a 16-year-old and was also selected to Canada's team for the world junior championships. After the Flames had lost so many of their veteran defencemen, they viewed him as a blue-chip prospect.

On July 4, 1999, Regehr's pro career literally came crashing to a halt in a horrific car accident that was not his fault. He suffered terrible damage to his legs, the keys to his hockey career. A two-inch bolt was driven through the bone of his right knee as the floorboard, rendered jagged by the impact, had impaled his legs onto the seat. Both of his legs were broken. After doctors inserted rods in both legs, Regehr lay on his bed, looked up at the ceiling and prayed. "The main thing I tried to do was look at the positives of the situation. I was still alive," he said.

Regehr would not be able to skate for at least four to six months. Calgary's promising prospect would be lucky to play at all, let alone in the NHL. But his legs healed faster than anyone thought they would. By September, he was ready to get back on the ice — and he went to Calgary's training camp. He signed a contract with the Flames and went down to Calgary's farm team in St. John, New Brunswick, for a two-week conditioning stint. He played his first pro game only four months after his near-death experience.

On a Thursday night in the nation's capital, Regehr suited up for Calgary, giving meaning to a game too early in the regular season to count for anything else. Coach Brian Sutter said Regehr played a mistake-free game as the Flames prevailed 4-3 in overtime. "Sometimes things happen to make a person stronger," said Regehr. "I'm very appreciative of what I have now. I know things can change in an instant." The rebuilding Flames were also grateful to have him.

In the second half of the season, Fred Brathwaite became the Flame's inspiration. He was the sixth goaltender that the team used. Four others had suffered injuries and another one played only three games on an emergency basis. Calgary had actually signed Brathwaite, then a member of Canada's national team, to make up for a shortage of goalies on their farm team. After a disastrous road trip on which their goalies struggled, the Flames decided to bring in Brathwaite for a look-see. Brathwaite did not just emerge as the team's new starter — he posted the best goals against average in the NHL for a while. But Brathwaite's strong, sometimes spectacular, play still could not get the Flames into the playoffs. They failed to qualify for the post-season again the next year.

President Ron Bremner decided to clean house. General manager Coates, head coach Sutter, and assistant coach Rich

Preston were all fired. Although they had just tried to negotiate a trade for a top player — rumoured to be Gilmour — the owners vetoed it. The deal, said Sutter, would have propelled the Flames into the playoffs. Al MacNeil, who had served as an assistant coach under Sutter for three years, thought the head coach's dismissal was unfair. He too believed the Flames were on the verge of making the playoffs. Fed up with how far the Flames had fallen from their glory years, MacNeil quit the team in protest. Incredibly, the Flames' longest-serving and loyal employee was gone. And the Flames missed the playoffs again. Calgary handed the general manager's reins to Craig Button, a young executive from the Dallas Stars.

New coach Don Hay was fired with 13 games remaining in the regular season, and replaced by Greg Gilbert, a former assistant. The Flames missed the playoffs one more time. However, before the start of the next season, the owners asked Al MacNeil to return to the organization and resume his former role as a jack-of-all-trades executive. Again showing his loyalty, he quietly obliged after spending a year watching junior games and cleaning out his files at home.

Nonetheless, the Flames stumbled from the start and again failed to qualify for the 2000-01 post-season. Up in the radio booth, Peter Maher longed for the day when the Flames would give him something to yell "yeah baby" about again.

In June 2001, the Flames obtained goaltender Roman Turek in a deal that was viewed as a commitment to turning Calgary into a contender. The lanky goaltender from

Strakonice in the Czech Republic was soon due to become a free agent and would be in line for a salary in the $5-$6 million per year range. Turek's early success helped fans forget about their beloved Brathwaite, who went to St. Louis in the trade that brought the Czech goaltender to Calgary.

Calgary's owners also replaced President Bremner with Ken King, a former newspaper publisher. Acknowledging that he had no previous experience in pro hockey, King promised to let Button and his staff run the hockey side. He would concentrate on business operations. "It's about the hockey," said King, suggesting that the franchise's survival depended on a team that was successful on the ice.

For the first time in several seasons, Calgary zoomed out of the starting gate. Riding Turek's hot goaltending hand, the Flames posted 13 wins, four losses — including two in overtime — and three ties in their first 20 games. Turek was rewarded for his outstanding play with a new four-year contract worth a US$19 million. The goaltender became the highest paid player in Flames history.

After attending the Canadian Olympic team's training camp in September, Iginla also joined the Flames in excellent condition. He served notice that he and the Flames intended to shine this season.

Almost immediately afterwards, Calgary's fortunes nosedived. The Flames went winless between November 17 and December 3. Over the next two months, the Flames recorded only seven wins — even though Iginla counted 12 goals and

6 assists in November to earn honours as NHL player of the month. Turek was suddenly colder than the Arctic, but coach Gilbert continued to use him, leaving Vernon to stew on the bench in what would be his final NHL season.

Iginla still enjoyed some good news in December: he was named to Canada's Olympic team. Three months later, after losing to Sweden in the opening game, Canada rallied and advanced to the Olympic final against the U.S. Iginla scored two goals and added an assist as Canada beat the Americans 5-2. Thanks to Iginla's fine play, Canada won its first Olympic gold medal 50 years to the day after the Edmonton Mercury's gave Canada its last one. Iggy was now a household name across the country.

Iginla's dream season continued when he returned to the Flames for the resumption of the NHL regular season. Playing with more confidence than ever before, Iginla notched his 50th and 51st goals of the season in early April. He became the first Flame to score 50 goals since Gary Roberts way back in 1991-92.

"Yeah, baby!" shouted Peter Maher — for the first time in several seasons — up in the radio booth.

Iginla finished the campaign as the NHL's top scorer with 52 goals and 44 assists. No other NHLer scored 50 that season. He garnered the Art Ross Trophy for most points in the NHL, the Rocket Richard Trophy for most goals, and the Lester B. Pearson Award as the most valuable player as judged by players. He also finished as the runner-up to Jose Theodore for the Hart Trophy following a rare split decision. However, all Iginla's awards were bittersweet. He became one of the few players in the NHL's modern era to win the scoring title even though his team failed to qualify for the post-season.

However, the Flames were beginning to show signs of real progress. Iginla and his linemate Craig Conroy, and a young defence corps were maturing together as a team. Conroy had tallied 75 points in a breakout offensive a year after being considered a checker for several seasons. Calgary's playoff chances looked good for a change. They looked even better in October, when the Flames acquired centre Chris Drury, considered one of the best young offensive players in the game, and solid two-way centre Stephane Yelle for Derek Morris, forward Jeff Shantz, and speedy winger Dean McAmmond.

With their linemate McAmmond gone, both Iginla and Conroy started the 2002-03 season slowly. Calgary won only three games in the opening month of October and started November by losing six straight. By late November, the Flames had only five wins to show for the entire season. Newspaper reports speculated almost daily on when the coach would be fired.

In a surprise move, team president King joined the team during a five-game road trip. On December 3, as the Flames prepared to play their final game of the trip in Denver, King contacted Gilbert in his hotel room and told him that his tenure with the Flames was over. For the second time since

2000, the Flames were about to go through a mid-season coaching change.

There was just one problem. Calgary had no permanent replacement for Gilbert.

Chapter 8
A New Bench Boss

Two days before the Flames axed Gilbert, the San Jose Sharks had canned coach Darryl Sutter. Although the Sharks were mired near the bottom of the conference standings and riddled with injuries, the firing caught Sutter by surprise. He had never posted a losing record since he began his coaching career. But he took the heat for San Jose's slow start to the season. Rather than sulk or stew at home, Darryl took his wife Wendy to the annual National Finals Rodeo in Las Vegas, saying, "It was something I always wanted to do." The trip to Vegas was just Sutter's way of dealing with adversity — which he had faced many times before.

Sutter had been Chicago's 11th choice, 117th overall

from the Lethbridge Broncos of the Western League in the 1978 entry draft. According to his brother Rich, Darryl's low selection stemmed from a serious knee injury, which had not been treated properly. Upset with being drafted so late, Darryl had instead signed with a team in Japan, where he counted 41 points in only 20 games. "He was the Darryl Sittler of hockey in Japan," recalled his brother. After returning to North America and signing with Chicago, Sutter won the American Hockey League's rookie award in 1980. He then joined the Blackhawks on a permanent basis. In eight seasons in Chicago, he scored 40 goals once and at least 20 goals in five consecutive seasons. The Blackhawks twice advanced within one series of the Stanley Cup finals with Sutter as captain.

Most of the time, he played in constant pain because of numerous knee operations. It eventually hurt to watch him play, said Rich, because he was trying to do on one leg what most players do on two. After the 1986-87 season, Darryl reluctantly announced his retirement, at the age of 29. He immediately launched a new career as a coach in the Blackhawks organization. He guided the Indianapolis Ice to an International League title, then returned to Chicago as an assistant coach. In 1992, he helped the Blackhawks reach the Stanley Cup finals, for the first time in more than two decades. After Sutter took over as head coach the next year, Chicago became a perennial Stanley Cup contender. In 1995, Sutter suddenly quit.

He decided that his then two-year-old son Christopher, who was born with Down Syndrome (an ailment that affects motor skills and IQ) needed him more than his team did. "I didn't agonize over it," said Sutter. "It was reality, it was the right thing. I had put myself ahead of my family for 17 years. My responsibility is as a father, first and foremost."

After two years at home in Viking, Alberta where — thanks to a satellite dish — he watched more games than ever before, he resumed his coaching career behind the bench of the San Jose Sharks at the start of the 1997-98 season. He inherited a 62-point club, which had missed the playoffs in four of the previous six seasons, and transformed it into a Stanley Cup contender. Under Sutter, the Sharks made the playoffs in each full season that he served. He became only the second coach in NHL history, behind the New York Islanders' legendary Al Arbour, to improve his team's point total in five straight seasons. The results were even more impressive, because the Sharks faced many injuries and contract disputes. Darryl rarely had a full roster to work with.

So Sutter may have been surprised but he was not worried when he was dismissed by the Sharks. He figured he would get another job sooner or later. While Sutter was vacationing in Vegas, Calgary's president Ken King appointed the ever-loyal MacNeil as interim coach. MacNeil only expected to be behind the bench for one or two games. He focused on getting the team ready for the new coach. The veteran Flames executive wanted to make sure that Calgary stayed in the fight for the playoffs.

Meanwhile, speculation about who would become the permanent Flames coach abounded. One report had Jim Playfair, head coach of Calgary's farm team in St. John, New Brunswick, on the verge of being hired. Playfair said he would only take the job if he was guaranteed to keep it the following season. When the *Calgary Herald* reached Sutter by phone, he said he would be interested, but so far it didn't look like the Flames were. December dragged on and Calgary still did not have a new coach. King refused to discuss who was being considered for the job. Behind the scenes, he quietly began negotiations with Darryl Sutter.

Despite the rumours and the uncertainty, MacNeil kept the team on an even keel as they posted victories over Colorado, Vancouver, Nashville, and Minnesota, a team managed by former Calgary GM Risebrough. It was clear that players were enjoying the game again — and the team was enjoying one of its best months in recent memory. MacNeil's supposedly brief coaching gig lasted 11 games as he finished with a 4-5-2 record.

Finally, on December 28, 2002, the Flames named Darryl Sutter as the 13th coach in its franchise history. The Flames post was a good fit for Darryl, said Rich Sutter, because he looked forward to moving his family back to his home province. During his first news conference, Sutter vowed to give the team an identity that the players would try to live up to every day — a winner's identity. In January, he guided Calgary to six wins, seven losses, and a tie. The Flames' turnaround was not surprising. After all, they had improved — temporarily as it turned out — under a new coach before. The question was: How long would the good times last under Sutter? In February, Calgary won only two of 13 games.

Despite the slump, the new coach continued to get good reviews. However, as the NHL's March trading deadline approached, fans, reporters, and players started to wonder how Calgary would fare. Rumours of potential trades surfaced and Iginla quietly worried about his future. The former NHL scoring leader was now the club's highest paid player at $7 million per season. The Flames might consider dealing him for a few players to save money. As the deadline drew nearer, he became more and more nervous. He wanted to stay in Calgary and help finish the rebuilding job that had started with the trades involving Nieuwendyk (for Iginla himself), Fleury, Suter, and others from the 1989 championship team.

The trading deadline came and the Flames kept Iginla. In fact, they dealt for a player who had helped him in the past — Dean McAmmond — and who hopefully would help Iginla re-kindle his offence of a year earlier. The Saddledome was buzzing the next day as Calgary prepared to play the Toronto Maple Leafs. The excitement stemmed from the arrival of former Flame Doug Gilmour, whom the Leafs had re-acquired at the deadline from Montreal for a draft pick. Gilmour was returning to one old team while playing against another former team. The other ex-Flame, McAmmond, had worked out with the Flames in the morning and was also looking forward to playing with his old Calgary teammates again.

As game time approached, though, word spread that all was not right with the McAmmond trade. The GM had unwittingly broken a rarely necessary rule in the collective bargaining agreement. Once a player was traded, he could not be traded back to his former team within 12 months of the original deal. Less than half a year had elapsed since McAmmond was traded to the Avalanche. The league later ruled that McAmmond would have to sit out the rest of this season.

Sadly, Gilmour also suffered misfortune. Early in the second period, Flames winger Dave Lowry, who had his back to the play, collided with the former Toronto captain in the neutral zone. Gilmour crawled to the bench with a severe knee injury that ended his season — and his career.

Fortunately, another trade that Calgary made did go through as planned. The Flames acquired Shean Donovan from the Pittsburgh Penguins for a couple of minor-leaguers. On the surface, the deal appeared to be a salary dump as the Flames unloaded two contracts in exchange for one. Donovan had counted only nine points in 52 games with the sad-sack Penguins. The Timmins, Ontario, native had started his NHL career under Sutter in San Jose in 1994-95.

Since he had played for Sutter before, Donovan's acquisition suggested that the coach was gaining greater influence within the Flames organization. However, the trade was questionable. Based on his career stats, the offensively challenged Flames could not expect Donovan to do much more than check. Before he left Pittsburgh, his career had apparently reached rock bottom. Fans could only hope that Sutter knew something about him that other coaches did not. After donning the Flames' uniform, Donovan again struggled to produce. However, his lone goal in a Calgary uniform proved to be the overtime game winner against Marty Turco, the league's top goaltender. Maybe Sutter had inside knowledge after all.

Although he wasn't scoring much, Donovan was helping the Flames win. After a terrible February, Calgary posted winning records in the final two months of the season, giving Sutter a respectable 19-8-8 record with the team. But for the first time in his NHL coaching or playing career, Darryl Sutter missed the playoffs.

At the end of the season, more changes loomed. Sutter received the added duties of general manager. Now, in addition to coaching the team, he would have to build the team. He would also draft, trade, and sign players, hire scouts, and oversee off-ice training schedules. As the Flames attempted to climb the proverbial mountain, almost every important decision would fall on Sutter's shoulders. Fans had to wonder, what did he know about managing a hockey organization?

Sutter's biggest challenge in the off-season was to sign

Chris Drury. Since his arrival the previous October from Colorado, reporters had speculated that Drury did not want to play in Calgary. Although he claimed that he liked Calgary, his usually glum facial expression suggested that he wanted to play elsewhere. As a result, the Drury deal threatened to become an albatross like the Gilmour trade of a decade earlier. After the strong finish to the regular-season, at least from the perspective of selling tickets, Calgary could not afford to have another key player hold out. May and June came and the Flames boss grew tired of what he viewed as an impasse. On July 3, 2003, Sutter traded Drury to the Buffalo Sabres in return for defenceman Rhett Warrener and forward Steve Reinprecht, whom the Sabres had acquired earlier in the day in a separate deal with Colorado.

Warrener didn't waste any time displaying his love for the Flames. On the day of the trade, the Shaunavon, Saskatchewan, native happened to be in Calgary for the annual Stampede, the exhibition that attracts a million visitors from around the world. He showed up for a news conference at the Saddledome on the Stampede grounds sporting a black cowboy hat and told reporters how much he was looking forward to playing in Calgary. In actual fact, he was just glad to be playing. A few months earlier, the defenceman had been involved in a bizarre incident. He was quarantined because he had been potentially exposed to the deadly Severe Acute Respiratory Syndrome (SARS), through his roommate's sister. Fortunately, Warrener showed no symptoms and doctors cleared him to re-join the club.

At the age of 27, Warrener became Calgary's oldest — and most experienced — defenceman. Drafted by Florida Panthers in the second round in 1996, he had achieved more than most of the players drafted ahead of him in the first round. Most of the 1996 first-rounders were not even in the NHL. After entering the league as a teenager, Warrener was already an eight-year veteran — and he had played in two Stanley Cup finals with Florida and the Buffalo Sabres.

Reinprecht was another example of a player who excelled after not being expected to do much. Perhaps because of his previous injuries, the scouts had overlooked the six-foot-one and 190-pound Edmonton native — even though he fit the NHL's prototype of a big, hard-working, and talented forward. Despite being a high scorer in junior, midget, and college, where he was also a four-time all-star with the vaunted University of Wisconsin Badgers, Reinprecht was not drafted. After being named as the Western Collegiate Hockey Association's player of the year and an all-American, he signed as a free agent in March of 2000 with the Los Angeles Kings. In the 2000-01 season, he finished fifth among rookie scorers with 15 goals and led all first-year players with five short-handed tallies. But he would stay with the Kings for only 59 games that season. Colorado insisted that he be included in the blockbuster deal that brought former Los Angeles all-star defenceman Rob Blake to the Avalanche on March 22, 2001. As a result, Reinprecht, like Fleury, became one of the few players to win the Stanley Cup as a rookie.

In his first major trade, Sutter had pulled off a sleeper. The deal worked financially and, more importantly, on the ice. Warrener and Reinprecht could step into Calgary's lineup immediately. Unlike previous deals, the Flames would not have to wait for future draft picks to develop. The future was now. In addition to acquiring players with talent and experience, Sutter had obtained players who knew how to win.

Meanwhile, two players acquired earlier — Yelle and Martin Gelinas — had also won Stanley Cups. In fact, Gelinas had reached the finals with three different teams. As a teenager, as part of the 1988 trade that sent Wayne Gretzky to Los Angeles, Gelinas won a Stanley Cup with the Edmonton Oilers. He also helped the Vancouver Canucks reach the 1993-94 finals, and his strong play enabled the upstart Carolina Panthers advance to the final in 2001-02.

Gelinas, Yelle, Reinprecht, and Warrener could serve as role models for the homegrown Flames who had little or no playoff experience. So could another player, who, just because of his position, was probably the most important Flame of all — Roman Turek. The goaltender had won a Cup title with Dallas in 1998-99 as a backup to Ed Belfour. He had also helped St. Louis reach the Stanley Cup semi-finals in 2000-01. But he had not performed well in Calgary since his hot start in 2001-02, just before he signed his big contract. The 2003-04 season offered Turek a chance to redeem himself.

Despite Turek in goal, Calgary opened the campaign

Oleg Saprykin, Calgary vs. Toronto, September 17, 2000.

with a humiliating 4-1 loss to Vancouver. Then, in the second game of the regular season, San Jose forward Alyn McAuley crashed into Turek, his knee colliding with the goalie's head. Turek was forced to leave the game, until doctors determined that he did not suffer a concussion. He soon returned to the lineup — but his comeback was short. A week later, only a minute and a half into the first period against Buffalo, he attempted to stop a shot by Ales Kotalik. Turek injured his knee and was again forced to the sidelines. This time, he would miss at least a month because of a sprained medial collateral ligament. Suddenly, the Flames had a major hole in goal.

The team's other goalie, Jamie McLennan, a career back-up, had spent the entire 2001-02 season in the minors because he could not crack the lineup of the parent Minnesota Wild. No other NHL team wanted him. Dany Sabourin, officially a rookie, was called up to take Turek's place on the roster. After three full seasons in the minors, he had no NHL experience. First-year minor pro Brent Krahn, a former Calgary Hitman drafted in the first-round in 2000, showed great potential, but was definitely not ready for the NHL. He was also recuperating from reconstructive knee surgery, which had kept him out of action almost two seasons.

With McLennan and Sabourin sharing the load, Calgary won only four games in October. In November, the losses continued. What a difference a year didn't make. The Flames were playing as poorly for Sutter as they had for Gilbert. On November 15, the Flames lost 2-1 in overtime to the Oilers in Edmonton — and Sutter came home unhappy.

The very next day, he traded a conditional second or third-round 2005 draft choice to his old team, the Sharks, for Miika Kiprusoff. "What do I like about him?" asked Sutter in response to a reporter's question. "He's an experienced NHL goaltender who's not 40 years old." Kiprusoff hardly looked like a saviour. Despite his coy comment, Sutter knew that "Kipper" could rise to a challenge. When Sharks starter

Evgeni Nabokov was injured in the first round of the playoffs against St. Louis, Kiprusoff had stepped in as a last-minute replacement. He stopped 39 shots as the Sharks beat the Blues 3-2. He became the first Finnish goaltender to win a Stanley Cup playoff game; he allowed only three goals in his first five NHL post-season contests.

Although he had posted a respectable 7-6 record in 2001-02, Kiprusoff played poorly in 2002-03 so fell to third-string status under new San Jose coach Ron Wilson. So far in 2003-04, Kipper had not played a single game with San Jose. If they had wanted to send him to the minors, the Sharks would have to put him on unrecallable waivers. Any other NHL team could pick him up without having to supply any players in return. Since he wasn't playing, and his previous season's record was shaky, his value on the trade market was low. By dealing him to the Flames for a draft choice, at least San Jose could get someone for him. And the Flames did not have to surrender a regular for someone who could best be described as an experiment.

Although Kiprusoff had not played that season in San Jose, he had practiced — almost every day — and learned under Sharks' goaltending coach Warren Strelow. Although rarely in the public eye, Strelow had helped turn San Jose into a goaltending mecca. In addition to Kiprusoff, he had tutored Nabokov, who was healthy again and had become one of the NHL's most consistent goaltenders. Strelow had also tutored former San Jose farmhand Johan Hedberg, who backstopped the Pittsburgh Penguins to an improbable berth in the Stanley Cup semi-finals in 2000-01. Two decades earlier, Strelow had even tutored Jim Craig as he helped the U.S. capture the 1980 Olympic gold medal.

Strelow also knew what it was to suffer. Instead of skates, he wore spiked shoes on the ice because he had lost a leg to diabetes. He was also on a waiting list for a kidney transplant. If Kiprusoff thought he had difficulties, he only had to look at his coach and friend for inspiration. On the evening before Kipper departed for Calgary, Strelow called him and gave him some final words of advice. He also warned members of San Jose's management that Kipper could come back to haunt them.

Sutter did not give Kipper a chance right away. The goalie had to watch as Calgary beat Toronto 3-2 in overtime on November 18 with McLennan in goal. On November 20, in his first game as a Flame, Kiprusoff stopped 22 of 23 shots as Calgary beat Montreal 2-1. It would be the first of many 2-1 victories — and first-star selections — as the Flames suddenly started reeling off wins.

In the first week of December, Kipper posted a 4-0-0 record and 1.00 goals against average, as the Flames beat his former Sharks team, Vancouver, Minnesota, and Pittsburgh. After a road loss to Minnesota, the good times continued for the rest of the month. Thanks to Kipper, who combined a butterfly style with the long-lost art of blazing across the crease, the Flames posted a 10-2-2 record in December.

Kipper, in goal for nine of those 10 victories, was named NHL player of the month. He also helped the Flames cope with a lack of scoring.

Iginla was struggling to reproduce his heroics of a year earlier, when he helped Canada to a gold medal at the Salt Lake City Winter Olympics. In his first 21 games, he had scored only five goals. Observers were starting to wonder whether the pressure of being named Calgary's captain was starting to get to him. At the age of 26, Iginla became the first black captain in the NHL. Craig Conroy had stepped aside in training camp, feeling Iginla was the best choice for the team.

As long as Kiprusoff was hot, it did not really matter whether Iginla was cold. Calgary kept winning and the early-season goaltending woes were all but forgotten. Turek was still out of the lineup with a knee injury. Contrary to the originally announced diagnosis of a month's recovery time, he had already been out two months. Calgary still remained in the top eight in the conference. A playoff berth, seemingly remote at the start of the season, was beginning to look more realistic. And then disaster struck the Flames again.

Kipper sprained his knee. The team announced that he would be out a month. With Turek still out of the lineup, McLennan, inherited the job by default. It was time for another unsung hero to pull the Flames through difficult times.

At the start of the season, Sutter had put McLennan

on waivers, attempting to see whether any other teams wanted to take him off Calgary's hands. There were no takers. For months, especially after Kiprusoff arrived, people had wondered how long "Noodles," as he was known to his teammates, would stick around. McLennan, a good-natured, happy-go-lucky type, was a big fan of the rock group KISS. He even painted pictures of Gene Simmons on his mask. But he knew he could kiss away his job if he didn't perform at this crucial time.

Noodles had joined Calgary in the summer of 2002 from the Minnesota Wild organization, in exchange for a lowly ninth-round draft choice. In his first season with Calgary, McLennan managed to record only two wins in the 22 games in which he appeared. Noodles vowed to do whatever necessary for his team. If he had to sit, he would sit. If he had to play — which he clearly wanted to do — he would play his best. Fans just wondered whether his best was good enough. Noodles, however, was yet another Flame who had faced adversity before. In May 1996, after spending a season in the minors, McLennan had come down with bacterial meningitis, a disease that attacks the lining of the brain. McLennan's kidneys shut down; he spent two weeks in hospital and lost 30 pounds. He spent the following season in the minors following his recovery, but the Blues signed him as a free agent. He posted a sparkling 16-8-2 record in 1997-98 and was awarded the Masterton Trophy. The Masterton goes annually to the player who exemplifies perseverance, sportsmanship, and dedication to hockey. And, McLennan would display those qualities again in 2003-04.

Although he was in the lineup when Kipper got hurt, McLennan was also quietly nursing a serious injury of his own. About two weeks earlier, in a game against Boston at the Saddledome, Noodles had taken a high, hard shot on the chest pad. Almost immediately, the goaltender staggered to the bench. After catching his breath, he returned to the Calgary net. Despite his injury, McLennan posted a shutout and was chosen as first star as Calgary blanked the Bruins 5-0.

Once he started playing in place of Kipper, it became obvious that McLennan was not in good health. At one point, reporters noticed that he could barely lift his catching glove. McLennan acknowledged that he was hurting, but he declined to give details on his injuries, attributing them to the wear and tear of playing. A few weeks later, McLennan revealed that he had been suffering from a broken sternum — an injury that might have kept others in bed. The sternum helps to protects the heart, lungs, and major blood vessels from damage. "Everything is tied into your chest," McLennan said weeks later. "The more you played, the more your muscles would spasm. I had a tough time holding my stick sometimes. The bottom line was I was going to play unless the doctors ruled it out."

Thanks to him, the Flames still stayed above .500 in the first two weeks of January as they counted three wins and a tie in their first six games of the new year. With McLennan playing in pain and Kiprusoff still another month away from returning, the Flames had no choice but to turn back to their former starter Turek.

In his first game back after missing 39 games, the Flames lost 3-2 to Dallas. But Turek earned a third-star selection as Calgary thumped Anaheim 5-1 and counted his 25th career shutout against Nashville. Still, Turek could not manage to win two games in a row. By then, Iginla was helping to keep the Flames in the playoff hunt.

Iggy recorded his first hat-trick on home ice February 3 and quietly moved into eighth place among NHL goal scorers. "Hopefully, this is the start of a run for me and my line," said Iginla. His comments would prove to be prophetic. Iginla did, indeed, start a marvelous run — around the same time that Kiprusoff returned from his injury. On February 10, after missing 19 games, Kipper launched the Flames on a four-game winning streak. It was their longest of the season.

Three straight losses followed. The long-awaited postseason berth was still in doubt. It was time again for Kiprusoff to work his magic — and he did not disappoint. On February 24, Calgary blanked Colorado 2-0. In the next 12 games, the Flames lost only three games. During that time, Sutter acknowledged that Calgary had put Turek on waivers. With the trading deadline approaching, the move was an obvious attempt to see whether any teams were interested in trading for him. But Turek would not leave the Flames.

Instead, in a move that saddened fans and players alike,

Noodles was traded at the deadline to the New York Rangers. The move spoiled a wonderful ride for the disappointed McLennan. He had looked forward to being part of Calgary's first playoff qualifier since 1995-96. McLennan's disappointment was Chris Simon's delight. As a result of the deal, he left the Rangers, who were already assured of missing the playoffs, to come to Calgary.

Simon, an Ojibway from Wawa, Ontario, was one of few First Nations players in the NHL. He had won a Stanley Cup with Colorado and helped Washington advance to the Cup finals. "Ron Wilson [then Washington's coach] was the first coach that I ever had that told me that I was a hockey player that was tough," said Simon. "I owe a lot of credit to him for giving me the confidence to become the kind of complete player that I'm trying to be." Simon's career had since stalled with weak teams in Chicago and the Big Apple. Although still known primarily as an enforcer, he also displayed an offensive touch. Sutter placed him on Calgary's top line with Iginla and Conroy.

Simon's intimidating presence gave Iginla and Conroy more room to work their offensive creativity. After acquiring Simon, the Flames tied Edmonton 1-1 and doubled Ottawa 4-2. Marcus Nilsson, acquired from Florida at the trading deadline, scored twice. After tying Nashville 4-4 in Tennessee, the Flames blanked St. Louis 3-0, dumped the Detroit Red Wings 4-1, and blanked the Columbus Blue Jackets 2-0.

Calgary stayed in sixth place, but a playoff spot was still

not guaranteed as the end of the regular season approached. On March 20, Calgary hosted Nashville in a return engagement but the Predators prevailed 3-1. With two seconds left to go in the game, after Nashville had scored an empty-net goal, Sutter sent out Krystof Oliwa, who immediately stirred things up. A brawl ensued. Even Kiprusoff dropped his gloves and fought Nashville netminder Tomas Vokoun. A day later, Sutter, who usually preached discipline, was suspended for two games for not controlling his team. Oliwa was tagged for three games by the NHL.

The next night, the Dallas Stars humiliated the Flames 4-0. This time, it was Simon who was suspended for two games. He was also fined $36,585.37 — for kneeing Dallas defenceman Sergei Zubov. It looked like the Flames were starting to unravel — at the worst possible time.

The Flames split road games in Phoenix, where they won 4-0, and San Jose, where they lost 3-2. On March 27, the Flames hosted the Los Angeles Kings, who they were battling for a playoff spot. The upstart Kings had stayed in the hunt all season long despite a plethora of injuries to several stars, including Adam Deadmarsh and Ziggy Palffy.

Simon returned from his suspension, looking to make amends for his mistake. In the second period, he committed another one. With the Flames trailing 1-0 early in the second period and on a power play, the puck came to Simon in the goal mouth — but he kicked it in and the goal was disallowed. But moments later, Simon re-directed a Jordan Leopold shot past L.A. goaltender Christian Huet, to create a 1-1 tie. After former Flame Jeff Cowan gave the Kings a 2-1 advantage, Conroy scored near the midway mark.

Both teams were scoreless in the third and went into overtime with a possible playoff spot on the line. Just a minute into the extra session, Calgary's Shean Donovan grabbed a loose puck near the Flames blueline and raced down right wing on a two-on-one with Conroy. Donovan looked over at Conroy, who wound up to one-time a pass. But with an L.A. defenceman in the middle and Huet leaning slightly, Donovan fired the puck over the goalie's glove as he stacked his pads. The goal gave Calgary a 3-2 win and effectively eliminated the Kings from the post-season.

"The whole way down, the puck was rolling a little bit and I was thinking pass and at the last minute I got a shot away," said Donovan. "I ended up getting it in, so it was nice." It was Donovan's first goal since February 1. As he had done on penalty shots earlier in the season, he slammed himself into the corner glass — and the crowd roared.

Iginla assisted on both of Calgary's regulation-time goals, earning his 500th and 501st career points. The milestone did not mean much to the Flames at this point — because a playoff spot was still not a done deal. The Flames could clinch a berth with a win over Phoenix at home.

That day, March 20, Flames co-owner Harley Hotchkiss, also the chairman of the NHL's board of governors, woke up at 5 a.m. in Toronto to fly to New York for league meetings.

The expiration of the collective bargaining agreement in September was a hot topic of discussion. He couldn't miss the meeting. Neither did he want to miss the Flames' potentially memorable night. When the meeting concluded, he raced out of the room, hopped a cab to the airport, and called his hotel's concierge. "You're not going to make it," she said. "You get me a boarding pass — and watch me," replied Hotchkiss. He even arrived at the Saddledome in time to have dinner. The crowd, cast in red shirts, was abuzz as the Flames and Coyotes, already eliminated from post-season contention, hit the ice.

Phoenix goaltender Brent Johnson was looking to redeem himself after recently joining the Coyotes in a trade. From the get-go, it was obvious that Johnson was having a strong night. But so was Kiprusoff, as he thwarted several early Phoenix chances. Before the first period ended, Regehr fired a pass across the goal mouth to Iginla, who fired the puck on net. Johnson foiled him. The puck was visible; sticks flailed at it and it went in. Although the goal was originally credited to Simon, officials later gave it to Iginla. "Simon came in and was whacking away and I initially thought he got it, " said Iginla. "But he told the ref he didn't and [officials] reviewed [the videotape]. I guess he gave it to me. It was very nice of him to be an honest guy. I didn't see it and, luckily, it went in."

It proved to be a critical goal — because nobody else could turn the red light on behind Johnson or Kiprusoff the rest of that night. "You can put it in the win column. Playoffs! Yeah, baby!" shouted Peter Maher over the radio and the Internet.

The best part, said the game's hero, Iginla, in the jubilant Calgary dressing room, was that the Flames did not have to rely on mathematics to get the post-season berth. "It feels good to win and not have to rely on another team," said Iginla. "This is the way we would have wanted it."

Iginla was just glad to be there. The Calgary captain recalled his anxiety of a year earlier when he thought he would be traded at the deadline. "I was really hoping I'd stay for a lot of reasons," said Iginla. "I really wanted to be here when we turned the first corner. I feel very fortunate that they've kept me here. It feels awesome. We've worked hard. We know this isn't the Stanley Cup or anything like that — but it's a huge step in growing as a team, getting better and, also, working towards winning one."

There was still one more bauble for Iginla to grab before the regular season ended. On the final Sunday, during a meaningless loss in Anaheim, he scored a goal to finish in a tie with Rick Nash of Columbus and Ilya Kovalchuk of Atlanta. All three finished with 41 markers to share the Rocket Richard Trophy. Meanwhile, Kiprusoff completed the regular season with a 1.69 goals against average — the best in the NHL's modern era.

Chapter 9
Back to the Stanley Cup Finals

The Flames drew the Vancouver Canucks in the first round of the 2003-04 Stanley Cup playoffs, evoking memories of their first-round triumph in 1989 — the last time they had advanced beyond the opening series. On paper, the third-place Canucks were the better team, but they were a team in turmoil. Late in the regular season, one of their stars, Todd Bertuzzi, had been suspended indefinitely for breaking the neck of Colorado's Steve Moore. Questions also surrounded the team's goaltending. Veteran netminder Dan Cloutier was looking to redeem himself following the Canucks' elimination at the hands of the Minnesota Wild a year earlier.

The Canucks took the first game 5-3 at GM Place. Calgary evened the series with a 2-1 win in game two — the first of many 2-1 games to come. When defenceman Sami Salo lost track of the puck after batting down a high shot in the Vancouver zone, rookie Mathew Lombardi whipped it home. Iggy scored the other goal.

Vancouver prevailed 2-1 in game three on Matt Cooke's winner. However, Vancouver suffered a major blow with 29 seconds left in the first period. After stopping an Oleg Saprykin shot, Cloutier lost his balance and fell backward, twisting his leg. He was out for the series. Johan Hedberg replaced Cloutier and performed admirably the rest of the night. Game four was no contest as the Flames blanked Vancouver 4-0 at the Saddledome.

Calgary also scored an important psychological victory. Temperamental Canucks coach Marc Crawford — the same coach who had kept Gretzky out of the shootout in the 1998 Winter Olympics at Nagano, Japan — decided to replace Hedberg with rookie Alex Auld. The Canucks had specifically acquired Hedberg in case something happened to Cloutier, but Crawford was abandoning him after only his second game as the starter. In game five, Iginla tipped home a shot with just under 15 minutes left in regulation to give the Flames yet another 2-1 win. They could clinch the series at the Saddledome two nights later.

Vancouver jumped out to an early, seemingly insurmountable 4-0 lead. The Flames rallied to tie the score 4-4 heading into overtime. Neither club could score for two extra periods. Early in the third extra session, as the Canucks were coming out of their zone, Vancouver captain Markus Naslund whacked Iginla's stick, knocking it out of his hands and behind him. As he tried to back up, Iginla tripped and fell on his bum as the Canucks raced up ice. The Calgary captain hustled back — without his stick — but Brendan Morrison scored to give the Canucks a 5-4 win and force a seventh and deciding game.

Again, the teams went to overtime with the score tied 2-2 after regulation. The extra session would not be nearly as long this time. Gelinas banged in Iginla's rebound 1:06 into extra time, giving the Flames their first series win since 1989. It also marked the second major series-winning goal for Gelinas. A couple of years earlier, he had netted the overtime winner when the Carolina Hurricanes eliminated the Toronto Maple Leafs in the Eastern Conference finals.

The Flames headed to Detroit for the second round. The Flames were clearly the underdogs against the Red Wings, who had finished first overall in the regular season. The Wings featured such stars as Steve Yzerman, Brendan Shanahan, former Flame Brett Hull, and yet another player the Flames had given up on — Robert Lang, who had been invited to training camp one season but wasn't signed.

Calgary shocked the Wings in game one at Joe Louis Arena as Nilsson converted Gelinas' pass from behind the net in overtime. The Flames skated to a 2-1 win. Yzerman stole

Martin Gelinas, Calgary vs. Toronto, January 13, 2004.

the show in the second game, scoring twice as the Red Wings romped to a 5-2 decision. The Detroit captain also accidentally clipped Flames defenceman Rhett Warrener near his right eye, sending him to hospital with blurred vision. But, back in Calgary, Iginla's second-period goal gave the Flames a 3-2 win in the third game — and a 2-1 series lead. Gelinas contributed two assists as all of the scoring was completed in the first 5:46 of the middle frame. The Wings played without veteran defenceman Chris Chelios. Saprykin, one of the smallest players on the ice, had sidelined him with a hit in the second game.

In game four, Gelinas and Villie Nieminen scored 18 seconds apart to help the Flames overcome a 2-0 deficit. Detroit still prevailed 4-2, evening the series again. With only three seconds left in the game, Nieminen rammed Detroit goaltender Curtis Joseph into his net and received a five-minute charging major and game misconduct. With his bone-headed actions, Nieminen, acquired from Chicago late in the regular season, broke up one of Calgary's most effective lines. He, Donovan, and Nilsson had all scored goals in three of the first four games.

The Flames didn't miss Nieminen in game five as Kiprusoff worked his goaltending magic. Conroy's goal with 3:53 left in the second period was the only goal that Calgary needed. The Flames skated to a 1-0 victory on the strength of Kiprusoff's 31 saves. "He made the saves. I don't know if he saw every one of them," Detroit coach Dave Lewis told reporters. "He made some big saves against a team with big-time goal scorers."

But the Wings suffered a major blow in the second period. Detroit's Mathieu Schneider fired a shot that ricocheted off Calgary defenceman Warrener's skate in front of Kiprusoff. It hit Yzerman squarely in the face as he stood to the left of the net. Yzerman, who doesn't wear a face shield, immediately sprawled to the ice, kicking his legs in pain. He was gone for the series with a left eye injury. "I think everybody on the bench was stunned," said Lewis.

On the day of game six in Calgary, the Red Wings' dressing room was like a funeral parlour as they faced the prospect of playing without their inspirational leader Yzerman. The Wings were also still without Chelios for the fourth straight contest. Kiprusoff and Joseph waged a goaltender's battle and there was no scoring in regulation time. Amazingly, with only 46.9 seconds left in the first overtime, Gelinas again notched the series winner as he banged in a loose puck from the side of the net. "They had more skill, but we worked extremely hard and it paid off," Gelinas said afterwards. "Everybody's been chipping in at different times and it's been fun."

The fun-loving Flames advanced to the Western Conference final against a team that could not help but evoke bad memories for Sutter and Kiprusoff — the San Jose Sharks. Sutter would have to prove that he was a better coach than the guy who replaced him, while Kiprusoff would have to outperform Nabokov. Donovan was also out to prove that San Jose had made a mistake by trading him. Grizzled veteran Dave Lowry was facing one of his old clubs, too, and former Flame Tim Hunter was now an assistant coach with San Jose, adding more flavour to an already interesting match up.

The Flames shocked the Sharks by taking the first two games in San Jose. But the Sharks retorted by winning the next two games in Calgary to even the series. Sutter replaced Kiprusoff in the second period of Calgary's 4-2 loss in game four. Kipper responded by shutting out the Sharks 3-0 back in

San Jose. The underdog Flames were now only one win away from qualifying for the Stanley Cup finals.

The Flames prepared for another close battle. Overtime — or "Marty Gelinas time" — would not be necessary this time, but the same ol' hero came through again. Gelinas notched his third series-winning goal as the Flames beat the Sharks 3-1 to the delight of the Saddledome faithful. Thanks to Kiprusoff, the Sharks scored just once in the final seven periods of the series.

After the game, Sutter and Iginla returned a call to Prime Minister Paul Martin. Martin wished the Flames luck as they returned to the final for the first time in 15 years. With no more Canadian teams left in the playoffs, the prime minister dubbed the Flames "Canada's team." Could the Flames carry the whole country on their hard-working shoulders?

Calgary's opponent in the final was the upstart Tampa Bay Lightning, which had finished first in the Eastern Conference. Tampa featured former Flames Martin St. Louis, who had already won the Art Ross Trophy for most points and was leading the playoff scorers. Cory Stillman, Chris Dingman, and several others who had once played in the Calgary organization were now playing for Tampa. At one point or another, several players in both clubs had been teammates with Calgary's farm club. Many had remained friends but, with the Stanley Cup at stake, all friendships were on hold until after the season.

In game one, Tampa's white-towel-waving fans were in

a frenzy after WWF wrestler Hulk Hogan's daughter sang the national anthem. Iginla gave them less reason to cheer when the Flames were shorthanded in the second period. The Calgary captain scooped up a loose puck, whipped by fallen defenceman Pavel Kubina and raced in alone on Lightning goaltender Nikolai Khabibulin. Iginla fired a wrist shot but Khabibulin —nicknamed the "Bulin Wall" — got his catching glove on it. The puck went straight up in the air as the outstretched goalie fell to the ice. Iginla alertly stopped behind the left edge of the net, spraying up a huge wave of snow, but Kubina now circled wide on the right side. Iginla waited for the puck to fall and then tapped it into the net past the helpless Khabibulin. The shorthanded marker — Iginla's 11th goal of the post-season — stood up as the winner as Calgary won 4-1.

In game two, the Flames received an emotional lift as Lowry miraculously returned to the lineup after missing 43 games with an abdominal injury. At one point earlier in the season, Lowry had been helping the coaches on the bench. Reporters speculated that his playing career was over. The Lightning still struck back in the second game and prevailed. Tempers flared because Tampa players ran Kiprusoff a few times. "We got out-worked, out-hustled, and out-muscled. All kinds of outs. And now we are out of Tampa Bay," said Nieminen.

The Flames returned to the Saddledome and promptly blanked the Lightning 3-0. One goal was earned by Simon, who was starting to play like his old self after missing 10 games because of a knee injury. Donovan and Iginla got the other goals while Kiprusoff recorded his fifth playoff shutout. After his goal, Simon did his impression of Donovan and excitedly slammed into the corner glass. Donovan could not do his usual celebration dive because he was mauled by his teammates.

However, the Flames had little reason to celebrate in game four as early penalties cost them dearly. With the Lightning enjoying a five-on-three power play, Tampa forward Brad Richards, a native of Prince Edward Island, ripped a slapshot over Kiprusoff's catching glove just 2:48 into the game. The goal stood up as the winner. The Lightning remained undefeated for every game in which Richards had scored — in the playoffs or regular season. "This one hurts because it was a chance for us to go up 3-1," said Iginla. "It's a tough one to take. We didn't find a way to score."

It was also tough to take because of another careless late penalty by Nieminen. With a little more than four minutes remaining, he ran Lightning star Vincent Lecavalier from behind. "Definitely a penalty," said Sutter. "It's called a five-minute penalty because they react to the player going down. It's [really] a two-minute penalty." For the second time in the playoffs, league disciplinarian Colin Campbell suspended Nieminen.

The next day, Sutter reacted the same way Wayne Gretzky had done during the 2002 Olympics. There was a conspiracy against Canada's team, Gretzky claimed, after his team's disappointing start. During a press conference in Tampa Bay, Sutter commented on the penalty calling. "We have lost three players total to injuries ... there was a total of two minutes called. So fine, we know what we're up against," said Sutter. "We're the underdog...We're the little team that wasn't supposed to be here and a lot of people don't want us to be here and to make sure that we're not successful. We know that." Sutter was still upset that former Flame Stillman had not been suspended for a hit from behind to Nilsson's head in game one.

NHL vice-president Campbell defended his decision. "Nieminen used his forearm to deliver a forceful hit from behind to the head of his opponent," said the news release. "This hit was more severe than any of the other plays that were brought to our attention during the final. This was a hit that clearly crossed the line and was directed at the head. Even if Lecavalier is able to play in game five, this type of hit must be subject to supplemental discipline."

Even though he didn't change Campbell's mind, Sutter's ploy helped galvanize a city. Back in Calgary, Flames fever was reaching its highest pitch. Flames flags flew on vehicles throughout the city while some diehard fans painted their vehicles in Calgary's colours. More than 30,000 Flames' jerseys had been sold and retailers were having a hard time getting them from suppliers. One chain ordered all of its stores outside Calgary to send Flames' jerseys back to Cowtown as soon as possible. But even fans in Edmonton and Vancouver were snapping them up.

Business was also booming at bars on Calgary's 17th Avenue — which had become known as the Red Mile — and other pubs throughout the city. For the first time ever, the James Joyce Pub on Stephen Avenue Walk and The Joyce on Fourth had TVs installed.

The Flames needed all the help they could get from their enthusiastic fans — because injuries had taken an extreme toll on the team. Denis Gauthier had been out for weeks with a knee injury while Mathew Lombardi was out with concussion-like symptoms. Toni Lydman, Simon, and several others had missed extended periods of the post-season. Reinprecht had been out since the regular season because of shoulder surgery.

All the fan hoopla inspired the club in game five. The Flames came out with a much better effort in Tampa Bay and won 3-2 as Saprykin put in Iginla's rebound in overtime. The Calgary captain had lost his helmet in a scramble but still rifled a shot on goal. Iginla was practically unstoppable that game as he fired six shots, scored a goal, and set up the winner. The Flames just needed one more win to claim the Stanley Cup.

After the game, the Red Mile was again teeming with fans of all ages and backgrounds. The fans sensed that the Flames were on the verge of making history. Surely the Cup was coming to Calgary.

Could Iginla take them to the promised land the next game, enabling the Flames to parade with the Cup on home ice? Before the sixth game, NHL officials had carted the Stanley Cup to the Saddledome in a crate. They unpacked it as millions of fans across the country watched "Canada's hockey team" on *Hockey Night in Canada.*

Unfortunately for the Flames, the Lightning capitalized on their very first power play chance. With Jordan Leopold in the penalty box for interference, Richards got the puck at the goal line about 20 feet to the left of Kiprusoff. He launched a wrist shot that struck the goalie and caromed into the net at 4:17. No problem, fans figured. Richards' lucky streak had to end sometime.

Calgary's Chris Clark reassured fans by creating a 1-1 tie at 9:05 of the second period. He popped home a pass from Nieminen, who was back in the lineup after sitting out his one-game suspension. But the dreaded Richards tallied again. He corralled a rebound and fired it between Kiprusoff's legs at 10:52 of the middle period. It was his second power play goal of the game and 12th tally of the playoffs. Nilsson atoned for his error a few minutes later. He put in a pass from Saprykin to tie the game.

With about five minutes left in regulation time, slightly blurry TV replays showed that the puck crossed the Lightning goal line as Gelinas — looking for his fourth series winner — charged the net. Had he scored, the Cup waiting in the Saddledome would have been Calgary's. Play continued.

When the whistle finally blew, the on-ice officials, oblivious to the play, did not call for a video review. Neither did the Flames.

The score remained 2-2 after 60 minutes, but neither team could score in two overtime periods. Calgary fans settled in for a nail-biting wait. But in the opening seconds of the third overtime, Richards deflected Tim Taylor's point shot. The rebound came to former Flame St. Louis. He fired a snap shot that brushed Kiprusoff's blocker arm — and squeezed into the net. Tampa won 3-2 just 33 seconds into O.T. and evened the series.

Calgary's sure-thing Cup was suddenly no longer a sure thing. "We're all dead," St. Louis told ABC after the game. "I was too tired to celebrate. It's just nice to be out there and give ourselves a chance to bring it [the Cup] back." Iginla had been held to just two harmless shots in the game. As the series shifted to Tampa, the Flames were a banged-up club too. Donovan, hurt earlier in the season, could not play. Several others were either out of the lineup, or nursing aches and pains.

At the beginning of the seventh and final game, Calgary appeared to be overmatched. Scoring chances were few and far between as the Lightning stuck closely to Iginla. Tampa's Ruslan Fedotenko staked Tampa to a 1-0 lead in the first period and struck again in the second, giving the hosts a 2-0 edge after 40 minutes.

Just when things looked hopeless for the Flames, midway through the third, Conroy scored on a slapshot from just inside the blueline. For the rest of the period, the Flames blitzed the Tampa net. Khabibulin was unbeatable. The final buzzer sounded with Calgary pressing for the equalizer. The Lightning had claimed their first Stanley Cup in their 12-year history with a 3-2 win.

"In the end, we ran out of gas," concluded Sutter. Unofficial team spokesman Conroy added, "We had two chances, one at home, and we didn't get it done." As the Flames dejectedly shuffled off the ice, the hopes and dreams of their fans went with them.

Calgary's supporters did not stay dejected for long. Two days later, more than 20,000 of the loyal old and new Flames fans, some arriving at dawn, packed Calgary's Olympic Plaza. "This team has totally won the hearts of the city," said one fan, Cameron Shank, echoing the delighted crowd. "Some of these players no one knew... and every last one of them has become a hero."

As each of the old and new heroes was introduced to raucous cheers, some of the Flames players in white Stetsons had tears in their eyes. As they experienced the historic occasion, they praised the fans. "This is truly unbelievable," said Iginla, flashing his megawatt smile. "You guys helped to make this year and this run the time of our lives."

Thousands of people savoured the moment, bonded by a team that had made a miraculous run. Some of them could remember the club's good, and bad, times from years past.

Like the best Calgary teams that had gone before them, Iginla and his teammates had triumphed over incredible adversity. All of the fans at Olympic Plaza that day would remember the Flames of 2003-04 forever — and look forward to more exciting times in the future.

Acknowledgments

In the late 1980s and early 1990s, I covered the Calgary Flames for the *Calgary Herald*. In recent years, I have covered the team for Canadian Press and *Business Edge*. Over that time, I have observed some of the most memorable moments in Flames history. This book helps re-create those unforgettable moments. In addition to capturing Flames' history for posterity, my aim with this collection was to show how the Flames have contributed to some of the most important events and advancements in NHL history.

This book is dedicated to late Calgary Flames TV broadcaster Ed Whalen, a good friend, who loved the team more than anyone I ever met, but died before the Flames recovered from their seven-year funk.

Special thanks to Altitude's hockey editor Stephen Smith for asking me to write this tome and to Joan Dixon for her editing efforts. Thanks also to Kara Turner and Stephen Hutchings of Altitude Publishing for patiently waiting for my manuscript as the Flames completed their Stanley Cup drive in 2003-04.

This book was relatively easy to write because of the memorable work of some other writers and friends, including Gyle Konotopetz, who lent me his files, Eric Duhatschek,

Alan Maki, Tom Keyser, George Johnson, and Eric Francis. This book was also made easier because of help from some people in the Calgary Flames front office. Thanks to Peter Hanlon and Bernie Hargrave for arranging accreditation to games and practices at very busy times. Special thanks also to Peter Maher, Al MacNeil, and Ken King for granting my interview requests.

Last but not least, thank you for reading this story. This book took on extra meaning for me, because I wrote it while I was in the process of moving to Vancouver, my hometown, for business and personal reasons, after living in Calgary for many years. I moved to Calgary specifically to cover hockey and as a result developed many lasting friendships. This book will ensure that I never forget them.

Photo Credits

Cover: Jeff Vinnick/Hockey Hall of Fame; Paul Bereswill/ Hockey Hall of Fame: page 65; Dave Sandford/Hockey Hall of Fame: pages 97, 113.

About the Author

Monte Stewart has written about the National Hockey League since the 1980s. From 1987-93, he covered the Flames for the *Calgary Herald.* He continues to write about the team for various newspapers and magazines. His articles on hockey and other topics have appeared in such publications as *A Century of the National Hockey League, Hockey Today, The San Jose Mercury-News, Business Edge, Profit Magazine, The Daily Oil Bulletin, New Technology Magazine* and *Chicken Soup for the Preteen Soul.*

This is his second book. He is also the co-author of *Carry On: Reaching Beyond 100,* the autobiography of late Calgary centenarian Tom Spear. Stewart has also edited several books and articles and taught journalism, writing, and Internet-related courses at the Southern Alberta Institute of Technology, the University of Calgary, and other post-secondary institutions. After living in Calgary for almost two decades, Stewart returned to his hometown of Vancouver in the spring of 2004.

OTHER AMAZING STORIES

ISBN	Title	Author
1-55153-943-8	Black Donnellys	Nate Hendley
1-55153-947-0	Canada's Rumrunners	Art Montague
1-55153-966-7	Canadian Spies	Tom Douglas
1-55153-795-8	D-Day	Tom Douglas
1-55153-982-9	Dinosaur Hunters	Lisa Murphy-Lamb
1-55153-798-2	Edmonton Oilers	Rich Mole
1-55153-968-3	Edwin Alonzo Boyd	Nate Hendley
1-55153-996-9	Emily Carr	Cat Klerks
1-55153-973-X	Great Canadian Love Stories	Cheryl MacDonald
1-55153-946-2	Great Dog Stories	Roxanne Snopek
1-55153-797-4	Great Stanley Cup Victories	Rich Mole
1-55153-942-X	The Halifax Explosion	Joyce Glasner
1-55153-958-6	Hudson's Bay Company Adventures	Elle Andra-Warner
1-55153-969-1	Klondike Joe Boyle	Stan Sauerwein
1-55153-980-2	Legendary Show Jumpers	Debbie G-Arsenault
1-55153-964-0	Marilyn Bell	Patrick Tivy
1-55153-953-5	Moe Norman	Stan Sauerwein
1-55153-962-4	Niagara Daredevils	Cheryl MacDonald
1-55153-790-7	Ottawa Senators	Chris Robinson
1-55153-945-4	Pierre Elliott Trudeau	Stan Sauerwein
1-55153-981-0	Rattenbury	Stan Sauerwein
1-55153-991-8	Rebel Women	Linda Kupecek
1-55153-956-X	Robert Service	Elle Andra-Warner
1-55153-952-7	Strange Events	Johanna Bertin
1-55153-954-3	Snowmobile Adventures	Linda Aksomitis
1-55153-950-0	Tom Thomson	Jim Poling Sr.
1-55153-788-5	Toronto Maple Leafs	Jim Barber
1-55153-976-4	Trailblazing Sports Heroes	Joan Dixon
1-55153-977-2	Unsung Heroes of the RCAF	Cynthia J. Faryon
1-55153-792-3	Vancouver Canucks	Justin Bedall
1-55153-948-9	The War of 1812 Against the States	Jennifer Crump

These titles are available wherever you buy books. If you have trouble finding the book you want, call the Altitude order desk at 1-800-957-6888, e-mail your request to: orderdesk@altitudepublishing.com or visit our Web site at www.amazingstories.ca

New AMAZING STORIES titles are published every month.

Comments on other *Amazing Stories* from readers & reviewers

"Tightly written volumes filled with lots of wit and humour about famous and infamous Canadians."
Eric Shackleton, *The Globe and Mail*

"The heightened sense of drama and intrigue, combined with a good dose of human interest is what sets Amazing Stories *apart."*
Pamela Klaffke, *Calgary Herald*

"This is popular history as it should be... For this price, buy two and give one to a friend."
Terry Cook, a reader from Ottawa, on ***Rebel Women***

"Glasner creates the moment of the explosion itself in graphic detail...she builds detail upon gruesome detail to create a convincingly authentic picture."
Peggy McKinnon, *The Sunday Herald,* on ***The Halifax Explosion***

"It was wonderful...I found I could not put it down. I was sorry when it was completed."
Dorothy F. from Manitoba on ***Marie-Anne Lagimodière***

"Stories are rich in description, and bristle with a clever, stylish realness."
Mark Weber, *Central Alberta Advisor,* on ***Ghost Town Stories II***

"A compelling read. Bertin...has selected only the most intriguing tales, which she narrates with a wealth of detail."
Joyce Glasner, *New Brunswick Reader,* on ***Strange Events***

"The resulting book is one readers will want to share with all the women in their lives."
Lynn Martel, *Rocky Mountain Outlook,* on ***Women Explorers***

AMAZING STORIES

EDMONTON OILERS

AMAZING STORIES

EDMONTON OILERS

Stories from the City of Champions

HOCKEY

by Rich Mole

PUBLISHED BY ALTITUDE PUBLISHING CANADA LTD.
1500 Railway Avenue, Canmore, Alberta T1W 1P6
www.altitudepublishing.com
1-800-957-6888

First published 2004

Publisher	Stephen Hutchings
Associate Publisher	Kara Turner
Series Editor	Jill Foran
Editor	Megan Lappi

We acknowledge the financial support of the Government of Canada through the Book Publishing Industry Development Program (BPIDP) for our publishing activities.

Altitude GreenTree Program 
Altitude Publishing will plant twice as many trees as were used in the manufacturing of this product.

We acknowledge the support of the Canada Council for the Arts which in 2003 invested $21.7 million in writing and publishing throughout Canada.

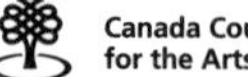

National Library of Canada Cataloguing in Publication Data

Mole, Rich, 1946-
Edmonton Oilers / Rich Mole.

(Amazing stories)
Includes bibliographical references.
ISBN 1-55153-798-2

1. Edmonton Oilers (Hockey team)--History.
I. Title. II. Series: Amazing stories (Canmore, Alta.)

GV848.E36M64 2004 796.962'64'09712334 C2004-903749-8

Printed and bound in Canada by Friesens
2 4 6 8 9 7 5 3

This book is dedicated to all the hockey entrepreneurs who take the risks and make it happen.

Contents

Prologue

It was 1990. Mark Messier, the captain of the Edmonton Oilers, faced the biggest challenge of his young career. He needed to carry the Edmonton Oilers through the playoffs to the team's fifth Stanley Cup victory without "The Great One" by his side. The Oilers had not been able to do it the year before. Two teams had met to battle for the 1989 Stanley Cup, but the Edmonton Oilers had not been one of them. Messier and the others had consoled themselves with the simple fact that making the finals — and winning them — was no piece of cake in a league of more than 20 teams.

The Oilers' playoff run got off to a rocky start. But after being down 3-1 in their series against the Winnipeg Jets, the Oilers were finally able to turn things around and pull the tough series out of the bag. Then, it was on to round two. Playoff pressure was bad enough. Making it worse, Messier knew that he lived in the shadow of the team's former captain and "spark plug" Wayne Gretzky. But he also knew that his team wasn't just good — they were great. Now it was time to prove it.

Messier pulled on his skates, laced them tight, and got ready to meet his former captain, Wayne Gretzky, and the L.A. Kings. It was game one, round two, of the 1990 Stanley Cup playoffs.

Chapter 1
New Team in a New League

he biggest news story in National Hockey League (NHL) history was announced with a one-word headline — EXPANSION. In September 1967, after years of uneasy speculation and stonewalling from profit-conscious team owners, the NHL doubled its size, transforming itself from a 6-team eastern league to a 12-team league that embraced cities on both coasts and as far south as St. Louis, Missouri.

Edmonton: A Hurtin' Hockey Town

Lost in the excitement of new expansion teams in cities such as Philadelphia, Pittsburgh, and Los Angeles was the *other* story — the story of disappointment and disillusionment in Winnipeg, Cleveland, and Edmonton. In the years that immediately followed, these cities found themselves shunned by the suddenly expansion-shy NHL. All of them argued they should be big-league towns. Nowhere believed that as fervently as Edmonton, because once upon a time, the city had been a big-league town with its own professional hockey team.

Supported by the Detroit Red Wings, the Western Hockey League's Edmonton Flyers had given the city a fabulous 10-year hockey run, starting with their first championship season in 1952-53. Those had been wonderful years for a President's Cup winning team of great players bound for NHL careers. The roster had included future big league stars such as Al Arbour, Norm Ullman, Johnny Bucyk, and goalie Glenn Hall. Flyers coach Bud Poile, a former Stanley Cup winning Maple Leaf, suggested that the Western Hockey League (WHL) form a western division of the NHL. Perhaps the WHL could form a second big league to compete with the NHL.

However, when Poile left Edmonton to coach the San Francisco Seals, he took Edmonton's dreams of big-league glory with him. The Flyers went into a tailspin and failed to make the Western Hockey League playoffs. Unimpressed, Detroit withdrew its support and Edmonton was forced to drop out of the league. Calgary was forced to do the same. Any hopes WHL backers had of becoming a part of the NHL or forming a rival league were dashed when the now-tiny WHL folded. Any dreams Edmonton had of being part of the only existing professional league died, too. Edmonton was a hurtin' hockey town.

When Edmonton hurt, William "Wild Bill" Hunter hurt. As the force behind Edmonton's Junior A team, the Oil Kings, Bill Hunter wanted the big league more than most. Hockey had been in the redhead's life since his father had managed a team in Saskatoon. When Hunter made the transition from a North Battleford sporting goods store operator to a Regina hockey team owner, it seemed a natural progression. Then he moved to Edmonton.

Hunter had backed the Oil Kings after their 1962 Memorial Cup victory. Within three years, the Oil Kings won the Cup again. While Hunter took great pride in the performance of his Oil Kings — seven consecutive runs at the Memorial Cup was extraordinary — there was always the feeling of what could have been, what *should* have been.

One day, Hunter received a call from Walt Marlow, a former Edmonton hockey nut who was now a sports reporter for the *L.A. Herald Examiner.* Marlow was home to visit his father and wondered if Hunter had a few minutes to spare. When Marlow and Hunter met, Marlow got straight to the point: he wanted to know what Hunter thought about the new hockey league that had just been formed. Even though he was co-owner of one of the most successful Junior A hockey teams in Western Canada, Hunter hadn't yet heard about the World Hockey Association (WHA). It didn't take long for the Oil Kings co-owner to see the possibilities. It took him even less time to start promoting it, with the kind of evangelical passion that had become the Wild Bill trademark.

Before long, Marlow had introduced Hunter to the men behind the WHA: Gary Davidson and Dennis Murphy. The two Californians instantly recognized Hunter's significance. This was a man who not only knew the game inside out, but also knew those who owned and managed the teams. He knew exactly who had the money it took to turn hockey dreams into reality. Hunter also owned a winning team (and the team's arena), in one of the cities shut out by the NHL. Davidson and Murphy couldn't believe their good fortune, and neither could Bill Hunter. Maybe the hurtin' was over.

Edmonton Momentum

Wild Bill Hunter was not only happy to lead the attack on the NHL, he was absolutely delirious about it. His frontline offensive was right there, in Edmonton. His battle tactic — a reorganization of the Oil Kings. The first order of business was to change the name of his team from the Oil Kings to the Alberta Oilers; the second was an injection of new players.

"Major league hockey at its best," Hunter's press release thundered, but then added, "any player who talks to me about placing the money for a three-year contract in the bank before he signs won't be talking to me ten minutes later." Hunter targeted former Flyers and members of his Memorial Cup winning Oil Kings, snatching many from NHL rosters, including former Oil Kings captain, Glen Sather.

The third order of business was a new hockey showcase

for the new team. A replacement had to be built for Hunter's small 5800-seat Edmonton Gardens, and fast. "If the city of Edmonton doesn't announce an arena in the next two months, we'll build one ourselves," he said. However, Hunter first needed to build support for the new team. It seemed simple enough. After all, this was a hockey town. All Hunter had to do was exactly what he did best: sell, sell, sell! As he began to build Edmonton momentum, Wild Bill Hunter was also building league momentum.

The term "press conference" hardly conveys the spirited rah-rah atmosphere of the rallies Wild Bill staged during those exciting days and nights. The media had always enjoyed Oil Kings press conferences, but now these loud, boisterous freewheeling media blitzes were newsworthy events in themselves. Bill had plenty of detractors, but he disarmed them. "I welcome criticism. I expect heaps of criticism. Criticism is healthy." He promised that the Alberta Oilers and other WHA teams would leave those "can't-do" naysayers in the dust.

"World Hockey Comes to Town," the new billboards shouted. "Follow the Crowd. Buy Now." Edmonton fans did what they were told. They started buying season tickets. Everyone felt they were buying more than seats in the Edmonton Gardens — they were buying a piece of a dream come true.

No Fun at All

Wild Bill Hunter's make-it-happen optimism notwithstanding,

nothing worthwhile is accomplished easily. In its early days, the World Hockey Association proved that particular rule over and over again. During the initial 1972-73 season, the WHA's Philadelphia Blazers made a big announcement: the Blazers would take on the NHL's Philadelphia Flyers. There was a little hitch, however. The Blazers' rink staff hadn't quite got the hang of making ice. Every time the players skated on the rink, the ice cracked. The game was called off.

In Edmonton, the ice was great, but the team playing on it wasn't. Hunter fired his coach and took on the job himself, but the Oilers finished out of the playoffs. Nevertheless, Edmonton — and all other 11 teams in the league — had actually completed their first season, which was more than many NHL honchos (and perhaps a few WHA owners) had expected.

As the 1974-75 season began, Bill Hunter watched as construction neared completion on the new Northlands Coliseum, the hockey showcase he had championed. That year, Edmonton made the playoffs, although they were quickly eliminated by the Minnesota Flying Saints, four games to one.

The following season, Hunter managed to lure a big-name veteran from the NHL, goalie Jacques Plante, although Plante failed to meet the expectations of the fans or the coach. A 3.32 goals-against-average was one reason for the team's less than inspiring 36-38-4 performance. Bill Hunter soon went back to work on the team's roster.

By the next year, hockey had become more work than fun for WHA operators. Some players returned to the NHL and losses mounted. A few months before, Team Canada, made up of WHA players, had lost a series to the Soviets. A losing image was not what the league needed at this tense time. Then, suddenly, WHA teams in Vancouver, Toronto, and Phoenix all disappeared in a sea of red ink.

Oilers owner Bill Hunter wasn't having much fun, either. Four different coaches — including himself — in four seasons hadn't made any difference to the success of the team. In spite of having the highest average attendance in the league (over 10,000), the team was still losing money. Wild Bill figured it was time to sell. The buyer was the Edmonton General Hospital's former chief of surgery and trust company owner, Dr. Charles Allard — an early Edmonton WHA backer.

It didn't take the good doctor long to realize he didn't like the team's losses or the public criticism that resulted. He liked the financial strain even less. A fast-moving, B.C. millionaire named Nelson Skalbania had been putting big-scale real estate deals through the Allard family trust company. When the doctor asked him if he would be interested in purchasing a hockey team, he said yes.

Share the Wealth, Share the Debt

The first thing a new WHA owner usually does after he buys a hockey team is formally announce that he's done the deal. Nelson Skalbania decided there would be a slight change in priorities. After he examined the team, its books, and its prospects (the Oilers had finished the season a dismal fourth in the five-team Canadian division), the West Coast entrepreneur realized it could be *years* before he saw a profit from the team. So, "quick-buck" Skalbania decided that the first thing he had to do was unload at least part of his hockey team. The questions was, to whom? The answer came quickly: his friend, Peter Pocklington.

The man he chose to share the potential wealth and the present debt — close to $3 million of it — was a fellow millionaire who had started selling cars while he was still a teenager in London, Ontario. Pocklington left classes at age 17 ("I was fired from school," he said) so he could concentrate on selling. Somewhere on the road to success he decided what he really wanted was to be wealthy. So that's what he set out to be, using the cash from car sales to do it. Peter Pocklington was the salesman's salesman. Running his first Ford dealership while barely in his mid-20s, he moved four times as many cars off the lot as his predecessor. A second, larger dealership soon followed. Then, Pocklington asked Ford to look for an even bigger one for him to buy. In 1971, Ford found one in Edmonton. Peter Pocklington moved west, at just about the time Wild Bill Hunter was revving up Edmonton's WHA engine.

As decisive as he was upon occasion (he signed the deal on the Edmonton dealership in about half an hour), Pocklington took the long view, nurturing along various investments for years, including real-estate properties in the American Sunbelt. Soon, he was acquiring and nurturing financial services and natural resource interests, as well.

When Skalbania asked him if he would be interested in buying a piece of Edmonton's WHA franchise, Pocklington agreed to talk. It was then that Nelson Skalbania held his unorthodox news conference.

One fateful evening in October 1976, as Peter and his wife Eva were enjoying dinner at the Steak Loft restaurant, the doors opened and Skalbania arrived with a gaggle of reporters in his wake. The bartering began.

When it was over, Pocklington's vintage 1928 Rolls Royce, two of his valuable oil paintings (both men were art collectors), and a mortgage note for $500,000 worth of real estate changed hands, along with a stunning ring that Eva slipped off her finger. "Worth at least a hundred thou—" Pocklington assured Skalbania. In return, Pocklington received 40 percent interest in the money-losing team and shouldered half the debt. Both men were happy with the deal.

Now that Pocklington and Skalbania were partners in hockey, the talk turned to the future. How long would it be before the Oilers could retire the debt? How long would it be before they could turn a profit? The question was not just how long, but simply *how*. Both men agreed on the answer to that question: when the letters "WHA" were replaced with the letters "NHL." It couldn't happen fast enough to suit Skalbania. That was too bad, as it was bound to be a long-term proposition — the kind he hated.

In spite of the long-term gamble that hockey teams represented, Skalbania had developed an itch that he just couldn't scratch. By 1981, he had bought a total of eight hockey teams, including Calgary's. One of the teams was a franchise in Indianapolis called the Racers. Like many other WHA teams, the Indianapolis Racers needed a lot of help. Gate receipts were lousy. That was no surprise — who wanted to pay to see a loser? Even some people who knew what Skalbania had paid for the team (one dollar, plus the debt) wondered about his decision.

The long-term problem, of course, was how to get the NHL to take in these teams. In the meantime, Skalbania desperately needed to find a way to get people to come and see his teams play. Maybe, just maybe, there was one solution to both problems. He needed a star attraction to interest both the fans and the NHL.

Chapter 2
The Kids

Wayne Gretzky was very upset. He called his dad from Sault Ste. Marie, where he was wearing number 99 for the Soo Greyhounds. He phoned home often to pour out his frustrations. His father, Walter, urged patience, although Wayne didn't have much patience left.

Sault Ste. Marie was a long way from Brantford, where Wayne Gretzky had lived with his family, had gone to school, and had tried (and failed) to live the life of an ordinary teenager. He had been out of the house, away from his hometown, his mom, dad, little brothers, and sister for more than two years, since he was 14. That was not a typical experience for a young teenager. Things had not been "typical" back home, either — not for a 10-year-old who could score 378 goals and win a season scoring title by a margin of 238. That was when the pressure, envy, and jealousy had begun. Four years later, Wayne was eager to leave, *had* to leave. Besides, big-time hockey was calling.

His first stop was the Metropolitan Toronto Hockey League's Young Nationals.

In Toronto, Wayne lived with the Cornishes. They were the family of a fellow player, so it was like a home away from home. In another and unpleasant way, life in Toronto felt just like life back in Brantford. Things got, well, difficult. Just trying to play for the "Nats" was a trial — or close to it. The league had a rule: Toronto boys only. So, the Cornishes made Wayne their legal ward. When the league wouldn't budge, they went to court. In the end, the league won the case. Wayne's response was to go back down to Young Nationals Junior Bs, to escape the rule and win rookie-of-the-year award. Yes, it was just like home.

His second stop was the Junior A Greyhounds in Sault Ste. Marie.

When he was drafted to the Greyhounds, Wayne enjoyed another home environment with the family of Steve Bodnar, a friend from his peewee hockey days. The Greyhounds GM Angelo Bumbacco was good to the boys on the team and to Wayne. So was the coach, Muzz McPherson. It was a great season: 70 goals, 112 assists, and trophies as best rookie and most gentlemanly player. Then, things got difficult again. This time it wasn't a problem outside the rink; it was a problem inside the rink.

Coach Muzz McPherson had resigned and Paul Theriault had taken over. Theriault had theories and he wanted changes. One change concerned Wayne's positioning in the play. Theriault wanted Wayne to be exactly wherever the action for the puck was the heaviest. That sounded pretty logical, but Wayne had been playing a different way for years.

Out in the backyard rink, Walter Gretzky had taught his son to skate away to where the puck was going to go, to *anticipate*. That way, when the puck arrived, Wayne would be there, waiting for it. Walter's way worked. Even before he left Brantford, people had been referring to Wayne as "The Great One." Virtually every time he went onto the ice, Wayne demonstrated that the word was more than simply a catchy adjective hung on his name.

Getting Good

For close to 15 years, young would-be, could-be hockey stars would stare up at a Wayne Gretzky likeness thumbtacked to their bedroom walls. They would lie on their beds, maybe after a practice or game, finger the newest Gretzky gum card, and wonder — how do you get that good?

Here's a secret. First, you have to start young.

One afternoon, two-year-old Wayne Gretzky was gazing at the TV, mesmerized by the flash and twirl of the hockey players on the screen and the rising crescendo of the arena crowd. Suddenly, Wayne's grandmother walked into the room and shut off the set. She was stunned when Wayne burst into tears, thinking he was being punished for being bad.

Little Wayne had barely begun to walk, but a few months later, during the winter, he was already on skates. Walter Gretzky, crouching down low behind his movie camera, captured images of his tiny son as he lurched around on the ice, grinning into the lens.

Far away, in the Quebec town of Lachute, at the rink next to Lowe's Dairy, it was the same story. Two or three times a week, the Lowe family would bundle their youngest into his snowsuit, and Clifford Lowe would take him to the rink, help him put on his skates, and then watch as three-year-old Kevin ventured onto the ice all by himself. A couple of years later, Kevin watched his older brother, Kenny, play goal. Kenny was already so good that he and his father sometimes talked about what it took to be a professional. Kevin heard his father say that if Kenny wanted to be a pro, he needed to act like one. Now was the time to start training. Kevin — one day destined to be a star Oilers defenceman — was listening.

Another secret: you have to have the right parents.

Just outside Portland, Oregon, kids would get together near Highway 26 to play hockey on a frozen pond. They always tried to play a little harder, a little faster, when Mark, his older brother Paul, and their dad would come down. The boys, even little Mark, were league players. However, it was Mark's dad, Doug, the boys wanted to impress. Doug was a *real* hockey player. He was helping WHL's Portland Buckaroos get to first place again for the third time. It was funny, though — although Doug would skate around a bit and shout encouragement, he would never actually play with the kids. They said it was because he was afraid he would hurt one of them. He was tough, went at it hard, and got all those penalties. Could he hurt someone? When they saw Mark Messier's dad play, the kids could believe it. Mark, who would one day be an Edmonton Oilers MVP, was already starting to play that way, too. He was only five.

Another famous hockey dad had played Junior B and knew exactly what it took. He didn't have it himself, but he thought maybe his son Wayne did. He was Walter Gretzky, an everyday guy with five kids, a house, a mortgage, and a job at Bell Canada. Later, many found it hard to believe that someone who appeared to be so ordinary could be The Great One's father.

They didn't know about the backyard rink Walter Gretzky had planned and built every winter, with a sprinkler rotating slowly in 20-below weather so the ice would be uniform and smooth. They hadn't been watching as Walter had shaved down the lightest hockey stick he could find to fit his little boy. They hadn't seen him shoot passes in Wayne's direction as the small youngster had hopped over sticks carefully positioned on the ice. They hadn't been there to hear the kind words of encouragement. In those early years, Walter's job, as he saw it, was to help Wayne find out if he had what it took to make it. He wanted to give the kid a chance.

In his book, *Champions*, Kevin Lowe says simply, "everything I learned in hockey since those childhood days goes back to what my father pushed me to do. I owe him a lot ...."

His family's commitment to the game began long before Kevin Lowe was born. By donating the rink's refrigeration plant, Lowe's Dairy had helped make skating and hockey a reality for many kids in Lachute.

A few days after Kevin was born, the Lowes were happy and relieved. It had been a difficult labour, but mom and the new baby boy were just great. Driving home from the hospital, Clifford informed his wife, Jessie, that he wouldn't be home after dinner that night. The rink had scheduled a meeting for that very evening. Clifford said he felt obligated to attend, but he also really wanted to attend. Jessie was put out. She wanted to know if hockey meant more to Clifford than his brand new son. The proud papa thought about it for a moment and then explained that Kevin might want to skate and play hockey someday. By going to the meeting, he would be working for them all.

"Little did I know how involved I would become with hockey," Kevin's mom later confessed.

A third secret: you have to want it more than anything else.

One valuable lesson Kevin, Wayne, Mark, and many other Cup-winning Oilers learned from their parents was one that applies to any goal worth pursuing on or off the ice, and that's commitment. Fortunately, when nothing matters as much as being out there with skates on your feet and a stick in your hand, commitment comes more easily.

Mark Messier and his brother Paul "wanted to play so badly," their sister, Mary-Kay, remembers. "They always wanted to go to practice. They played continuously for hours and hours." In fact, little Mark was barely old enough to be enrolled in elementary school when his lively imagination put him out on the rink, lifting the big, shiny, silver Cup above his head.

Back in Lachute, Clifford Lowe chatted with Kenny about hockey, discussing what the future possibilities were. His younger brother Kevin was listening, too. If Kenny wanted to be a pro, Clifford told him, he would have to eat, drink, and sleep hockey. School was first, followed by church, and then hockey. Little Kevin filed the information away.

However, Kevin quickly learned that some of the tests of his commitment would have nothing to do with what happens on the ice. In Lachute, the Lowes represented the English-speaking minority. Kevin's rapid rise in peewee hockey was rewarded early. He was made team captain. Clifford offered his congratulations and then suggested that with his new leadership role came new responsibility. It meant phoning the kids on the team, boosting their morale, and giving them instructions. It also meant a new, difficult level of commitment. The kids on the team were French-speaking and Kevin didn't speak the language. Although Kevin pleaded with his dad, Clifford was adamant — Kevin would have to learn French.

The next secret: you have to love it.

For Messier, Lowe, Gretzky, and future Oilers teammates Paul Coffey, Glenn Anderson, and Grant Fuhr, the love of the game was so great that anything — school or a part-time job — that kept them away from the rink was regarded as work. Playing hockey was different. Once the pads were buckled on, the skates were laced, and the guys stepped out onto the ice, the hours flew by.

"Nobody told me to practice three hours a day," Wayne Gretzky confided in his autobiography. "I practiced all day because I loved it."

The fourth secret: you have to have ability.

Most young people — and their parents — learn early on that without talent, satisfying achievements probably await off the field, court, diamond, or ice. Playing the game because you enjoy it is simply not enough. At the same time, latent ability must go beyond physical prowess and strength. If all of Wayne Gretzky's abilities were physical, he would have been "The Pretty Good One" instead of "The Great One." His skill and personality made him good. They also made him vulnerable to hockey's formidable bruisers.

"I'm Phyllis Gretzky," Wayne's mom told Bobby Hull in a hotel before one of his early games. "I don't want you hurting Wayne in those corners tonight," she warned him.

If the ability to mete out and endure physical punishment was what the game was all about, then Wayne's future was dim. The superlative athlete, however, had other abilities — mental abilities.

The top achievers on the team — any team — see the game differently than many of their teammates. What seem like isolated moves are perceived by the Messiers, Gretzkys, and Kurris of the world as components of very natural and obvious patterns. These mental abilities don't come naturally to most. It takes time and practice to hone those skills to near-perfection. (Ask any owner who wonders why he spent so much money on a young player who just isn't getting it fast enough!)

For most of us, the mental effort alone would be exhausting. Now couple that with full out, continuous physical exertion. For many players, the passion burns so brightly that there is a willingness to endure the drills and exercises over and over again. It is this conscious effort that makes a crucial difference to physical performance. Mental skills are important, but a dedicated work ethic can compensate for talents far more modest than those of Gretzky or Messier, and can elevate even an average player to moments of greatness.

"Absolutely," Wayne Gretzky told writer Peter Gzowski. "It's all practice. I got it from my dad. Nine out of ten people think it's instinct, and it isn't." When Wayne told Gzowski how hard it was, it was 1981. Wayne's real work, and those of his new teammates, still lay ahead.

The final secret: you have to be willing to pay the price.

After a quick pass to the scrawny 10-year-old with the

big ears, grim-faced parents took out their stopwatches to see how long it would be before Wayne Gretzky would release the rubber to somebody else, like maybe their own kid for once. It didn't matter that his team — and theirs — eventually won the game. It didn't matter that Wayne racked up 120 assists in 79 games. They had a name for someone like Wayne Gretzky: "Puck Hog." He wasn't the only one they yelled at. Up in the stands, the abuse hurled at Wayne Gretzky's father became so upsetting that his wife wouldn't even sit with him.

Life is full of desires and decisions. Peter Pocklington wanted to be wealthy. He wanted it badly enough that he simply made a decision to be rich. Getting to be an outstanding hockey player is much the same. Lowe, Messier, Gretzky, and many others wanted it so much that they simply made a decision to be the best.

Chapter 3
Gamesmanship

Gus Badali was Wayne's new agent. Gus knew that the NHL didn't take underaged players, but the WHA did. John Bassett, the owner of the Birmingham Bulls, offered Gretzky a one-year, $8000 contract. Badali shook his head. The Whalers offered an eight-year deal with a signing bonus of $200,000. Before Gus could put a pen in Wayne's hand, the Whalers, hoping to make it into the NHL, pulled out at the last moment. There was no use irritating the league because they had signed an underaged 17-year-old, right?

Wayne was becoming desperate. All he could think of was Gus Badali and the offer from the Birmingham Bulls. He phoned home again, begging his father to call Bulls owner John Bassett and get him out of Sault Ste. Marie.

A Foot Race to the WHA

Gus Badali had gotten his first look at Wayne Gretzky a year or so before, while he was playing for the "Junior Nats" in Toronto. Walter Gretzky had first heard about the newly established agent from other players' parents. When he asked Badali if he would be interested in a new client, Badali agreed to add Wayne to his small roster. By 1980, that roster would grow to 40 players, including Edmonton Oilers' first-draft choice, Paul Coffey.

Gus Badali was standing in the lobby of the Hotel Toronto when Nelson Skalbania stepped out of the elevator. Skalbania was there because the WHA was holding a meeting. Badali was there because a good player's agent goes where the deal makers gather and where connections are made. Of course Skalbania had already heard about Wayne Gretzky — who hadn't? His tip on the wonder boy came from none other than John Bassett, the man who had failed to sign him for his own team.

Badali wasn't surprised to see Skalbania at the hotel. The surprise came when Skalbania reached into his inside pocket, gave Gretzky's agent $1,000, and ordered him — well, offered a firm suggestion, anyway — to get the Gretzkys on a plane to Vancouver. Once they got out there, Skalbania implied, they could do a deal.

Skalbania's knowledge of Gretzky was merely by word-of-mouth. He had never watched him play, but for the moment, that was unimportant. He knew that if he had heard good things, the NHL executives had also heard good things. That was enough, right there. Still, a buyer had to have some demonstration of a player's abilities. So, after Nelson Skalbania drove the Gretzkys and Badali out to his palatial house in his Rolls Royce, the fun began.

Wayne smiled and nodded politely, but secretly, he was exhausted. He had not slept the night before and had just endured a four-hour flight in a cramped airplane. Now came the zinger.

"Hey, how about a little run?" asked veteran jogger, Nelson Skalbania.

Seven miles and one steep hill later, Wayne had managed (somehow) to pull away from the older but still physically fit businessman. After the two of them arrived back at the house, Skalbania felt quite confident. Wayne felt like he was at death's door. They all agreed to meet in Skalbania's office a few minutes later.

Now Skalbania had the confirmation he needed. It was obvious that Gretzky had the stamina he was looking for. Based on all reports, he would also be able to provide the kind of crowd-pleasing hockey needed to bolster the Racers' sagging revenues. Wayne Gretzky would definitely be an exciting addition to the Racers, or even to the Houston Aeros, another team Skalbania was thinking of purchasing.

Skalbania's more ambitious objective went far beyond getting a star performer for the Indianapolis Racers. He secretly wondered if that star performer, Mr. Wayne Gretzky, might just be the way to get the Racers into the National Hockey League. He knew that even if the NHL didn't want the team, they might be interested in its star performer. That was the real game. It always had been.

The NHL had already made an agreement with the Canadian Amateur Hockey Association to never entice a player under 20 years of age away from the amateurs. The player-starved WHA ignored the agreement and happily courted the young, hot players sweating it out on junior hockey teams. It was a good way to fill team rosters immediately and a great insurance policy for the future. Developing these young hotshots for three or four years meant the WHA could have a league full of superstars by the early 1980s.

However, the NHL threatened to lobby the federal government about the WHA scooping up all the underaged players. League executives whined about unfair competition. That threat tended to put a crimp in the WHA's style, because unfavourable opinions by the feds could mean funding cutbacks for hockey arenas. New hockey houses were absolutely critical to the existence of the new league. The WHA felt it had no choice. It, too, was forced to comply with the terms of the NHL's hands-off-youth agreement. However, team owner Nelson Skalbania knew that by openly defying the agreement and signing 17-year-old Wayne Gretzky, he would have something the NHL desperately wanted. The question was, did the NHL want it enough to merge the two leagues? Skalbania, Pocklington, and everyone else would soon find out.

Doing the Deal

When they were all inside his office, Skalbania looked at Gus Badali and boldly asked, "How much money do ya' want?"

They talked. They dickered a little. Badali had his eye on the paintings adorning the walls of Skalbania's home, but this would not be part of the deal. Peter Pocklington might be willing to give up some of his art, but Skalbania was not. Besides, money talks, and Skalbania's cash had plenty to say.

The dollars clicked into place: $100,000 for the first year, $150,000 for each of the next two years, and $175,000 for the fourth year. On top of this, there was also a signing bonus of $250,000. Over the four years, the total sum came to $825,000. That was certainly better than what Wayne's wages had been the summer before, doing road repairs for five dollars an hour.

There were smiles all around. Skalbania had done the deal, and now it was time to hold a news conference, although it wouldn't be in Indianapolis, the home of the Racers. Skalbania decided that Edmonton, a WHA town, would be the perfect place to make the signing announcement. He wanted to give the sports reporters back east something new and exciting to write about. It was also Peter Pocklington's hometown and Skalbania knew that Pocklington would love it.

However, there was still that small matter of a contract. As Skalbania's Leer jet roared away from Vancouver on its way to Edmonton, Skalbania told Wayne to write while he dictated. Wayne dug out a piece of paper, slid a lined page under a blank sheet to keep his lettering straight, clicked open his ballpoint pen, and started writing.

It was no ordinary hockey player contract. Aside from the fact that it was written in longhand aboard a Leer jet, and copied down by the player himself, this was a contract that would also be signed by Wayne's dad, who was watching all this with his wife. Wayne was too young to sign it by himself. The contract also differed in one very important way from others. It wasn't a player's contract. It was a contract for "personal services." The difference would become crucial when the leagues got together and started making rules about how many players teams could protect. In this contract, Wayne wasn't specified as a player at all.

It also wasn't specific about which team he would be playing for. Wayne might play for either Indianapolis or Houston. Skalbania liked keeping his options open. He had felt that way about buying the Houston Aeros, too. Skalbania leaned over, picked up the phone, and put a call through to Texas. The Aeros coach came on the line. Skalbania asked him what he knew about Wayne Gretzky. There was no enthusiasm on the other end of the line, just something about hearing that he didn't skate too well. Skalbania thanked him and hung up the phone. He signed the contract with Wayne Gretzky then and there but later decided to pass on purchasing the Aeros.

Eight games later, Nelson Skalbania knew that his short-term solution for Indianapolis wasn't working. He was still losing $40,000 a game. Wayne Gretzky was making a difference to the team, but he made no difference to a city that didn't really care about hockey. Skalbania phoned Wayne and gave him the news. He was going to be traded. He gave Wayne a choice: Edmonton or Winnipeg.

"Pick Edmonton," Gus Badali advised. If the NHL was going to take on any WHA teams, they would be looking not simply at the team, but at the city — the "market" the team was in. Edmonton (as Peter Pocklington knew so well) was hot. It had nothing to do with the popularity of hockey, but the oil, gas, and beef that kept the economy's temperature high.

Nelson Skalbania was not convinced. He decided they should explore possibilities in Winnipeg. Michael Gobuty was one of the Winnipeg Jets' owners. Before he made a decision, he asked others what they thought of Gretzky. Some of Gobuty's advisors were not altogether sold on the young hockey player, not for the money Skalbania was asking.

The final negotiations took place inside Gobuty's private jet. The two businessmen could not agree on the final price. Skalbania suggested they break the deadlock with a game of backgammon. Gobuty demurred. Backgammon, it seemed, was not his strong game. Skalbania shrugged. It wasn't his best game, either, but he wasn't about to tell Gobuty that. This was all about gamesmanship. They left Winnipeg without a deal.

Their next stop was Edmonton.

Like Nelson Skalbania a few months before, Pocklington

hadn't seen Wayne play. He asked his new coach, Glen Sather, if they wanted him. Sather had seen Wayne play, all right. At first, he hadn't been all that impressed. Then the coach had watched as the young, fast Indianapolis Racer had lived up to his team's name. Wayne had zipped around an Oilers defenceman and put the puck in the net. Had he just been lucky? That question was answered a mere 39 seconds later, when Gretzky raced down the ice and scored again. Sather took a harder look and made a mental note to get this kid if he could. Now, suddenly, the owner was handing him the opportunity. Sather didn't hesitate. He told Pocklington to buy Gretzky.

The deal included $300,000 in cash and a $250,000 note to be applied against the $500,000 Pocklington promised to pay Skalbania, should the NHL accept the Oilers into the fold. Caught short of cash a little later, Pocklington bought back his $250,000 note from Nelson Skalbania for just $100,000. In the end, Wayne Gretzky had become an Edmonton Oilers player for just $400,000.

A few months later, on Wayne Gretzky's 18th birthday, a little on-the-ice party was held for him at Northlands Coliseum. There was a cake, a bottle of bubbly, and a contract sitting on a small table set up for the benefit of photographers and fans. What Wayne signed that night was the longest and richest agreement in professional hockey history — a 21-year contract worth $3 million over the first 10 years alone. Wayne wouldn't be a player, you understand. Pocklington had adopted the Skalbania strategy.

"This contract is for personal services," he told the media. "There's no way anyone's going to touch him when we join the NHL."

Chapter 4 Building the Team

fter his halcyon days as a Memorial Cup winning Edmonton Oil Kings player back in 1961-62, Glen Sather had endured the long and winding major league road travelled by hundreds of other long-forgotten NHL journeymen. When the remnants of the Oil Kings became the new Alberta Oilers, Glen Sather thought he might play for Bill Hunter once again. Hunter drafted him but couldn't sign him. However, Detroit did. Nonetheless, Sather was not destined to play in Hockeytown but rather in Memphis, Tennessee, earning 48 points and 98 penalties. He might not have been a scorer, but he was a scrapper. At the very least, the time he had spent in the penalty box had been impressive.

Memphis was merely his first stop on that seemingly

endless road of NHL near-fame. Other stops: Oklahoma City, Boston (where Sather played two seasons and 13 playoff games without scoring one single point), and then Pittsburgh. He arrived in New York for the 1971-72 season, just as the Rangers became a Stanley Cup contender. Ironically, the Rangers played the Bruins, who took the Cup, and with it, any chances Glen Sather had of wearing that special ring. Glen hit the road again, bound for St. Louis, and after that, Montreal (one year too soon for their Cup series) and then Minnesota.

By 1975, 32-year-old Glen Sather was skating for an expansion team that would win only 20 games that season. Sather helped, posting nine markers and 10 assists. Just as the next season began, Edmonton — which had never dealt away his rights — came calling. It was time to go home.

Suddenly, newcomer Glen Sather was the Oilers captain. Then almost as suddenly — when it appeared that the Oilers would be edged out of the 1976-77 playoffs — Glen was offered the coach's job. "Offered" is putting it politely. The general manager, Bep Guidolin, told him that he could either watch the game from behind the bench (already setting Sather up as the scapegoat for another bad season), or watch it as a fan from behind the glass. Sather thought the space behind the bench looked just fine. Then, a miracle of sorts occurred. The Oilers won enough games — nine — to secure a playoff spot. However, they blew the semi-finals, losing five games to Houston. Peter Pocklington may not have liked what he saw on the ice during that series, but he certainly liked what — and who — he saw behind the bench. And so Glen Sather stayed and Pocklington sacked the GM instead.

The Beginning of the End

Early in the summer of 1977, as the Oilers' new coach attempted to put together some kind of plan for the coming season, leaders of the two leagues were cloistered in New York, attempting to forge some kind of merger. Three days of heated meetings had, it seemed, resulted in an acceptable formula. Six WHA teams would join the NHL and have a chance at the Stanley Cup. What did this mean to the Oilers? What impact would the decision have on the team roster? The questions were set aside for an even more important one: would the Oilers even exist by September? Then came more news from New York. If Edmonton was still playing next season, it would be as a WHA team. The proposed merger was off, killed by six intractable NHL owners.

So tenuous was the Oilers' lease on life that summer that the WHA drew up two 1977-78 schedules, one for eight teams and another for seven. When Peter Pocklington decided they were in, Glen Sather went to work again. One unpleasant task was to compensate for the loss of defenceman Robin Sadler, who turned his back on a two-year, $200,000 contract to return to B.C. and become a fireman. Sadler had not been enjoying himself. Sather could have told him that he wasn't the only one.

Glen Sather's first full season was just slightly better

than the previous one. Winning 38 games and tying three in an 80-game schedule, the Oilers placed fifth and qualified for a berth in the playoffs for the Avco Cup. Then, the father-son team of Gordie and Mark Howe came to town, along with the rest of the second-place New England Whalers, to show Oilers fans what real hockey was all about. In this particular series, real hockey was about winning four games out of five, which New England did very handily. The Whalers went on to meet the Jets in Cup competition. The Oilers went home for the holidays. It was another long summer for Sather as he prepared for the season to come.

Two circumstances made the next season particularly significant for the Oilers. One was the arrival of Wayne Gretzky in November 1979. Gretzky didn't come alone. He was part of a three-player deal. Also purchased from Nelson Skalbania were the Racers' young, promising goaltender Eddie Mio and sharp-shooting left-winger Peter Driscoll. That gave Glen Sather and the team more to play with. Nevertheless, the challenges continued. Earlier, Sather had courted Butch Goring of the L.A. Kings. The Oilers made what Goring called "a great offer." The Kings saw the Oilers and raised them, offering Goring US$250,000 for each of the next five years. He decided to stay in California.

Undeterred by that disappointment and others, Sather concentrated on developing the team, bolstering its defensive side so it could make sudden, offensive attacks to be led by Wayne Gretzky. Sometimes, from behind the bench, Sather

Wayne Gretzky

seemed ready to participate in those attacks himself. Although he was a prankster with his own squad, he demonstrated his old competitive streak from behind the bench. During games he quickly turned tough, yelling put-downs at opposing players as they skated by, and offering tart and pointed replies to comments shouted at him by the other team's fans.

It is easy to think of 1978-79 as "the Gretzky season," but another, bigger event was about to change everything for Glen Sather and Peter Pocklington. The 1978-79 season was to be the last one for the World Hockey Association. Encouraged by Nelson Skalbania's deal with young Wayne, which acted as a finger-in-the-eye to the NHL, Birmingham's John Bassett upped the ante and signed seven juniors. Obviously, the WHA was not taking the NHL's threats seriously. What it was taking, instead, were the young, talented players that an ever-expanding NHL would need to infuse new energy into its future.

Almost unbelievably, the Edmonton Oilers finished the season as league leaders. True, the WHA was just a six-team league (Houston and Indianapolis were gone before the season ended), but Edmonton's 48-30-2 season standing was Glen Sather's best yet. There was even more to celebrate. Edmonton's new found energy and aggressiveness gave the Oilers a seven-game victory over New England in the Avco Cup playoffs. Edmonton faced two-time, Cup-winning Winnipeg in the finals.

The first two games of the finals were played in Edmonton, but fewer fans showed up for each game than paid to see the average regular season game. As the puck went down on the first face-off of game three in Winnipeg, there were still plenty of seats available. The attention of hockey fans was on that "other series" between Stanley Cup competitors, Montreal Canadiens and New York Rangers.

There was another underlying reason for fan apathy: many feared this was the end. The concerns about the league's future had infested other teams, too. Many players went into the finals with doubts and misgivings. Where would they be this time next year?

The Oilers lost the first two games on home ice and were finally goaded into action by the high-scoring Gretzky to win 8-3 in the third game. The Great One scored the opening goal in game four and another in the second period to break a 1-1 tie. However, the Jets beat Oilers goalie Dave Dryden two more times to give Winnipeg a close 3-2 win. The Oilers roared back in game five, beating the Jets 10-2. Game six was an almost equally lopsided affair, ending with a 7-3 Avco Cup victory for the Jets. Thousands came out to cheer the champs as they rolled slowly down Main Street in Winnipeg, although many lining the parade route seemed to be cheering for something else. One banner read, "Next Year, the Stanley Cup."

The NHL held another vote to decide whether the two leagues would merge. With the voting complete, the 14-3 result was uncontestable. The contentious and costly contest between the two professional leagues was finally over. As a consequence, the WHA was history. In the end, the two leagues didn't call it a merger. They called it, more accurately, an NHL expansion. Only four of the strongest WHA teams would join the NHL: the Quebec Nordiques, the New England Whalers, the Winnipeg Jets, and the Edmonton Oilers. How did Edmonton hockey fans feel about the announcement of their new NHL team? The answer was unequivocal: they snapped up 15,242 season tickets in just 11 days — every single ticket available.

Those ticket revenues would soon come in handy. Edmonton — like other WHA-turned-NHL cities — would pay dearly for the privilege of inclusion in the one-and-only league. The price of admission was $6 million. There was another cost, too: manpower. Players in the four former WHA teams were soon up for grabs in a "reclamation" draft.

It is a testimony to the excellence of the Oilers' lineup that NHL teams took many players from its promising roster. Twelve players who had taken the team to the finals were lost, including, at first, Ed Mio and Dave Dryden. That left the Oilers without a starting goalie. With players taken from wing, centre, and especially defence, there wasn't a position that didn't suffer losses, either to league redistribution or to retirement. However, after more than a year of league indecision, at last Glen Sather knew exactly where he stood: up to his neck in team reconstruction. His first order of business was to retrieve the best of those who had been lost.

Team Builder

It could have been worse. With a keen eye and razor-sharp strategy, Sather recaptured some of his high-scoring players, including second- and third-place point-getters, right-winger Blair MacDonald, and centre Brett Callighen. Then he managed to snatch back goalies Eddie Mio and Dave Dryden.

Of the 16 players Sather selected during the expansion draft that soon followed, only four made the roster — defencemen Pat Price (from the New York Islanders), Lee Fogolin (from Buffalo), and Doug Hicks (from Chicago). Pittsburgh Penguins player Colin Campbell (destined to become the New York Rangers' coach) would have a brief, one-season stay in Edmonton. Sather's personal reclamation program also brought back Risto Siltanen and Oilers tough-guy Dave Semenko. Sather and his scout Barry Fraser then began to formulate their strategy for the entry draft in August.

In the first round of the next draft, the Edmonton Oilers would pick 21st from a long roster of promising players from the Oshawa Generals, Lethbridge Broncos, Niagara Falls Flyers, and other training-ground teams. The list was considerably shorter by the time Fraser announced the Oilers' choices. It was one of the prices to be paid for entry into the NHL. Former WHA teams were relegated to the final pick positions. Already gone were great players that included Duane Sutter, Rob Ramage, Mike Gartner, and Ray Bourque. Finally, number 21 was announced and the Oilers picked Kevin Lowe of the Quebec Remparts. Sather called Lowe's mother and told her that he was "thrilled to have him."

Acquiring Lowe had been no snap decision. That's not the way Sather and Fraser worked. The actual draft was the end of the selection process. Weeks before, names had been discussed and lists had been made. Lowe rated high with Fraser.

"We had him eleventh on our list," Fraser said later. "When his name came up, we didn't think about it for a minute." They didn't think about it on that particular day, anyway. On draft day, the scouting, the interviewing, and the thinking had already been done.

The Oilers had given up their second-round pick in order to retrieve Semenko. Then came the third round, with a 48th pick. Edmonton chose a player who had escaped the serious notice of other scouts. That was understandable — in 52 WHA games, he had just one goal and 10 assists. So, why were the Oilers interested? The answer to that went back to the previous March, when Sather had first seen him play. The kid was big, strong, and good in the corners. Sather told others that if Mark Messier was available in the summer, he would "take him in a minute." Soon, Messier was part of the team.

Then came the fourth round. The decision had already been made, although it hadn't been a quick one. Urged to look closely at Glenn Anderson, Sather asked Fraser if he knew what he was doing. "This kid is going to be in the Hall of Fame someday," was the scout's self-assured reply. Fraser had seen the 19-year-old from B.C. do it all at the Canadian Olympic team's training camp. He knew Anderson excelled at scoring, playmaking, and speed skating.

Sather was convinced. He urged the tall, speedy goal-getter to join them immediately. At first, Anderson hesitated. He wanted to finish the national team program first. Fortunately, that wasn't going to be a problem for the Oilers

— they would happily wait for a talent this promising.

The following year, at the Montreal Forum, where 2500 fascinated spectators attended the first public draft, Sather and Fraser put two cornerstones of their future Stanley Cup winning team into place. In the first round, in a sixth pick, Sather chose the Kitchener Rangers' Paul Coffey. Coffey was the kind of offensive defenceman Oilers team-builders were looking for. In The Great One's opinion, he had "maybe more speed than any defenceman who ever lived."

In the fourth round, Sather and Fraser had the opportunity to pick someone else they had been looking for — and had found — sometime before. Subtle scouting and an excellent eye for talent had put Finnish Olympic team member Jari Kurri on their list months before. The Oilers had to wait until Kurri won the silver medal in the 1980 World Junior Championships, but the wait — as with Anderson — would be worth it.

"We could never have waited until the fourth round if everybody knew what we knew," Fraser chuckled. "He'd have gone real high." It was another Sather steal.

Halfway through the first NHL season, goalie Dave Dryden retired. A fast trade with Quebec meant that Ron Chipperfield would be replaced with starter goalie Ron Low. The coach and the scout were still looking for more netminding talent and found it in Victoria, B.C. and, of all places, Billings, Montana. They had watched Grant Fuhr play a number of times for the Victoria Cougars and had carefully

Paul Coffey

studied Billings Bighorn goalie, Andy Moog. Moog became an Oilers player in the sixth pick of that year's draft, and in the 1981 amateur draft, Fuhr joined the team. In training camp, Fuhr was so good that Sather sent Andy Moog down to Wichita in the Central League for a brief remedial stint.

Finally, in the spring of 1981, Pat Price was traded for another player Sather had lost back in the insanity of the reclamation draft: right-winger Pat Hughes.

They were all energetic, talented men with great potential. Now what was Glen Sather going to do with them?

Style Setter

Acquiring Wayne Gretzky or other strong players didn't represent a "Sather strategy" as such. It was merely the initial phase of a bigger, more ambitious one. The next phase meant building a team around his key offensive star — but what kind of team, and what kind of play?

Then, as now, attitudes were influenced by conventional wisdom. In the 1970s — the era of the goon — intimidation and threats of violence from the brawlers-and-maulers were common tactics. Wayne Gretzky, for one, was no fighter, and he certainly didn't need to be. What Glen Sather was about to do was flaunt conventional wisdom. In this, he was not alone.

"What's the league waiting for, somebody to die out there?" protested L.A. Kings' marksman Marcel Dionne.

The Montreal Canadiens — those kings of finesse — had led the way in 1976, defeating the league's self-appointed intimidators, the Philadelphia Flyers, to win the Stanley Cup. The Habs' victory over Philadelphia's "Broad Street Bullies" was, as Serge Savard put it, "a victory for hockey."

A change was in the air.

There was also a lesson to be learned from the three-time Avco Cup winning Winnipeg Jets. In its last two seasons, the Winnipeg Jets had put as many as eight Europeans on its player roster. This might have been foresight on the part of the Jets' organization, but more than likely it was simply desperation. Up against the NHL's financial clout, penny-pinching WHA teams were forced to get their players from anywhere they could — including overseas.

Glen Sather had been impressed with the likes of Anders Hedberg, Ulf Nilsson, and other European players in the WHA. The point, Glen Sather knew, was not to import these players and then attempt to retrain them to play North American style hockey. To some extent, the Jets embraced a European style — a winning style — of playing. That was another point not lost on Glen Sather. He liked the style and he liked winning. In 1979, during a trip to Finland and Sweden, he found more to like. He especially liked what he saw as he watched youngsters play peewee hockey. He liked the swift passing, the sudden switching of sides, and the use of attacking defencemen. Glen Sather brought it all back with him — the flow, the finesse, and most of all, the speed-skating offence.

Now, it seemed, he had some players who might master the style, and, by the 1980-81 season, three that already had: Finnish centre Matti Hagman, left-wing Jari Kurri, and defenceman Risto Siltanen.

Managing the Team and the Media

The ideal situation for a team-builder such as Glen Sather was to undertake the construction work in relative obscurity. Perfecting plays based on innovative strategies was best done in secret. Not only did a lack of outside attention help focus energy and effort, but it allowed the strategies to remain safe, even when executed before thousands of spectators. Used against different teams in different places, these strategies were rarely fully realized in single — or even consecutive — games.

Fortunately during this time, the press helped Sather out by providing almost no coverage of the fledgling Edmonton team. Sports writers were too busy writing and voicing their opinions about Montreal, Boston, New York, and Philadelphia — the Stanley Cup contenders of the era. In 1978 and 1979, the glare of the media spotlight was brightest in the biggest of the big-league cities. Out in the west, Edmonton was an ideal construction site, where Sather, Gretzky, Messier, and the rest skated in relative obscurity. It wouldn't be until later, in the early 1980s, that the Oilers, and especially Wayne Gretzky, would sweat under the full heat of the media lamp.

In September, new arrivals who had been drafted from minor league teams earlier in the spring congregated in Wild Bill Hunter's nondescript Edmonton Gardens for rookie camp. The rookies were carefully scrutinized, with observations recorded in Barry Fraser's "Player Evaluation Report." Each rookie's skills — skating, puck handling, passing, checking, and more than 70 other components were rated on a scale of one to nine. There was the rare "one" ("reject"), but more than a few "two's" ("reject with one good quality"). Most merited an overall three or four. The season before, Wayne Gretzky had scored a nine. Sather, Fraser, and assistant coach Bryan Watson weren't the only ones watching.

The veterans straggled into the Gardens to see the new guys play (a single season in the professional league qualified you as a mature player in this outfit). Sitting at rink side, these wise, old pros would shake their heads, smile, and snicker. A week later, the smiles were gone as Watson put them through their grueling paces at the veterans' camp in Jasper. It was no laughing matter.

As a master strategist and planner, Sather was prepared when the media shifted focus a season or two later (and then felt foolish, when Edmonton blew the first-round 1982 playoffs to L.A.). In the early days, those who travelled to Edmonton, including the media, found themselves quickly won over by the adroit and charming Oilers manager.

To the players, Glen Sather was many things. He was fair, taking a player aside to let him know how he felt about an abysmal level of play, rather than chewing him out in front of his teammates. He could also be quietly ruthless, often in a particularly creative way. One year, Mark Messier had arrived at the wrong airport in Edmonton for a flight with the team. He called Sather to say he would be late. Sather told him that was no problem — he'd find a ticket waiting at the counter when he arrived at the right airport. The team would fly on ahead. Messier got the ticket all right, destination: Wichita, Kansas, where the Oilers' Houston farm team was playing. Sather let Messier suffer for his mistake, setting him adrift for close to two weeks before throwing him a lifeline.

They called Sather "Slats." He was a prankster. By all accounts, in those early days, Glen "Slats" Sather made it fun: buckets of cold water for the guys as they took hot showers, shaving cream in their hairbrushes, and talcum powder sprinkled in their hairdryers. He was also generous (he and Anne Sather had hosted Wayne Gretzky during his first three weeks in Edmonton), offered plenty of praise, and was clear about his expectations.

"One day we're gonna be in the NHL," Sather told Wayne not long after he arrived, "and one day you are going to be captain of this hockey team. Remember I told you that."

He was also a benign manipulator. No surprise: Slats had studied psychology in college.

Gretzky had long-since moved out of the Sather home and was rooming with veteran Ace Bailey and his wife. Kevin Lowe, on the other hand was new, alone, and away from Quebec for the first time. Sather suggested Gretzky and Lowe get together (although "ordered" is the more accurate term, as Lowe remembered). It worked. Gretzky was an eating machine and Lowe, ironically, was a terrific cook. Even better, teammates Doug Hicks and Dave Lumley lived next door. Mark Messier would drive down from his parents' home in nearby St. Albert to hang out. Glen Sather must have smiled. Not all teamwork is forged in the arena.

Later, Kevin Lowe remembered how positive Sather was. More than positive, he could be downright inspirational. On the eve of the finals with the New York Islanders, the team was tense. For months, the players had been reliving the agony of a resounding defeat and the loss of the Stanley Cup the year before. Sather could sense the paranoia.

"You guys are the best team in the NHL!" he exhorted. "If you just use your heads and play the way we're telling you to play, you're going to win and you're going to win easy." It wasn't just what he said, it was the way he said it.

"When he spoke I got goose bumps," recalled Lowe. "I wanted to get out onto the ice right away."

It was psychology at work.

Chapter 5
Growing Pains

Halfway through that first 1979-80 NHL season, Edmonton was third from the bottom of the standings. It was time for a shakedown. Some of the "shaking" went on between the older Oilers players and the newcomers. Sure, Wayne Gretzky was good, but so what? He needed to be better. That was the way veteran defenceman Pat Price and goalie Jim Craig figured it, and they both told Wayne so. As Gretzky skated near the crease, a frustrated Craig, smarting from a two-goal deficit, snarled, "Gretzky, just who do you think you are, anyway?"

Gretzky, it seemed, knew exactly who he was. In the next half hour, he scored three goals to win the game. Both Price and Craig were gone from the team within a couple of seasons.

Six games from the end of the season, the team rallied and were within one spot of qualifying for the playoffs. Messier's brief stay down in Houston was the kind of "shakedown" maneuver that, although not planned, had had a positive effect not only on Mark, but on his teammates, too. The second was the trade that had brought goalie Ron Low west from the Quebec Nordiques. Low regularly made great plays in the crease. All his teammates on the ice had to do was put the puck past the other goalie, which they were already doing with increasing regularity.

Later that year, Gretzky made it clear again who he thought he was — someone out to beat Marcel Dionne in the scoring race. In Edmonton's final (and winning) regular season game against Colorado, it wasn't looking good until Wayne assisted on the tying goal and shot in the game-winning marker, his 51st. Gretzky had little trouble with Sather's offensive concept — 51 goals and 137 points were proof of that.

His team had needed the win against Colorado, because now they were in the playoffs, but Wayne figured he still needed the points, even though he had racked up 23 of them in the last 11 games. What he really needed was at least one more goal, because at the end of the night, after the Kings had played their game, and all the goals and assists were added together, both Dionne (53-84-137) and Gretzky (51-86-137) claimed 137 points. The player to break the tie would be the one who had scored the most goals. That meant Dionne would carry away the Art Ross Trophy. Wayne's consolation prizes: the Lady Byng, for most sportsmanlike player, and the coveted Hart Trophy, as most valuable player.

The Three-Game Playoffs

Edmonton was a new team in the playoffs, and there was a new rule for them to play by. The Oilers would play a first-time, best-of-five preliminary round series. Early in the second half of the season, there was little doubt which team they might meet after the regular season. For months, the Oilers had been watching a tough bunch of grinders and goal-getters with a blend of disbelief and dismay. By late winter, the Philadelphia Flyers had played 53 consecutive games without a defeat.

"It was a magical ride," said the new Flyers coach, Pat Quinn, in wonder.

However, the string of victories had ended abruptly with a seven-game losing streak, just about the time the Oilers finally took off. The Flyers posted a lacklustre 3-5-5 in their last 13 games of the season. Maybe there was hope.

"We were scared bleepless going into the playoffs," recalled Philly goalie Phil Myre. Oh, if the Oilers had only known!

Game one was a seesaw affair. Edmonton battled back after an early, two-goal deficit, after Ron Low belatedly found his confidence in the crease. The Oilers took a third period 3-2 lead. A 30-foot drive by Flyers player Rick MacLeish evened the score. Eight minutes into overtime, Flyers captain Bobby Clarke bounced the puck off Low's pad and into the net. The second game was an even more decisive 5-1 Flyers' victory. In the third game, spurred on by screaming fans in Edmonton, the Oilers pulled ahead with goals by Messier and Gretzky in the first. Then it was overtime again, when Ken Linseman circled around Oilers defenceman Pat Price, and beat Ron Low for the winning 3-2 victory. Suddenly, after a brief, first-round, three-game playoff series, the Edmonton Oilers' first NHL season was over.

Two Steps Forward ...

... was followed by one step back, or so it seemed in those early Oilers seasons.

As the 1980-81 season began, the team was still in its formative stage, with individuals learning to play, and in some cases to live, with each other. It was even tougher for the team's trio of Finns. Kurri barely spoke English. The language barrier tended to make the Finns a team-within-a-team. Glen Sather knew it, although he didn't have time to dwell on it. He was happy enough that Jari and Wayne both spoke the language of hockey fluently. Then there was the duo of Kevin Lowe and Lee Fogolin. It was as if those two were joined at the hip out on the ice. That was the way it should be for two defencemen, and that was the way Glen liked it.

The "Glen-and-Barry" headhunting team was in high gear. There were more bright newcomers. Defenceman Paul

Coffey was so unsure about how long he would be putting on an Oilers uniform that he was still living at the Edmonton Plaza Hotel. Right-winger Curt Brackenbury had come from the Quebec Nordiques just a few weeks before.

The Oilers were the youngest gang in the NHL. Few were married. As the second, big-league season began, Coffey, Gretzky, and Messier were still teenagers. Jari Kurri was barely 20, Kevin Lowe was just 21, and Risto Siltanen was 22. Twenty-five-year-old defenceman Lee Fogolin, Doug Hicks (a league veteran of eight years), and captain Blair MacDonald, 26, were decidedly middle-aged by comparison. Goalie Ron Low — at age 30 — appeared to be the team's designated "old man."

"Who was your childhood idol?" an interviewer asked right-winger Glenn Anderson.

"Wayne Gretzky," the wisecracking 20-year-old Anderson replied.

At the beginning of that season, they were playing badly. Twenty-one teams were eligible for a shot in the playoffs that year. That meant just five teams — the league's very worst — would be out of the running. It looked like the Oilers would be one of them. Even at that early stage of the season, it was time to stop thinking and start doing.

Glen Sather took a deep breath and then took stock. Maybe it was time to get rid of a few players. The team was playing so badly that the recently promoted general manager and president wondered whether it was only players he needed to get rid of. Maybe he needed to get rid of coach Bryan Watson, too. That would be tough. Bugsy was a good friend.

First, however, it was back to the minors for a handful of players. Then, after the team lost nine out of 10 home games, Sather and Pocklington said goodbye to Bryan Watson — with two years' salary to cushion the blow. Assistant coach Billy Harris would stay exactly where he was. The former Toronto mainstay had skated for the mighty Leafs in the 1950s and 1960s and had seen a lot of Stanley Cup action. If there was one thing this club needed, it was people who had seen a little of that and knew what it was like to go all the way. Glen Sather decided not to go coach shopping. Instead, he walked out of the front office and moved back in behind the bench. That's how bad things were.

As September moved through October and into November, things didn't get much better. After a brief flurry of victories, including, to the delight of hometown fans, a 10-3 win over Chicago, the Oilers lost eight of the next nine games. That winter, Edmonton couldn't even beat teams it was *supposed* to beat — ones in the bottom half of the standings. They were whipped by Minnesota and then beaten by Washington.

The team was plagued by injuries. Injured earlier in the season, Ron Low's hand had healed at last. Then, during a warm-up with the farm team, the puck smashed his hand — the *same* hand. Low shaved his beard off in disgust and sat out the rest of the season. In January, the Oilers were beaten badly 5-0 by the Montreal Canadiens. That hurt, but for Eddie Mio, the pain was physical. He was carried out on a stretcher after Rejean Houle sent the puck crashing into his facemask.

Inexplicably, however, in the midst of all these horrors, the Oilers were able to shellack the Canadiens 9-1 on home ice a few weeks later. There was no doubt that the Oilers had something going for them. Too bad they couldn't find it more often.

The new coach began retooling his team. As winter moved into spring that second NHL season, there were more goodbyes (including Dave Semenko, Don Murdoch, Ron Low, and later captain Blair "BJ" MacDonald). Some were gone just briefly and some forever.

Mark Messier was on Sather's list of trades. In hindsight, because we know what Messier eventually achieved, this seems shocking. However, at the time, nobody knew for sure what he could do, although Sather had a pretty good idea. He also knew Messier was nowhere close to achieving his potential. Sather couldn't afford to wait. He had a long talk with Mark. The word "demotion" might not have been overtly mentioned, but the possibility was certainly there. Messier was told to stay home at night and reminded about Sather's famous bed check.

While on the road, nobody knew when Glen would check the players' beds. The season before, big Dave Semenko had tiptoed down the hotel corridor one hour past the eleven o'clock curfew, opened the door of his room, and found Slats sitting inside, grinning up at him. "And did you have a good night?" was all the coach said before he quietly let himself out.

After the conversation with Sather, Mark went home and had a long conversation with himself. By mid-February, he was a changed player.

At this point in the season, some of the players were starting to come around, and some of the best ones were getting even better (Wayne Gretzky had just posted 100 points), but the team itself still needed some work. Unfortunately, the NHL wasn't about to give the Oilers — or any team — time off to improve their performance. It was time to "face the music," so to speak. The team was about to play the St. Louis Blues.

The Blues were the league's number-one team. They had won 24 of their last 27 games, and boasted netminder Mike Liut as one of their own — the man many were already calling the season's MVP.

In the second period, with the score tied 2-2, things began to happen. Right-winger Curt Brackenbury hammered a shot at the St. Louis goal. Liut made the save, but, as usual, Wayne Gretzky anticipated the rebound. He pounced on the puck, zipped it past Liut, and the Oilers pulled ahead. Mark Messier and Glenn Anderson then worked together to make it 4-2. On the bench, the Oilers' tension started to ease. In the third period, captain BJ MacDonald dropped the puck back to Paul Coffey, who dashed over the blue line and backhanded it past an increasingly frustrated Liut to make the score 5-2.

Then, something miraculous happened. People who were in the stands that night remember it and still talk about it. Wayne Gretzky put in another one. Barely nine seconds later, he followed it up with one more. The crowd was on its feet, applauding wildly. Liut acknowledged Wayne's feat in his own way, by simply skating off the ice. As Liut's replacement, Ed Staniowski, hunkered down between the pipes, you had to wonder, just what he was thinking? If he thought the worst was over, he was wrong.

Fewer than three minutes passed before Gretzky put in another goal. The kid wouldn't — or couldn't — stop. He shot in another one! Were these the fastest four consecutive goals in NHL history? At the time, nobody knew for sure, but the record Wayne Gretzky tied that night — most goals in a single period — had been set 47 long years before by Leafs player Harvey "Busher" Jackson (in some ways, the Wayne Gretzky of his day).

The Oilers won that night. In 1981, any win was a great win for the Oilers. But this wasn't just any win, and St. Louis wasn't just any team. The Oilers had just whipped the number one team in the league, 9-2.

After handing the Blues that crushing defeat, the Oilers went on to win only four of the next 10 games. The victories were fabulous, rekindling faith in the team, but many of the defeats were humiliating. Where was the consistency?

Getting Better

At the beginning of the season, the Oilers had basically been, "Wayne Gretzky and those other guys." By early March, however, there were half a dozen new sports celebrities wearing white, blue, and orange. They had names people knew and spoke of with conviction and excitement: Messier, Coffey, Anderson, Moog, Kurri, and Lowe. There was talk about "the team of the future." However, right now, there was another playoff series coming up. This one was against the Montreal Canadiens.

The Oilers didn't have to look at the Canadiens' roster to know who they were up against. They knew these men. They were winners of four straight Stanley Cups: Guy Lafleur, Steve Shutt, Serge Savard, and Guy Lapointe. Back in Montreal, the playoffs were a given; the Cup victory simply expected. It was an annual cultural tradition. This was the team Edmonton faced. This was the team that a basically unproven goalie faced. This was Andy Moog's moment. As it turned out, it was also the team's moment.

Inside the Forum, the Habs' holy shrine, youthful Oilers dashed around aging superstars. The first game was a decisive win: Oilers 6, Canadiens 3. In game two, Coffey and Siltanen scored in the first two periods, giving the Oilers a one-marker lead. The Canadiens watched as all but one of their 30 shots were turned aside by Andy Moog. Kurri found the Montreal net again in the third period to make it a 3-1 victory for the Oilers.

"We Believe in Miracles" read the huge banner on the wall of Northlands Coliseum, inviting ticket holders inside for game three. Over 17,000 Edmonton believers chanted "Andy! Andy! Andy!" and watched Moog play a thrilling game of "keep out," while teammates, spurred on by a Gretzky hat trick, humiliated the Habs 6-2. The front page of the *Edmonton Sun* simply repeated what everybody else was saying: "INCREDIBLE!"

In Unionville, New York, during the next series, the Islanders brought the high-flying Edmonton squad back down to earth. It was a bumpy landing, with a pair of 8-2 and 6-3 losses for Edmonton. Back in Edmonton, again inspired by a Gretzky hat trick, the Oilers beat the Islanders 5-2. A 4-4 tie sent game four into overtime but Islanders defenceman Ken Morrow tipped the puck in past Andy Moog at 5:41. The Long Island crowd held its collective breath as the Oilers moved ahead 4-2 in game five, then cheered as their home team closed the gap 4-3. Four minutes before the end of the game, the singing began on the Oilers' bench.

"Here we go Oilers, here we go! Here we go! Here we go Oilers, here we go!"

Glen Sather shrugged and laughed. It seemed that every time the team got into trouble, they'd start to sing. That was okay by him.

"I think it was Mark Messier who started it," Paul Coffey recalled. "It just felt right to start singing," he remembered, laughing. Andy Moog kept the puck out during those last, long minutes of the game. Imagine that: the Canadian youngsters would be going back to "Edmonchuck," dragging the Stanley Cup champs along with them for game six.

The Oilers held the Islanders at bay until into the second period, and then the 1-1 tie slipped away. Mark Messier put Edmonton on the scoreboard again, but the Islanders Bryan Trottier and Dave Langevin put Gretzky against the boards while Denis Potvin and Mike Bossy put the puck past Andy Moog. When the game ended 5-2, so did the Oilers' chances at the Stanley Cup.

Wayne Gretzky was truly disappointed. Yet, there were compensations. He won his second Hart Trophy as most valuable player by five votes (Mike Liut, the runner-up had his own disappointments), and, at last, he had beaten Marcel Dionne in the scoring race 164-135.

"Gretzky makes me feel like an old man," said the Kings sharpshooter with a sigh.

Chapter 6
The Turnaround

For Andy Moog, it was one of the worst things that could have happened. Just weeks after his playoff triumph against Montreal and his outstanding showing against the powerhouse New York Islanders, his future was threatened by a newcomer to his own team. His name was Grant Fuhr.

The Final Offensive Play

What Sather the strategist wanted was a goalie so rock solid that the Oilers defencemen — especially Paul Coffey — no longer felt compelled to hang back to protect a lead or stem an attack. The defencemen needed to feel free to dash up the ice and join the offence. Fuhr, Sather felt, was that goalie. Moog was still extremely valuable, a key component in the two-goalie system that fast, furious hockey demanded. So, Moog wasn't going anywhere. And that, he eventually realized, was the problem. For the rest of his career with the Oilers, Moog would live life in the shadow cast by the great Grant Fuhr. In four seasons, Moog would perform in only 11 playoff games.

Watching rookie Fuhr in that first season, assistant coach Billy Harris was reminded of the poise and cool of legendary Maple Leafs netminder Johnny Bower. Considering that Johnny was a 10-year pro in his 30s during his NHL rookie year and Fuhr was barely 20, fresh from the minors, this was high praise, indeed. Fuhr's style was something of a throwback, too. In peewee hockey, the Alberta-born Fuhr had been coached by "Mr. Goalie," the great Glenn Hall, who had won his Stanley Cup ring with the Chicago Blackhawks 20 years before. Living a quiet, retired life on his farm, Hall had taught Fuhr his trademark butterfly style.

Fuhr's toughness was exceptional. When the pressure was on, or when the score was close, Grant Fuhr didn't merely reach out to snag the puck with his glove or knock it aside with his stick. He would *lunge* for it. He would commit his entire body to keeping the rubber out of the crease. A man with incredible hand-eye coordination, he routinely made miraculous saves.

His temperament was puzzling. Gretzky wondered more than once if he ever got excited. Nothing seemed to rattle Grant Fuhr. Errors by defencemen might cost the team goals and

Grant Fuhr

Fuhr his statistics, but he never berated his teammates. Before big games, you wouldn't have found him slumped in the dressing room, moody and morose, or chattering away nervously. Instead, Fuhr could be found striding across the golf course, a smile on his face. "It clears the head," he would say.

Before long, the Oilers had the confidence to play a hell-bent-for-leather, cowboy-style offence. They knew they had a "pardner" back in their own zone who would "keep the barn door closed." Now they could take chances and be riskier in their play. More and more, it was fast-skating, quick-passing defenceman Paul Coffey who led the charge into enemy territory. Glen Sather was a happy man, while stoic Andy Moog remained patient and understanding … at least for the time being.

Gretzky's Personal Best

Just seven games into the 1981-82 season, lantern-jawed Mark Messier told reporters that his team would finish first in their division. That meant beating Vancouver and Colorado, the team's Alberta rivals, the Calgary Flames, and the L.A. Kings. Reporters were skeptical.

All the major players on the team started scoring well, doing their bit to help Messier make good on his prediction. None did as much as The Great One. During the Oilers' 39th game of the season, Wayne Gretzky scored four times against the Philadelphia Flyers in Northlands Coliseum. It was the fourth goal — a quick shot three seconds before the final siren — that really counted, not so much for the game they had already won minutes before, but for the record book.

Gretzky had started his internal countdown at the beginning of the game, as had most of the crowd. The first goal was number 47 of the season, the second was number

48, and the third, number 49. Then, as the clock continued ticking, there was nothing for about 10 minutes. Gretzky was desperate. Grant Fuhr stopped a loose shot and pushed it toward Glenn Anderson at the red line. Gretzky dashed past him.

"Pass it to me! Pass it to me!" he shouted. Anderson did as he was told.

With most of the crowd on its feet, Wayne pelted up the ice, fired, and watched Philly netminder Pete Peeters go sprawling as the puck hit the back of the net. By scoring his 50th goal in the 39th game, The Great One had bettered the 50-goals-in-50-games record set almost 40 years before by Maurice "Rocket" Richard. Mark Messier and the rest of the players mobbed Wayne before he could skate off the ice.

For many who had been watching Wayne for years, this moment came as no surprise. Seven years before, back in Sault Ste. Marie, one of the owners of the Soo Greyhounds had placed a long-distance call to his professional hockey-playing son. The son's name was Phil Esposito.

"There's a boy here who will break all your records one day," Esposito's father had told him. "He's only 14 and he's playing Junior in the Soo. His name is Gretzky. Wayne Gretzky."

At the time, Esposito had been dubious. "Well, that's great, dad. But he's only 14. Let's wait and see."

Even before the game, fans had stopped speculating about 50-in-50 (the feat seemed fairly likely) and had started speculating about Gretzky's ability to equal Phil Esposito's league record of 76 goals by season's end. Wayne began to speculate about it, too. He made it his objective to beat Esposito's record, with goals against Detroit. Unfortunately, it didn't quite work out that way. Esposito was there, in Detroit, watching the potential record breaker. Nobody had asked Esposito to go, it was just the right thing to do. At the end of the game, Wayne Gretzky had tied — but not broken — Esposito's record. Was he disappointed? Esposito waved off the thought.

"I wanted to be here," he said simply. "I want to be wherever it is he scores his seventy-seventh."

"Wherever" meant Buffalo, where the Oilers would meet the Sabres and where Wayne Gretzky, with 17 games still left in the season, would meet his destiny.

The game was tied 3-3. Winning the game was the team's focus. Number 77 could wait. Somebody — *anybody* — needed to put the puck in the net! Buffalo goalie Don Edwards decided to make Gretzky work for it, stopping four of his shots. Then, the Oilers — and their star player — finally got what they both wanted. The 77th came late in the third period with an elementary wrist shot by Gretzky. With minutes still on the clock, time stood still as the Oilers smothered him. The crowd gave him a standing ovation and Phil Esposito — perhaps remembering the prescient phone call from his father seven years before — personally presented the puck to the man who had beaten his own "personal best."

Oh, and yes, the Oilers also won the game 4-3.

And still it would not end.

There were five games left in the season when the Oilers took to the ice in Calgary. Making an assist on a goal by Pat Hughes, Wayne Gretzky reached another objective: a point total of 200 in one season. Why stop a good thing? Minutes later in the same game, he had another assist, and then, two more goals. At season's end, Wayne Gretzky's final tally was 212 points, 92 goals, and a third Hart Trophy.

Those in the Shadows

Wayne Gretzky made a lot of headlines that season, but he wasn't the only one who helped the Edmonton Oilers climb from fifteenth to second place in the league standings in the space of one season. It took an entire team to do that, young men who played in the shadow of a hockey phenomenon and were proud to do so.

"It doesn't bother me at all," Mark Messier told reporters who asked how he felt about the adulation surrounding Gretzky. "Everybody on this team is going to get their day; it's only a matter of time."

Sporting his big, wide grin, Messier told his teammates, "There's nowhere for us to hide out there, so let's play with reckless abandon!"

In spite of a November ankle injury that bothered him for most of the season, that's exactly what Messier began to do. Others followed his lead. Messier and the other "reckless"

Oilers — Anderson, Coffey, Kurri, and Lowe — were racking up more than a point a game. The end result: 417 goals by the end of the season, something no single team in NHL history had ever achieved. Anderson's point total skyrocketed from 53 to 105. Coffey's bounced from 32 to 89. With 86 points, Kurri, beat his previous season's total by 11.

In the second-to-last game of the 1981-82 season, Gretzky set Messier up for two goals against the L.A. Kings. After the second one, which came less than 30 seconds from the end of the game, Messier did a little dance of glee and there wasn't a face in Northlands Coliseum that wasn't smiling with him. Messier had just scored his 50th goal of the season.

The team made good on Mark Messier's prediction of divisional leadership and came just eight points short of becoming overall league leaders. The team that edged them out was none other than the New York Islanders. It was a portent of things to come.

Soon, it was playoff time. No sweat, the Oilers concluded, given the team they would face in round one. Messier, Coffey, and the others boldly started thinking about who they would meet in round two.

After a first-game loss of 10-8 in round one against the L.A. Kings, the Oilers were incredulous. Wasn't this the lowly fourth-place team in a five-team division? Wasn't this the same team they had beaten seven times in eight games, some by scores as silly as 11-4 and 10-3? This was the L.A. Kings, for pete's sake! Surely game one had to have been an aberration. The score in game two was Oilers 3, Kings 2. That was more like it, but it had been close, with the final Gretzky goal coming in overtime.

Game three in Los Angeles had the standing-room-only crowd in a frenzy. By the end of the second period, things had quieted down substantially as it looked like Grant Fuhr would lead Edmonton to a 5-0 shutout. Early in the third period, the Kings finally managed to squeak one by him, although the L.A. team's owner had already walked out in disgust. Three more L.A. goals soon narrowed the gap, and the crowd suddenly found its voice again. By the end of regulation time, the game was tied and suddenly the Oilers were fighting for a win. Mark Messier gave it his best, but his shot went over the net. In the face-off that followed, the Kings' Doug Smith won the draw. Then, Daryl Evans took the puck and pushed it past Grant Fuhr to give the Kings a 6-5 win.

In game four, it was another close call (3-2) for the Oilers, but a win was a win. There was nothing close about game five, however. It was Kings 7, Oilers 4, in Edmonton, no less. That meant the Kings were off to round two and the Oilers were off the ice until the next season. The *Edmonton Journal* sent the team away for the summer with a terse two-word farewell message: "THEY CHOKED!"

Season of Achievements

The story of the Oilers' 1982-83 season is told well through the achievements of its most valuable players, as well as its statistics. Wayne Gretzky set another record, this one for scoring in consecutive games (the first 30 of the season), which is one reason why he led the league again in scoring with 71 goals and 196 points. Those goals and points were reason enough to give Gretzky his fourth straight Hart Trophy. Messier scored four goals in a single game for the first time in his career and earned a 48-58-106 total, the seventh best in the entire league. The Oilers were divisional leaders (a ridiculous 28 points in front of second-place Calgary) and boasted a new record of 424 goals that placed them just four points behind the league-leading Boston Bruins.

However, none of the Oilers were wearing Stanley Cup rings.

The team was an enormous draw in its hometown, of course, but also, unlike any other team, it had become a huge attraction, playing for 94 percent capacity crowds wherever it landed. Put another way, Wayne, Jari, Mark, and the rest were putting about 1400 more bums in seats at every game than the league average — and contributing about $16,000 extra for the *other* team every time they skated out into someone else's arena.

Behind the Statistics

There were other chapters in the Oilers' tale that turnaround season. Glen Sather was feeling the strain of his multiple roles as general manager, coach, and president. He needed help. The team engine was running full out, but the last playoffs had revealed that it still needed fine-tuning. The team welcomed former defenceman John Muckler as coach. He was the perfect foil for Sather. While Glen was the passionate motivator, Muckler was the cool-headed analyst — exactly what the team needed.

A good year for the team, 1982-83 was, ironically, a lacklustre year for the goalie people had placed so much faith in. In hockey lore, it's called the "sophomore jinx," the second-year slump that many goalies endure. Fuhr's second-season goals against average skyrocketed up to an embarrassing 4.28. By the new year, he was hearing boos from Edmonton fans as he skated on and off the ice after another bad game. Glen Sather and John Muckler agreed on the "tough love" approach that had worked so well with Moog and Messier. Grant was moved down to the Moncton Alpines for 10 games and Andy Moog was out in front of the Oilers' net once again.

Finally, the Finals

The headlines of the venerable *Hockey News* provide a very succinct summary of the three playoff rounds that the Edmonton squad played that year:

"Oilers Waste Little Time Disposing of Winnipeg," was the first headline.

"Oilers Easily Extinguish Calgary's Flames," exclaimed the second.

"Oilers Make It Look Easy Against Hawks," extolled the third.

The Oilers, at last, had gone all the way to the finals. The New York Islanders were waiting.

The season had not been kind to the Islanders. The three-time, Stanley Cup winners were sixth in overall league standings. In the playoffs, however, they had found firm footing and were ready to do battle for the Cup once again. "They" were a squad of seasoned NHL veterans, led, in part, by Mike Bossy, the right-winger who had been the first player in 36 years to score 50-in-50, and the first one to do it in his *rookie* year. It was just the first of four years in which he would achieve the feat. His outstanding performance in the playoffs the year before had earned him the Conn Smythe Trophy. Together with left-winger Clark Gillies and centre Bryan Trottier, "Hawse," as Bossy was known, was ready for another Stanley Cup.

"We wanted that fourth Cup ... to win it by beating Edmonton, already regarded as the NHL's next great team," Bossy wrote later in his autobiography. "We were old and confident, they were young and cocky."

However, it quickly became obvious that Islanders goalie Billy Smith was the man to beat. Smith was a superb playoff netminder, but as excellent as his play was in the finals, it was the "Hatchet Man's" mind games that made the difference. Psychology, not simply physical prowess, allowed the Islanders to beat the Oilers and carry away their fourth

Stanley Cup. That year, the Oilers saw a Billy Smith they had never seen before. Although Smith had been a Dr. Jekyll-like goaltender all season long, the playoffs brought out Mr. Hyde.

Snarling and slashing, Smith challenged the Oilers shooters constantly, leaving the crease, and in spite of his bulky hockey pads, swaggered aggressively into *their* territory. A slash on the leg of Glenn Anderson brought howls of protest from the Oilers' bench. "Suspend him," Sather screamed. Smith just laughed.

Smith coupled a belligerent attitude with outstanding ability. Every time he slapped aside the shots of Lowe, Kurri, Messier, and Gretzky, he slapped aside the team's chances at the Cup. Smith held the high-scoring Edmonton Oilers to only six goals in the entire series. Even the great Gretzky was held scoreless. For his efforts, Smith took home the Conn Smythe Trophy that his teammate, Mike Bossy, had won the year before.

Down with tonsillitis, Bossy saw game one on a TV suspended above his hospital bed. What he saw was a goalie duel between "Smitty" and Andy Moog. Moog was fantastic as he tried desperately to compensate for the lame performance of the Oilers players out in front. However, Smith had all the support he needed (with goals by Duane Sutter and Ken Morrow) to shut Edmonton out 2-0.

"PUBLIC ENEMY NUMBER ONE," shouted the front-page headline in the *Edmonton Journal.* In case there was any confusion, the story was also accompanied by Billy Smith's photograph.

Bossy was on the ice in game two, and surprisingly so was Glenn Anderson.

"Wasn't Anderson hurting?" Billy Smith sneered after the game. "I thought it was his funeral today."

In a way, it was. The Islanders had just buried Anderson and the rest of the Oilers, taking game two 6-3.

Another slash and Wayne Gretzky fell to the ice, another apparent victim of vicious Smith. He was soon back on his skates, shouting and pointing his stick at the goalie. Smith calmly lifted his goal stick to eye level, a few feet from Gretzky's face. The result was a five-minute slashing penalty for Smith. Later, an angry Dave Lumley took revenge and speared Smith in the throat. The best — and worst — was yet to come.

In New York, the Islanders scored four goals in the third period to end a game-three tie and win 5-1. Anxious, it seemed, to enjoy their summer, the Islanders didn't wait long to dominate in game four. Bossy led the scoring with the first of three goals in the first period. While the Oilers struggled to catch up, a frustrated Glenn Anderson skated in front of the net and grazed Smith's mask. Smitty crashed to the ice and lay writhing in front of the goal. The whistle blew and Anderson was out of the game for five long minutes on a high-sticking penalty. Smith struggled to his feet and managed to keep the puck away, giving the Islanders a 4-2 win and the Stanley Cup. It wasn't just the Cup they had won, as the Edmonton Oilers did not need to be reminded, but the Cup in a four-game sweep!

It was a proud and very public moment when Billy Smith accepted the Conn Smythe Trophy at the league's formal presentation. Flashbulbs popped and TV cameras zoomed in. Suddenly, the expected acceptance speech turned into a final, verbal "slash" at the Oilers. There, behind the microphones, Billy admitted that he hadn't really been all that badly hurt in game four — not hurt at all, in fact. He had, he confessed, just faked it.

"I did the same thing to Anderson as Gretzky did to me," he said, without the slightest hint of remorse. "I threw myself on my back on the ice and squirmed around. I want the world and all of Canada to know that two can play at that game."

Chapter 7
The Sweetest Victory

Glen Sather was pleased to formally announce what the media gathered before them already knew. The president of the Edmonton Oilers was very proud and pleased to formally introduce five-time Stanley Cup winner, Kevin Lowe. After 18 seasons in the NHL, Lowe was to be the team's new assistant coach.

The newest member of the Oilers coaching staff graciously answered questions. After all the time he had spent with the club, one reporter asked what his most memorable event was. That was easy. Kevin Lowe remembered the day like no other: the day his bright, brash team had battled its way through a repeat Cup series with New York to beat the once-mighty Islanders and take the Stanley Cup home to

Edmonton for the very first time. It was a day unlike any other, a day he knew would probably never come again. Lowe didn't hesitate: "May 19, 1984," he said, overcome with emotion.

A Sobering Season

Although he had left the core of the team intact, Glen Sather had also begun making serious and significant decisions. The first was moving Mark Messier from wing to centre. Messier responded to the challenge and played tougher and harder, like he had never played before. Even a six-day suspension couldn't stop him. Another decision was to trade Tom Roulston to Pittsburgh for centre Kevin McClelland. Pittsburgh had been so unimpressed by McClelland's two goals and four assists after 24 games that they had shipped him off to a farm team. Sather and Fraser were still after potential and they saw it in "Mac." The team also welcomed Grant Fuhr back into the fold.

Other things, such as strategy, did not change. Speed and finesse were the order of the day, as they had been since the Oilers had first become an NHL team. Other teams were watching and learning, too, giving the aggressive offensive line the name "Five Up." Killing penalties was easier when you dedicated two of your best men (Gretzky and Kurri) to the task. Why had nobody else thought to do the same?

The fine 1982-83 season had been, in retrospect, merely a prelude to the one that followed. For most of the last half of the 1983-84 season, while the team was playing and winning, its players were mentally preparing themselves to meet the Islanders. So great was the commitment to beat the Islanders that 28-year-old Lee Fogolin voluntarily turned over his captaincy to Wayne Gretzky. Where there was once youthful, playful banter, there was now purposeful discussion.

They called him "Captain Video." According to Roger Neilson, the former head coach of Toronto, Buffalo, and Vancouver, teams simply couldn't see enough video and film. He had used the medium not only to scout other players, but also to instruct those he had coached, helping them prepare for other teams. Fired the year before by the L.A. Kings (he had the Oilers to thank for that), Neilson had watched Edmonton's humiliation in the finals and thought Glen Sather could use his help. Sather thought so, too. Soon, Neilson went to work, watching, replaying, and then editing tapes of the Islanders into a formidable "best of" collection. It wasn't long before the team began to see results.

Four games into the season, the Oilers were 4-0. Wayne Gretzky thought that maybe the team could average six goals a game throughout the season. They already had two "eights" in those first few games. As the days went by, the Oilers added a "10," an "11," and a "13." In the space of four games, the Oilers kept those high numbers, beating Washington 11-3, Pittsburgh 7-3, Winnipeg 8-5, and Quebec 7-4. After 52 games, the Oilers' average was 5.78 goals per game.

Wayne "Streak" Gretzky couldn't stop scoring. When his scoring hit 40 consecutive games, people started to take notice. The Daoust skate manufacturers had produced a blue and orange skate for the Oilers. Now they were afraid that if Wayne put them on it would end the streak, so they held the skates back. The Titan manufacturers had a new plastic-injected stick. Wayne tested it and loved it. Again, Titan refused to let him use it in games because it might end the streak.

How Sweet It Is

Later that season, the Oilers watched the video and film clips to get ready for their biggest challenge of all. They saw that Billy Smith had trouble behind the net. They made lists of Islanders they knew they would have to prepare for, both mentally and physically. They talked strategy, including how to get players such as Bryan Trottier off his game. They wondered if they could possibly beat the Islanders twice in the first four games, or better yet, in the first two right there in Edmonton.

More than anything, however, they simply wanted to wipe that smirk right off Billy Smith's face. There was no question that it was really Smith who had beaten them. So, Glen Sather played it safe. Grant was in, and, once again, Andy Moog was out. The pressure mounted, but it was toughest on Wayne Gretzky, who had been held scoreless during the last series.

A first-round playoff victory against the Winnipeg Jets was a given. The second round proved to be something else.

The Calgary Flames weren't going to be snuffed out by the Oilers the way they had been in the previous playoffs. Coffey was down with the flu, and Wayne Gretzky was less than great. His parents came to cheer him on, happy to do anything that might work. It took a nasty seven-game series to quench the Flames. By that standard, the last round against Minnesota was a walk in the park, a stroll that led straight to the finals and a rematch with the Islanders.

It had been a lazy, self-satisfied summer and the Islanders had started talking about a "Drive for Five" (five Stanley Cups in a row) to tie the Montreal Canadiens' record. Looking back at it a few months later, Bossy, Trottier, and the others couldn't help feeling disappointed with a season that should have been good enough for them to clinch their division championship again. Expectations were high, but the team's energy was low.

The Oilers' plans were coming to fruition. In a reversal of Smith's first-game shutout in the previous series, Edmonton took the first game 1-0 in Unionville, Long Island. They seemed to be able to anticipate everything the Islanders were going to do. This was Grant Fuhr's show, co-starring newcomer Kevin McClelland, who scored the lone goal in the third period. Preparing for the second game, the Oilers were both relieved and excited. The Islanders were not.

The NHL's schedule change preyed on the minds of the New York players. Already tired, they were frustrated because the usual home game pattern of 2-2-1-1-1 had been altered to save plane fare. Now it was 2-3-2.

"I didn't like that we had to play the middle three games in Edmonton," Mike Bossy remembered. "After falling behind one game to none, I liked it even less."

In game two, Bryan Trottier scored just 53 seconds into the game. Clark Gillies, who had only scored 12 goals all season long, produced a hat trick and the Islanders skated off with a 6-1 win.

And Wayne Gretzky was still scoreless in the series.

In game three, the fans in Northlands Coliseum came alive, and the Oilers responded. In the second period, the Islanders were leading 2-1 until the Oilers scored three goals — the first in a solo dash by Mark Messier, and, with less than one minute remaining, two more just 18 seconds apart by Anderson and Coffey. In the third, Messier scored again and McClelland added one more less than half a minute later.

"Worn out, tired, hurt, and discouraged," Mike Bossy sensed that they were finished. In comparison, the Oilers grew more confident with every period. The 7-2 victory was a costly one, however. Grant Fuhr was caught behind the net and smashed into the boards by two other players. The Oilers' star goalie was taken away with a sprained shoulder. Nonetheless, the Oilers had been practicing those "high numbers" all season long and had gotten to like them, so they repeated the 7-2 score in the fourth game, with Andy Moog in goal to keep the other side of the scoreboard low. At last, The Great One scored, not once, but twice. There was no stopping them now.

Nobody on the team wanted to go all the way back to New York. It was time to put an end to the series, right then and there, in Edmonton. Andy Moog was in goal. The start was ominous, with an Islanders' power play less than a minute into play for the most ridiculous of reasons: too many men on the ice. Kurri and Gretzky, the magic men of Edmonton, provided two goals in the first period and Billy Smith skated slowly away to be replaced with Roland Melanson. The crowd was delighted, screaming, "We want Billeeee!"

Ken Linseman scored on a power play assisted by Gretzky and Charlie Huddy. Within five minutes, on another power play, Jari Kurri scored with assistance from Paul Coffey and Glenn Anderson. Now it was 4-0. The Islanders fought back in the third period, with Pat LaFontaine scoring twice for New York within the first minute. Under great pressure, Moog continued to make excellent saves, until, with 3:15 left, Pat Flatley crashed into the goalie, who lay motionless on the ice. While Flatley went to the penalty box, Moog staggered to his feet. The stunned crowd let out a sigh of relief. With less than 30 seconds of play left, and the New York net wide open, Dave Lumley grabbed the puck on the face-off, and shot it down from the Edmonton end into the open net to make the fifth and final goal.

Fans leapt onto the ice, balloons floated and bounced, and Wayne Gretzky had a tug-of-war with souvenir-hungry fans who wanted his stick. When New York and Edmonton players met each other in two passing lines, in the post-game ritual, the Islanders were doing more than shaking hands. Some of them knew they were passing the Stanley Cup to the next dynasty.

Chapter 8 The Dynasty is Forged

Just before the start of the 1984-85 season, the focus of Canada's hockey fans was not on the NHL, but on the Canada Cup series. There was a lot at stake. Three years earlier, the Soviets had beaten Canada to win the Cup. Glen Sather was the team's new coach and GM and he picked the league's best players for the team, many of whom also played for the Oilers. They included Grant Fuhr, four Oilers defencemen, and three forwards: Anderson, Gretzky, and Messier. Sather's controversial selections provoked a storm of criticism, although the criticism soon melted away as the Oilers and their teammates soundly beat the Soviets and then went on to win the best-of-three finals against Sweden, 5-2 and 6-5. It was a very gratifying way to start the new season.

The Oilers continued their winning ways, playing 15 straight games without a loss and celebrating their scoring champs Wayne Gretzky (73 goals) and Jari Kurri (71 goals). Finishing second in the league, the season was also rewarding in other ways. Paul Coffey won his first Norris Trophy and Kurri took away the Lady Byng. Gretzky won the Hart once more, as well as the Art Ross Trophy and the Lester B. Pearson Award.

The "Sather-and-Fraser" team went shopping again. In the fourth-round draft, they chose Esa Tikkanen, a Finnish player destined to have a very exciting start to his NHL career. The team then advanced to what would be a record-setting series of playoffs, setting a total of 25 NHL records, as they beat the L.A. Kings, Winnipeg Jets, and Chicago Blackhawks. They were in the finals again, this time facing the "bad boys" of the 1970s, the Philadelphia Flyers. Ten years later, of course, not many of those "bad boys" were still on the ice. Dave "the Hammer" Schultz, Andre "Moose" Dupont, Reggie Leach, and Bernie Parent were now just memories. Like Glen Sather before him, player-turned-GM Bobby Clarke had been rebuilding the Flyers, with the likes of defenceman Mark Howe, 50-plus-goal-scorer Tim Kerr, new Swedish netminder Pelle Lindburgh, and captain Dave Poulin.

In game one of the Stanley Cup series, Gretzky was scoreless as the Oilers were beaten soundly 4-1. Play was so bad that coaches John Muckler and Glen Sather refused to let the team see the films of the games.

"It's scary how well we're playing," Philadelphia's Mark Howe admitted. "We were just all over them."

What the Flyers needed (and perhaps the Oilers, too), was a little surprise. So, in game two, Wayne Gretzky had a new partner in the line, newcomer Esa Tikkanen. In game two, the Oilers reversed their fortunes, posting a 3-1 win. Back in Edmonton for game three, Gretzky performed magnificently, making seven shots on goal and scoring three in the first period alone to take the game 4-3. Game four began with a sudden onslaught by the Flyers, who leapt into a 3-1 lead before the first period was over. Glenn Anderson tied the game by the end of the second period. In the third, Rick Tocchet dashed from the penalty box straight to the Oilers' goal on a breakaway. Grant Fuhr brushed off his effort, and allowed Wayne Gretzky an opportunity to put the team ahead with two more goals. The final score was 5-3.

The fifth game was almost anticlimactic, with the added attraction of seeing team leaders Glen Sather and Mike Keenan shout back and forth as the Oilers ran away with the game (8-3) and the team's second Stanley Cup.

Another League-Leading Season

The 1985-86 season started well but then went horribly wrong. In an early game with the Flyers, with the score 2-2, Mark Messier was taken out of the face-off circle for jumping the gun (or the puck). When he complained about the call, he was given a two-minute penalty. His absence, and the resulting power play, cost the team the game.

Right after Christmas, the NHL arranged a game with the Russians in Edmonton.

Coming off the Christmas break (replete with turkey and wine), the Oilers were no match for the Soviets. The Oilers lost 5-3 in another high-profile game. Nevertheless, the team wrapped up the season as league leaders with a stunning 56-17-7 record.

We All Make Mistakes

Round one of the playoffs against the Vancouver Canucks was the most lacklustre playoff series the Oilers had experienced in their short NHL history. It was no contest as the Canucks bumbled around on home ice before a crowd that was at less than half its full capacity. Round two, against the Calgary Flames, was a rude slap in the face. So far, the Flames hadn't worried the Oilers. During the season, Edmonton had won five of six games against Calgary and had tied the sixth. Nonetheless, the Flames' sole 9-3 win late in the season had given the Flames an enormous psychological boost going into the playoffs.

Back home in Edmonton for round two of the playoffs, the Oilers were stunned when Calgary beat them soundly once again, 4-1. The Flames, buoyed by the performance of their young goalie, Mike Vernon, grew even more confident. The Oilers managed a 6-5 win in game two but needed overtime to do it. The Flames came back 3-2 in game three.

The Oilers soon stopped the talk about "an upset" by the Flames with a solid 7-4 win in game four. The series was tied, but if the Oilers weren't worried, they should have been. In Edmonton, disbelieving fans watched the Flames singe the Oilers 4-1. Back in Calgary, Flames fans were ready for their team to shut down Edmonton in what they hoped would be the final game. The Oilers felt confident they would be back in Edmonton for game seven. And they were. They extended the series on a 5-2 win.

At the Coliseum for game seven, the game was tied 2-2 after a Flames early 2-0 lead. Then, Edmonton's rookie defenceman, Steve Smith, accidentally banked an errant puck off of Grant Fuhr's leg for a goal on his own net that broke the tie and ended the Oilers' season prematurely. Players on the bench looked up in disbelief.

"What the hell happened?" asked slack-jawed John Muckler. "How is the puck in the net?" Surely there had to be time to get another goal and take the game into overtime. It was not to be.

Peter Pocklington walked over to talk to the tearful player, who was sitting in isolation in the dressing room, but Smith was inconsolable. Nonetheless, the media was waiting and it was time for Steve Smith to take it like a man. It was a dismal and dispiriting end to a season that had held such promise for the team. Now that promise belonged to Calgary, as the Flames prepared for their first Stanley Cup finals.

Up Where They Belong

That summer before the 1986-87 season, the players wondered nervously what changes coach Glen Sather had in mind. There had to be changes after that awful climax to the previous season. Sather did the best thing he could have, at the time, and that was absolutely nothing. All the right talent was in all the right places.

Unfortunately, in Sather's eyes, one "talent"— Paul Coffey — wasn't demonstrating as much as he could have, and the coach said so publicly. However, neither one let their growing animosity hinder the team's fortunes as the season progressed. The embarrassing loss to Calgary focused the players on the task at hand — winning the Cup again. They were soon poised to do so, finishing first in league standings. Gretzky won the scoring championship, while Kurri finished second, and Messier placed fourth. Then, it was time for a Stanley Cup rematch with the Philadelphia Flyers.

It was also time for strategy. The Flyers' rookie goalie, Ron Hextall, was brilliant, but he also had a temper. Fuhr suggested they play rough in the Philly crease, to see if they could ignite that short fuse of his. (This was a legitimate tactic in the last Cup final to be played before the NHL expanded the semicircle crease and years before penalties could be imposed for goalie interference.) In the finals, however, it was the Flyers' goalie who interfered with the Oilers, as Hextall laid out Kent Nilsson with a slash to the back of his legs. Following a series of long, loud calls for his suspension, the league belatedly assessed an eight-game absence against Hextall, although it wouldn't take affect until the *following* season.

The score was tied in the first period of game one. Wayne Gretzky moved the Oilers ahead. A Flyers goal by Brian Propp, late in the second, tied the game again and gave fans an edge-of-their-seat thrill. Then it was Anderson, Coffey, and Kurri, and a 4-2 victory. In game two, another tied score left fans breathless, until Wayne Gretzky put one in the net. Two more Flyers' goals put them ahead in the second period. In the third period, in the face of an overwhelming offensive, Hextall stood firm. The Oilers outshot the Flyers 15-5, but it wasn't until Glenn Anderson snaked his way past the Philly defence that the Oilers registered another goal. Then it was Coffey to Kurri and in the end a 3-2 win for the Oilers.

It looked like three-in-a-row for the Oilers as they led 3-0 early in the second period of the third game. The Flyers rallied and won 5-3. The Oilers took game four handily 4-1 and then lost game five 4-3. Goaltender Ron Hextall kept the Oilers at bay and the Flyers took game six 3-2, forcing a seventh and deciding game. Back in Edmonton, Messier, Kurri, and Anderson made a "come-from-behind" effort to give the Oilers a 3-1 Stanley Cup victory. It was good to be back. Steve Smith got to hold the Cup, after all.

Nonetheless, Hextall's performance had been so fundamental to the Flyers' performance that he was given the Conn Smythe Award as the series MVP.

The "Coffey Break"

After assisting his team to win three Stanley Cup victories in the seven years he had been with the Oilers, defenceman Paul Coffey felt he deserved more respect. The most meaningful way to demonstrate that well-deserved respect, he figured, would be for Sather to tear up his contract and increase his paycheque. Sather refused to do that until the contract was finished.

At the time, Paul Coffey was one of the fastest skaters and highest-scoring defenders in the league. Incurring the displeasure of a player this valuable could have meant a potentially devastating loss. Concerned, perhaps, about setting a dangerous precedent for future negotiations with players, Sather decided to hold his ground. Soon, Peter Pocklington became involved, questioning Coffey's courage. After that, it was difficult for Coffey to come back.

After he missed the first six weeks of the season, Coffey was traded to the last-place Pittsburgh Penguins along with Dave Hunter and Wayne Van Dorp. In return, four players joined the Oilers, including Craig Simpson. The Penguins said they wouldn't negotiate a higher fee with Coffey, but they soon capitulated. Sather shook his head. Paul Coffey was a player, not a team. Negotiations between Glen Sather and Grant Fuhr's agent, Rich Winter, took a tense turn as well. Heated words escalated into a shoving match. However, Fuhr was soon back in the Oilers uniform with a new contract. Mark Messier was also coming back. Andy Moog, however, was a different story.

Discouraged at his lack of ice time since the arrival of Grant Fuhr, Moog took advantage of a new Olympic ruling that allowed professionals to play Olympic hockey. Moog joined the Canadian team during the winter Olympics. Sather then turned to Boston for a trade. The result was an exchange of goalies — Bill Ranford for Andy Moog. Along with Ranford came Geoff Courtnall. At the time, neither team could have guessed how that single trade would affect both their futures at the end of the season.

What started out as a difficult season off the ice also began as a more challenging season in front of the fans. Edmonton's games-won total was down to 44. For the second season in a row, the team posted an under-400-goal total. The Oilers dropped to second place in the Smythe Division behind the Calgary Flames, which became the number one team in the NHL. Out with an eye injury for 16 games, Wayne Gretzky missed out on both the Hart and Ross Trophies for the first time in eight years. Nonetheless, with Lowe, Fuhr, and the new line of Mark Messier (centre), Craig Simpson (left-wing), and Glenn Anderson (right-wing), Edmonton was still a team to be reckoned with.

The Strangest Finals

In round one of the 1987-88 playoffs, reckoning with the Oilers fell first to the Winnipeg Jets. Edmonton ended Winnipeg's Stanley Cup hopes quickly in five games. The result of round two was even quicker. The Oilers beat the much-touted Flames in just four games. In the third round, the Oilers met the Red Wings. The Red Wings were soon sent packing back to Detroit, smarting from an 8-4 loss in the fifth and deciding game. Meanwhile, the Boston Bruins had battled their way past Buffalo in six games, Montreal in five, and New Jersey in a long seven-game series to win the Wales Conference Championship. Edmonton and Boston, and as it turned out, Grant Fuhr and Andy Moog, would both play for the Stanley Cup.

Bruins coach Terry O'Reilly decided to start Andy Moog in game one. Spirited Oilers defence meant that the Bruins were able to get only 14 shots on Grant Fuhr, one of which lit up the scoreboard. The Oilers did better, winning the game 2-1. The number of shots-on-goal tells the tale of the second game. Edmonton besieged goalie Reggie Lemelin, levelling 32 shots against him, while Boston managed only 12 shots on Grant Fuhr. The Oilers had a 4-2 second-game victory.

One of the most spirited of the Oilers in the series was none other than Steve Smith, who played hard and fast as one of Edmonton's offensive defencemen, clearly outpacing Norris Trophy winner Ray Bourque. The "Flying Finn," Esa Tikkanen, was the hero of game three at the Boston Gardens, scoring a hat trick and contributing mightily to the Oilers 6-3 win.

Then, old age intervened. The aged veteran was not any of the players, but rather, the ancient Boston Gardens, which betrayed its own home team. Boston was playing a tight, hard-fighting contest and was leading 3-2 into the second period. After Craig Simpson put one past former Oilers goalie Andy Moog to tie the score, the lights went out. For a few minutes, there was total darkness. Then, the feeble glimmer of emergency lighting reached the rink surface, but it wasn't enough to complete the game. A combination of heat, humidity, and ancient equipment had brought a hard-fought Stanley Cup game to a standstill. The players and fans filed out.

NHL president John Ziegler met with officials and cited NHL bylaw 27.12c: "If for any cause beyond the control of the clubs, a playoff game should be unfinished, such game shall be replayed in its entirety at the end of the series, if necessary, and it shall be replayed in the rink in which the unfinished game occurred."

Everyone agreed.

When word of the decision reached the Oilers in their dressing room, they were relieved. They could go back to Edmonton and finish the series in style. Besides, nobody was anxious to return to Boston. In that ancient Boston Gardens, who knew what would happen next?

In Northlands Coliseum, the Bruins, with Moog in goal, played bravely in what was called game 4-A, leading 2-1 in the first period. Then, the Flying Finn scored in the second and the Oilers surged ahead. There were just 10 seconds left when Wayne Gretzky passed the puck to Craig Simpson, who angled it in past Andy Moog with a tenth of a second to spare. At the final siren, the score was 6-3 and the Stanley Cup was held high by the Edmonton Oilers, once again.

The Big Trade

In 1988, just weeks after the dynasty had won its fourth Stanley Cup in five years, the NHL held its annual congress in Montreal. Taking a break from the speeches and the planning sessions, Red Fisher, veteran *Montreal Gazette* sports reporter and broadcaster with CBC's *Hockey Night in Canada*, chatted with Vancouver Canucks coach Bob McCammon.

"Have you heard?" McCammon asked. "The Oilers are trying to deal him . . ."

By *him*, of course McCammon meant Wayne Gretzky — The Great One. Fisher hadn't heard. As quickly as he could, however, he buttonholed Edmonton coach John Muckler to ask him if it was true. Muckler said it was nonsense. Then he tracked Glen Sather down in his hotel room. He got virtually the same response.

A couple of days later, over breakfast, Canadiens president Ronald Corey mentioned Gretzky's name. Then the Oilers' marketing people mentioned "a big trade," although Fisher couldn't check it out, because many of them were already gone. Fisher phoned Sather again in Edmonton, who suggested he call Peter Pocklington. During their conversation, the Oilers owner told Fisher that his assumptions were ridiculous. Fisher decided to go on holidays.

Fisher was having a good time in Europe, although he couldn't get the rumours — and the denials — out of his mind. So, more than 9000 kilometres away, he sat down and began typing out a "what if" story.

On July 16, 1988, Wayne Gretzky stood inside Edmonton's St. Joseph's Basilica, the city's biggest church. Wayne was all dressed up, with a black tie and a white corsage. Usher Paul Coffey and everyone else — all 700 guests, in fact — were dressed up. The Great One and his fiancée, Janet, were about to be married. As the hour drew nearer, Paul and Wayne found a moment or two to talk. You could call it "small talk," except for the secret that Wayne soon shared with his former teammate. He confided that Peter Pocklington was trying to trade him.

About three weeks later, in Portugal, Red Fisher's telephone rang. On the other end was Montreal Canadiens sportscaster Dick Irvin.

"There's a press conference about to start in Edmonton," he told Fisher.

Mark Messier was on the golf course when he got the news. He had been phoning Wayne off and on for days, but his friend had not returned his calls. Wayne Gretzky likely knew just how persuasive Messier could be. This time was no exception. As soon as Messier found out about the impending trade, he tried to talk Gretzky out of the move, but to no avail. Next, it was Glen Sather's turn. Sather and Gretzky talked for an hour as the president tried everything he knew to dissuade him. It was no use — Wayne Gretzky's mind was made up. He would soon be on his way to Los Angeles.

Chapter 9
One More Time

Events often converge. In popular sports' history, the decline of the Edmonton Oilers began when a financially beleaguered owner decided to trade away his biggest asset to help counteract losses in his other businesses.

However, even before the trade was formulated, other seemingly unrelated challenges were threatening the team — the loss of a tremendous talent such as Wayne Gretzky was just the most public. Less public was the challenge of finding the new talent needed to continually renew the team's youth and vitality. Scouting prowess, once the domain of a select few, such as Barry Fraser, was now more commonplace. There were great players out there, but Edmonton wasn't getting them.

In the years following Esa Tikkanen's selection in 1983, luck and timing, those largely uncontrollable factors, had made the right picks an elusive thing for the Oilers. Many of the players selected in the drafts had played so fleetingly with the Oilers that they were soon forgotten. Some never played at all. It was little wonder that Peter Pocklington got fed up and bypassed Glen Sather altogether to enter into negotiations directly with Tikkanen. Sather preferred a more leisurely approach, which didn't suit Pocklington. Shaken by the almost-overwhelming negative reaction to the Gretzky trade, he simply wanted the new deal with Tikkanen to be concluded quickly.

Playing Past the Pain

Perhaps Glenn Anderson said it best. Starting the 1988-89 season without Wayne Gretzky, he said, was like mourning the death of a brother.

While clearly devastated, Mark Messier, now the captain of the team, attempted to rally the players, urging the team to get going and move forward into the new season. That was easier said than done. Yet, it had to be done, and early in the season it looked as if the Edmonton Oilers were going to do it. First they beat the Islanders, then trounced Winnipeg with a winning goal by Kevin Lowe. Then it was time to meet the Kings. In the pre-game skate, the Northlands' crowd gave their lost hockey hero a standing ovation and began chanting his name. It was a modest beginning for Gretzky — the Kings lost 8-6, and he assisted in just two of the six goals — but Messier scored twice against his friend's new team.

Messier's six-game suspension just a few days later, in the wake of a particularly punishing blow to Canucks player Rich Sutter, didn't help team morale, or performance. "Inadvertent," was the league's verdict, but the suspension was not revoked.

By mid-October, Glen Sather admitted that his team's performance had been less than stellar. It got worse. At the end of the season, Edmonton's record of 38-34-8 put them in third place in the Smythe Division. There was still a lot of power on the team, with high-scoring aces Jari Kurri, newcomer Jimmy Carson (received in the Gretzky trade), and, of course, Mark Messier. It was enough to send the Oilers to the playoffs once again. Their first round opponents: the L.A. Kings and Wayne Gretzky.

Inside Inglewood's Fabulous Forum, Mark Messier performed well in the series opener, with a goal and two assists, to lead his team to a 4-3 win. The Kings evened the series 1-1 the next night with a 5-2 victory, in which Gretzky scored one goal. Back in Edmonton for game three, many of the same fans who had stood and applauded The Great One at the start of the season now booed him in reaction to his complaints in the media about Glen Sather. Messier crunched Gretzky into the boards.

"The first thing that went through my mind? That Janet wouldn't like it," Messier laughed later.

The Oilers won, 4-0.

Kevin Lowe gave the team its winning goal in game four, smacking Messier's rebounded puck back into the net with less than half a minute left to play. The game was 4-3; the series was 3-1. In Los Angeles, Gretzky provided three points for a 4-2 Kings win and then L.A. won another in Edmonton, 4-1. Game seven in the Forum was a tense contest. It was tied up 3-3 halfway through and then it became the L.A. Kings' show. The final score was 6-3, a stunning triumph for Gretzky and his new team, and a demoralizing defeat for past friends and teammates.

Champions Again

The Edmonton Oilers had a lot to prove in the 1989-90 season, especially after the disappointing previous year. Peter Pocklington's cash-strapped ways meant that putting together a Cup-winning team was becoming more and more difficult. Many of the team's former Stanley Cup winners were now playing against the Oilers, instead of with them.

Had Wayne Gretzky's departure meant that much to the club's winning ways?

It hadn't, not according to Mark Messier, his heir apparent, or to Glen Sather, whose deftness in drafts and deals was still bringing new players on board, including young up-and-at-'em players such as Adam Graves and Joe Murphy. With these two new additions and Martin Gelinas, the Oilers had a line that had started to produce.

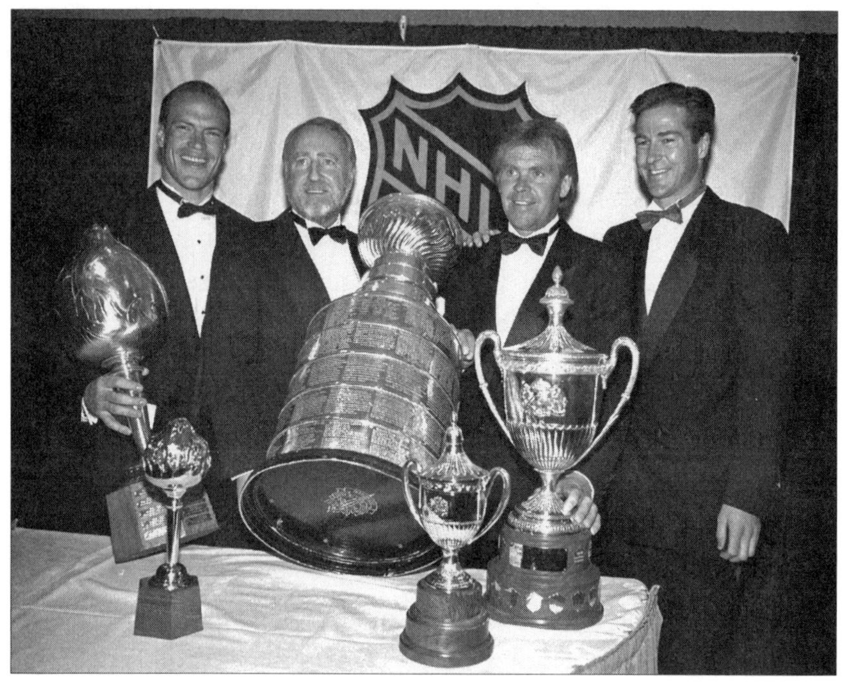

Left to right: Mark Messier, Peter Pocklington, Glen Sather, and Kevin Lowe at the 1990 NHL Awards

The number one power line of Mark Messier, Jari Kurri, and Esa Tikkanen was still devastatingly effective. When injuries sidelined Grant Fuhr late in the season, Bill Ranford was ready to take over in the crease. There was young blood, too. Adam Graves was a bright, fast addition to the team, and he scored often. Messier was more focused and energetic, clearly the leader Glen Sather needed him to be. The past was, well, the past. The present was fleeting. It was the future that Messier was focused on as he pulled his team toward his vision of another Stanley Cup victory.

Messier was still an excellent player. The 1989-90 season was his best yet: hat tricks on three different occasions added up to multiple points in 41 of the team's 79 regular-season games. At the end of it all, Mark Messier's 45-84-129 goal-assist-point record was a mere 13 points shy of Wayne Gretzky's own set of statistics. The Oilers finished second in their division that year, just nine points behind Calgary, fifth in the league, and better than the year before.

The playoffs went, well, the way Oilers' playoffs were meant to go. In round one, the Winnipeg Jets made the Oilers work for their series' victory. Behind three games to one, Messier marshalled the troops and Edmonton took the next three games. Next, it was time to dethrone the Kings. Oh, but how the mighty fall! The score in the first game was Oilers 7, Kings 0. In the second it was Oilers 6, Kings 1. Could it be this easy? In Los Angeles, the Edmonton squad rolled up two more wins, 5-4 and 6-5 in overtime. Six games later, the Oilers had beaten the Blackhawks and were soon playing for the Cup once again, against the Boston Bruins.

The first game against the Bruins was so long, it was as if the crowd had paid to see what baseball fans called a "twilight double-header." Close to an hour into overtime, most of the Edmonton first-stringers (and most of the Bruins) were clearly exhausted. Glen Sather decided to take Petr Klima off the bench and put him on the ice.

When Detroit had traded Klima for Jimmy Carson, the Red Wings had wished the Oilers luck with a player they considered to be lazy. However, as soon as Messier put him on the line between himself and Anderson, Klima suddenly found the inspiration he needed. That night, he made a powerful contribution, managing to score on former Oilers goalie Andy Moog to finish the longest game in Stanley Cup history.

The other games were shorter, but no less sweet, thanks in no small measure to goalie Bill Ranford, who, at the end of this momentous series would cradle the Conn Smythe Trophy. The second game ended with a resounding 7-2 win for the Oilers. Boston took game three 2-1 in Edmonton, and then the Oilers were back, with a pair of 5-1 and 4-1 victories.

Holding the Cup high, Messier slowly skated over to his parents, to share the moment with them. It had been a long journey from that frozen pond by the highway in Portland, Oregon. *Hockey News* was there, and the camera shutter clicked. The happy victory photo ran on the paper's cover, accompanied by a one-word headline: "REDEMPTION."

Of Men and Money

The next season started without Jari Kurri. Contract negotiations had not gone well. For a while, protracted negotiations with Glenn Anderson had many also doubting his eventual return.

However, there was another absence that was more

The Edmonton Oilers win the 1990 Stanley Cup.
Left to right: Kevin Lowe, Mark Messier, and Jari Kurri

keenly felt by the team. Grant Fuhr, who never seemed to lose his cool, had a problem. After successfully completing treatment, the star goalie was suspended for 60 games for cocaine use.

He just wanted to be a "normal guy," he later told *Edmonton Journal* reporter Dan Barnes. However, he wasn't "normal." He was Grant Fuhr, a trophy-winning goalie for the Edmonton Oilers. Looking for escape, Fuhr had found drugs.

"I led a double life," the future Hall-of-Famer explained.

It was just one of many problems that now plagued the team.

As the first years of Pocklington's financially constrained decade ground away at the once-mighty Oilers, it's not likely that either Peter Pocklington or Glen Sather saw the 1990-91 season as a new beginning. They might just as easily have felt it was the beginning of the end, as it had been with the collapse of WHA. However, unlike those earlier, happier days, there were now clouds on the Edmonton Oilers' hockey horizon.

By the mid-1990s, Glen Sather's champagne-and-caviar days were done. Nonetheless, the coach continued to soldier on resolutely into the new millennium, facing diminishing budgets and spiralling player costs.

Pocklington redoubled his efforts to unload the team. "Sold," announced the headline in the *Edmonton Journal* in March of 1997. Fans were fearful: would the team leave town? A year later, however, a group of Edmonton investors fashioned a solid financial solution that would keep the Oilers in Edmonton, where they belonged.

Bibliography

Allen, Kevin and Bob Duff. *Without Fear.* Chicago, Illinois: Triumph Books, 2002.

Bossy, Mike. *Boss.* Toronto, Ontario: McGraw-Hill Ryerson, 1988.

Carpiniello, Rick. *Messier: Steel on Ice.* Toronto, Ont. Stoddart, 1999.

Dowbiggin, Bruce. *Of Ice and Men.* Toronto, Ontario: Macfarlane Walter & Ross, 1998.

Fisher, Red. *Hockey, Heroes and Me.* Toronto, Ontario: McClelland and Stewart, 1994.

Fischler, Stan. *Golden Ice: The Greatest Teams in Hockey History.* Scarborough, Ont., McGraw-Hill Ryerson Ltd., 1990.

Falla, Jack, editor. *Quest for the Cup 1917-2000.* Toronto, Ontario, Key Porter, 2001.

Frayne, Trent et al. *Hockey Chronicles: An Insider History of National Hockey League Teams.* Toronto, Ontario: Key Porter Books, 2000.

Greenberg, Jay. *The Full Spectrum.* Toronto, Ontario: Dan Diamond and Associates, 1996.

Gretzky, Walter and Jim Taylor. *Gretzky.* Toronto, Ont., McClelland and Stewart, 1984.

Gretzky, Wayne and Rick Reilly. *An Autobiography.* New York: HarperCollins, 1990.

Gzowski, Peter. *The Game of Our Lives.* Toronto, Ontario: McClelland and Stewart, 1981.

Hesketh, Bob and Francis Swyripa, editors. *Edmonton: The Life of a City.* Edmonton, Alberta: NeWest Publishers Ltd., 1995.

Hunter, Douglas. *A Breed Apart: An Illustrated History of Goaltending.* Chicago, Illinois: Triumph Books, 1995.

Champions: The Illustrated History of Hockey's Greatest Dynasties. Toronto, Ontario: The Penguin Group, Penguin Books Canada Ltd., 1997.

The Glory Barons. Toronto, Ontario: Viking, 1999.

Jenish, D'Arcy. *The Stanley Cup: A Hundred Years of Hockey at Its Best.* Toronto, Ontario: McClelland and Stewart Inc., 1992.

Jones, Terry. *The Great Gretzky Yearbook II.* Toronto, Ontario: General Paperbacks, 1982.

Klein, Jeff. *Messier.* Toronto, Ontario: Doubleday Canada, 2003

Lowe, Kevin, Shirley Fischler, and Stan Fischler. *Champions.* Scarborough, Ontario: Prentice-Hall Canada, Inc., 1988.

McFarlane, Brian. *One Hundred Years of Hockey.* Toronto, Ontario: Deneau Publishers, 1989.

Strachan, Al, editor. *One Hundred Years of Hockey.* Toronto, Ontario: Key Porter Books, 1999.

Weir, Glenn et al. *Ultimate Hockey.* Toronto, Ontario: Stoddart, 1999.

Acknowledgments

The Edmonton Oilers' dynasty ran from 1984 to 1990. In the 15 years since Mark Messier led the team to its last Stanley Cup victory, no other team has come close to equalling its record. There are many who doubt any other NHL team ever will. Ironically, that fatalistic prediction has little to do with the ability of players. It has more to do with the ability of team owners to buy talent. Free agency minimizes the chances that team backers will be able to afford — and therefore, keep — the talent a team already has in place.

The evidence continues to mount. In the 1990s, only two teams managed more than a single Stanley Cup victory. Once in a while, there is a brief flare of hope that a modestly financed franchise can somehow — with luck, timing, and determination — break free of its financial limitations and go all the way. Edmonton hockey fans don't have to look too far over the horizon for proof of this possibility. Why, look at those former rivals, the Calgary Flames!

Such dominance by a single hockey team — a "dynasty" — has only rarely been achieved by a handful of teams, usually in a six-team league. However, the Oilers' rise occurred in a league of over 20 teams. Moreover, the feats of the Edmonton Oilers, and those of many of its individual players, are among the most astonishing in NHL history. It's surprising then that only a few books have ever been published about the Edmonton Oilers — a paltry selection when you consider that, for most of one entire decade, this particular team almost single-handedly defined professional hockey excellence.

Of that handful of books, fewer still tell the entire story. Most, including the engaging *Gretzky* by The Great One's father Walter Gretzky, end just as the team's Stanley Cup ascendancy began.

There are many books that relate the life and times of outstanding individual Oilers' team members (including two about Mark Messier, one about Dave Semenko, and many more about Wayne Gretzky). This may be one reason why the entire story of the *team* has never been told in a popular way. As Wayne Gretzky's phenomenal feats overshadowed those of his teammates so, too, have they dominated the bookshelves. Books about Gretzky, Messier, and others appear to tell the team's story. However, these are player histories, not Oilers histories.

Early in 1980, renowned and respected broadcaster and writer Peter Gzowski knew *something* was happening out in Edmonton. Wayne Gretzky, who Gzowski had met and interviewed some years before, encouraged him to come out west and see for himself. The result was a book called *The Game of Our Lives,* an elegant, game-by-game description of a single season for a team that, even then, seemed destined for greatness.

Champions is an autobiography of defenceman Kevin Lowe. It is a meticulously accurate historical record written by veteran hockey researchers/writers Stan and Shirley Fischler. Unfortunately, Lowe's first-person reminiscences, which do not begin until Chapter 13, end in 1988, somewhat prematurely as it turned out.

To learn more about the later years of the Oilers, one must turn to *The Glory Barons,* by one of the sport's notable chroniclers, Douglas Hunter. This excellent book places much of its focus on the "political and economic issues" that helped to create the team and then bring it to its knees.

All of these works, and others, were extremely valuable to me in my efforts to tell the story of the final dynasty.

Photo Credits

Cover: Paul Bereswill / Hockey Hall of Fame; Paul Bereswill / Hockey Hall of Fame: pages 73, 155; London Life-Portnoy / Hockey Hall of Fame: pages 45, 52; Doug MacLellan / Hockey Hall of Fame: page 112.

About the Author

BC-born author Rich Mole has enjoyed an eclectic communications career, as a former broadcaster, a freelance journalist, and, for 20 years, the president of a successful Vancouver Island advertising agency. A lifelong fascination with history has fuelled his desire to write about the times and people of Canada's past. Rich now makes his home in Calgary, Alberta.

AMAZING STORIES

by the same author

AMAZING STORIES™

GREAT STANLEY CUP VICTORIES

Glorious Moments in Hockey

HOCKEY

by Rich Mole

ISBN 1-55153-797-4

AMAZING STORIES

also available!

ISBN 1-55153-794-X

OTHER AMAZING STORIES

ISBN	Title	Author
1-55153-943-8	Black Donnellys	Nate Hendley
1-55153-947-0	Canada's Rumrunners	Art Montague
1-55153-966-7	Canadian Spies	Tom Douglas
1-55153-795-8	D-Day	Tom Douglas
1-55153-982-9	Dinosaur Hunters	Lisa Murphy-Lamb
1-55153-798-2	Edmonton Oilers	Rich Mole
1-55153-968-3	Edwin Alonzo Boyd	Nate Hendley
1-55153-996-9	Emily Carr	Cat Klerks
1-55153-973-X	Great Canadian Love Stories	Cheryl MacDonald
1-55153-946-2	Great Dog Stories	Roxanne Snopek
1-55153-797-4	Great Stanley Cup Victories	Rich Mole
1-55153-942-X	The Halifax Explosion	Joyce Glasner
1-55153-958-6	Hudson's Bay Company Adventures	Elle Andra-Warner
1-55153-969-1	Klondike Joe Boyle	Stan Sauerwein
1-55153-980-2	Legendary Show Jumpers	Debbie G-Arsenault
1-55153-964-0	Marilyn Bell	Patrick Tivy
1-55153-953-5	Moe Norman	Stan Sauerwein
1-55153-962-4	Niagara Daredevils	Cheryl MacDonald
1-55153-790-7	Ottawa Senators	Chris Robinson
1-55153-945-4	Pierre Elliott Trudeau	Stan Sauerwein
1-55153-981-0	Rattenbury	Stan Sauerwein
1-55153-991-8	Rebel Women	Linda Kupecek
1-55153-956-X	Robert Service	Elle Andra-Warner
1-55153-952-7	Strange Events	Johanna Bertin
1-55153-954-3	Snowmobile Adventures	Linda Aksomitis
1-55153-950-0	Tom Thomson	Jim Poling Sr.
1-55153-788-5	Toronto Maple Leafs	Jim Barber
1-55153-976-4	Trailblazing Sports Heroes	Joan Dixon
1-55153-977-2	Unsung Heroes of the RCAF	Cynthia J. Faryon
1-55153-792-3	Vancouver Canucks	Justin Bedall
1-55153-948-9	The War of 1812 Against the States	Jennifer Crump